English education,
social change and war
1911–20

To W.G.S. and M.A.S.

English education, social change and war 1911–20

Geoffrey Sherington

Manchester University Press

Published by
Manchester University Press
Oxford Road, Manchester M13 9PL

British Library cataloguing in publication data

Sherington, Geoffrey.
English education, social change and war, 1911–20.
1. Education – England – History.
I. Title.
370′.942 LA631.7

ISBN 0–7190–0840–9

Distributed in North America by
Humanities Press Inc
Atlantic Highlands
N.J. 07716, U.S.A.

Photoset in Plantin by
Northern Phototypesetting Company, Bolton
Printed and bound in Great Britain by
Biddles Ltd, Guildford and King's Lynn

Contents

Tables and illustrations

Tables

Illustrations

Abbreviations

Be.L., L.G.P.	Beaverbrook Library, Lloyd George papers (now located in House of Lords Library)
B.L., F.P.	Bodleian Library, H. A. L. Fisher papers
B.L., G.M.	Bodleian Library, Gilbert Murray papers
B.L.P.E., P.P.	British Library of Political and Economic Science, Passfield papers
C.U.L., C.P.	Cambridge University Library, Crewe papers
N.C.L., G.P.	Nuffield College Library, Gainford papers
N.L.S., H.P.	National Library of Scotland, Haldane papers
N.L.W., H.L.P.	National Library of Wales, Herbert Lewis papers
N.L.W., T.J.C.	National Library of Wales, Thomas Jones collection
P.R.O.	Public Record Office
U. of L., B.C.	University of Leeds Library, Brotherton collection

Acknowledgements

Research for this work was carried out initially with the financial and other assistance of McMaster University, Ontario. Whilst a student there I received advice and guidance from many individuals, including the late H. W. McCready, D. J. Russo and C. M. Johnston. Among others who have been encouraging and helpful in various ways, I would like to thank: Professors W. H. G. Armytage, Peter Gosden, Dick Selleck and Brian Simon, Dr Bill Stephens, Edgar Jenkins, and Bill and Leisha Fullick. Barbara Billington and Mary Black have done most of the typing, with help from Ann Webb and Dianne Kelsey.

For permission to cite from unpublished manuscript sources I am grateful to Mrs Mary Bennett and the Bodleian Library for the correspondence and diary of H. A. L. Fisher; the Trustees of the National Library of Scotland and Dr A. R. B. Haldane and his family for the correspondence of Lord Haldane; Mrs I. K. Jones for the correspondence of Herbert Lewis; Cambridge University Library for the correspondence of the Marquess of Crewe; the Trustees of the National Library of Scotland for the correspondence of J. Dover Wilson; the British Library of Political and Economic Science for the diary of Beatrice Webb in the Passfield Papers; Viscount Runciman for the correspondence of his father; and Lord Aberdare for the correspondence of W. N. Bruce. I would like to thank also the following institutions for permission to consult other sources: Nuffield College Library for the Gainford Papers; the Bodleian Library for the Gilbert Murray Papers; the University of Leeds Library for the Brotherton Collection; the Trustees of the former Beaverbrook

Library for the Lloyd George Papers; and the University of Wales Library for the Thomas Jones Collection. All reasonable efforts have been made to contact the holder of any copyright material. I apologise for any omission and would be grateful for knowledge of the fact. Crown copyright records in the Public Record Office appear by permission of the Controller of H.M. Stationery Office. The two cartoons are reproduced with the kind permission of the *Western Mail*.

Some of the research on which this work is based appeared previously in the *British Journal of Educational Studies*, *Journal of Educational Administration and History* and the *ANZHES Journal*. Parts of the material published in those journals appears by kind permission of the editors.

Finally, my wife Lisa and son Gregory have been ever tolerant with the wiles of a sometimes impatient author.

Introduction

This study is intended as a contribution to the debate over war and social change in the twentieth century. A related purpose is an attempt to further the understanding of early twentieth-century English education.

An earlier generation of historians believed that war undermined many of the values of civilisation and was therefore a counter to human progress.[1] The focus on 'total war' involving all citizens, particularly during the second world war, has led to a reconsideration of war as a force generative of social change. The work of Richard Titmuss on British society and the second world war suggested that the prosecution of the war effort led to the introduction of advanced and progressive social policies in order to maintain the morale and commitment of the mass of the population.[2] More generally Stanislaw Andrzejewski had earlier developed the idea of the 'military participation ratio', arguing that, throughout history, the more the general populace participated in war the greater was the force of levelling tendencies throughout society.[3]

In recent years the main proponent of the relation between war and social change has been Arthur Marwick. Marwick's *The Deluge* (first published in 1965) was a major attempt to assess the total effect of the first world war on British society.[4] Attempting to formulate a model of change, he has argued that war affects society through four 'modes' – as 'destruction', as 'test', as 'participation' (with increased social involvement and gains for the masses) and, finally, as 'an emotional and psychological experience'.[5]

This model is imaginative and enlightening but it has not gone unchallenged as far as British society and the first world war are concerned. Work during the 1960s suggested that many of the hopes of widespread social reform during the first world war failed through administrative problems, an 'ideological blindness' among reformers, and the still class-structured nature of British society. Prominent was Paul Johnson's major study of the planning of British reconstruction, although he wrote virtually nothing on educational reconstruction.[6] More recent monographs would seem to suggest that not only institutions but also visions and opinions remain less amenable to wartime change than historians have often imagined.[7]

Historians of education have also shown a fascination with the possible relation between war and specific educational change. War has often been seen as revealing deficiencies in the English educational system, and bringing about greater State involvement.[8] Most interest in the first world war has focused on the formulation and passage of the 1918 Education Act, the main piece of wartime educational legislation. (Marwick himself cites it as representative of measures designed to repair the damage of war[9]). One historian has attributed the major content of the 1918 Act to H. A. L. Fisher, the President of the Board of Education from 1916 to 1922.[10] Another administrative study has concentrated on the pressure groups supporting and opposing the Act, and also on its passage through Parliament.[11] From a somewhat different perspective D. H. Akenson has argued, in a short article based only on published sources, that there is a pattern between war and English educational change, whereby war helps enact pre-war ideas on education while peace undermines their fulfilment.[12]

Despite this interest in the 1918 Education Act (and it will be suggested here that all the existing literature fails to understand the origins and aims of this measure) there is no major study of English education and the first world war comparable to P. H. J. H. Gosden's recent work on the second world war.[13] The aim here is to examine the whole general field of English education both before and during the first world war and the immediate post-war period. The emphasis is on the formulation and attempted implementation of policy, although there is also consideration of the impact of war on the educational system itself. A number of issues feature prominently throughout this study. The place of religion in elementary education, the development of adolescent education and the role of the secondary schools, the place of scientific and technical education, the relation between the State and the universities, administrative problems of finance and teacher supply – these were matters of major concern. But the issues varied in intensity throughout the period under study, and not all held the same place of concern after the war that they did before. Hence there is no conscious effort to trace the development of all individual questions. Instead, the study concentrates on analysing the policy-makers' response to particular problems as they related to the varying flux of political, social and economic forces. It is hoped thereby to provide a fuller understanding of the nature and purpose of English education and English educational policy prior to, during and after the war of 1914–18.

The study is confined generally to England (the only exception being post-war policy for the universities, when State university grants were placed under the administration of a committee for the whole United Kingdom). Both Scotland and Ireland had, of course, their own educational systems and were under separate administrations. Wales, while tied to England administratively, had its own peculiar issues, particularly in regard to the question of language.

Furthermore, this is not a study of all wartime changes or attempted changes in English education. No effort is made to provide a detailed examination of the private sector or of the public schools (although their relation with the State is considered briefly). Similarly, internal changes within the universities are not discussed in great depth. Certain other areas, which were of State concern but outside the general supervision of the Board of Education, are excluded. Thus agricultural and army education are omitted and adult education is only touched upon.

One final word. All historians are aware, if not always conscious, of the presuppositions they bring to the study of the past. Research for this work started on the premise that the Great War was an important formulator of English educational change. The final result is somewhat different. Sometimes the sources themselves can enlighten as well as surprise us.

Notes

1 As two examples, see Quincy Wright, *A Study of War*, Chicago, 1942, and John U. Nef, *War and Human Progress*, Cambridge, Massachusetts, 1942.

2 Richard Titmuss, 'War and social policy', in *Essays on the Welfare State*, London, 1958, pp. 79–86.

3 Stanislaw Andrzejewski, *Military Organisation and Society*, London,

1954, pp. 33–8.

4 Arthur Marwick, *The Deluge*, London, 1965.

5 Arthur Marwick, 'The impact of the first world war on British society', *Journal of Contemporary History*, 2, 1968, pp. 60–3. See also Arthur Marwick, *War and Social Change in the Twentieth Century. A Comparative Study of Britain, France, Germany, Russia, and the United States*, London, 1974.

6 P. B. Johnson, *Land fit for Heroes, The Planning of British Reconstruction, 1916–1919*, London, 1968. See also Philip Abrams, 'The failure of social reform: 1918–1920', *Past and Present*, No. 24, 1963, pp. 43–64.

7 Martin Pugh, *Electoral Reform in Peace and War, 1906–1918*, London, 1978. See also J. M. Winter, *Socialism and the Challenge of War. Ideas and Politics in Britain, 1912–18*, London, 1974; Johnson, *Land fit for Heroes*, pp. 239–40; and Bentley Gilbert, *British Social Policy, 1914–1939*, Ithaca, N.Y., 1970, p. 1.

8 W. H. G. Armytage, 'Battles for the best. Some educational aspects of the welfare-warfare State in England', in Paul Nash (ed.), *History and Education*, New York, 1970, pp. 283–307; George Haines IV, 'The response to World War One', in *Essays on German Influence upon English Education and Science, 1850–1919*, Connecticut College, 1969, pp. 166–81; and R. J. W. Selleck, *English Primary Education and the Progressives, 1914–1939*, London, 1972, chapter one.

9 Arthur Marwick, 'The impact of the first world war on British society', p. 61.

10 D. W. Dean, 'H. A. L. Fisher, reconstruction and the development of the 1918 Education Act', *British Journal of Educational Studies*, XVIII, 1970, pp. 260–2.

11 L. I. Andrews, *The Education Act, 1918*, London, 1976.

12 D. H. Akenson, 'Patterns of English educational change. The Fisher and the Butler Acts', *History of Education Quarterly*, V, IX, 1971, pp. 143–54.

13 P. H. J. H. Gosden, *Education in the Second World War. A study in Policy and Administration*, London, 1976.

I

Edwardian education

English education in the first decade of the twentieth century was in shape much like the pattern of English society – hierarchical and class-structured. During the nineteenth century there had developed not so much an educational system as a series of separate parts, each bearing an uncertain relation to the others. The two nations described by Disraeli had been perpetuated through educational change. The main role of the State had been concerned with the provision of elementary education for the working class, mediating that provision through compromises with the established Church. Apart from enquiries and regulation of endowments, the schooling of the governing and middle classes had operated outside State control. In the modern industrial society of Edwardian England the legacies of these divisions remained.

The administrative structure of Edwardian education lay in the terms of the Act of 1902, which had created local education authorities throughout England and Wales. Owing to pressure of local feeling, even here there was no uniform system. Part II authorities, comprising the councils of counties and county boroughs, were to be responsible for both elementary and all forms of 'higher education'. Part III authorities, comprising the councils of boroughs over 10,000 in population and urban districts over 20,000 in population, were to be responsible for elementary education. As a further complication, a large number of boroughs and urban districts were granted limited spending powers in higher education. However, there was no provision for giving powers over higher education to expanding urban areas or to take away powers over elementary education from those towns whose population had declined. In general the 1902 Act left unclear the relation between the counties, which were responsible for both elementary and higher education, and those Part III authorities which were autonomous in elementary, but under the county for purposes of higher, education.

The most controversial features of the 1902 Act related to the new provisions for the funding and support of 'voluntary' denominational schools, almost all of which were Church of England or Roman Catholic. All elementary schools were required to have bodies of management. In schools provided by the local council the powers of the school management were to be defined by the appropriate local education authority. The body of management of the non-provided or voluntary schools, normally consisting of four foundation members chosen in accord with the trust deed of each school and two managers appointed by the local education authority, retained powers over the appointment and dismissal of teachers and over religious teaching. In financial terms the local authority was to accept responsibility not only for the pay of teachers in the voluntary schools but also for 'fair wear and tear' of buildings, while the managers were to provide the school building itself.

Many Nonconformists saw these measures as designed to preserve and strengthen the denominational schools by providing a firm base in local rate aid. There was particular concern over the issue of those voluntary schools, almost all Anglican, in areas where there was no other provision for elementary school children. These 'single-school areas' existed chiefly in rural districts and were a touchstone of what was seen as the continuing privileged position of the established Church. Lloyd George, himself forced to attend the local Anglican school in his youth, told the Commons during debate concerning the 1902 Act,

> The Church has over 12,000 schools in the country, which are mission rooms to educate the poor in the principles of the Church. In 8,000 parishes there are no other schools, and the whole machinery is there utilised to force the Nonconformist children into them.[1]

Despite continuing opposition to these arrangements for the denominational schools, including a ratepayers' strike in Wales, the passage of the Act of 1902 did lay the foundation for educational expansion. With the exception of the Roman Catholic sector, the voluntary schools, many of which were old nineteenth-century foundations, declined during the early twentieth century. By 1911 the majority of English children were being educated in council schools, many of which were founded in the decade after 1902.[2] Part II authorities also entered the field of secondary education by both aiding existing endowed grammar schools and other secondary institutions and building and maintaining their own secondary schools. By 1911–12 there were 833 secondary schools receiving State grants, including 428 'aided' endowed grammar schools and 381 council 'maintained' schools.[3]

The establishment of secondary schools was associated with changes in the recruitment of teachers. After 1907 the nineteenth-century system of pupil teachers, drawn from within elementary schools, was supplanted increasingly by schemes providing for 'bursars' or student teachers who had received a secondary education to the age of seventeen with concurrent or deferred teaching practice before passing on to a training college. A number of local education authorities also established training colleges. From 1900 to 1913 the number of teacher training colleges grew from sixty-one, most of which were denominational bodies, to over eighty, including twenty local education authority institutions, and eleven university departments.[4] Over the same period the proportion of teachers with a formal teacher's certificate (obtained by training in a college or sitting for an annual exam) grew from 55 per cent to 66 per cent of the total teaching body, while those who had undergone training in a college increased from 30 per cent to 40 per cent of the total.[5]

Improved status for teachers was not accompanied by a relative increase in pay. Teachers were very much in the lower bracket of, if not below, those Edwardian families who can be defined as 'middle class' by earning an annual income of £160 to £700. Of those with a teacher's certificate, in 1913–14, 93 per cent earned less than £200 per year, 81 per cent less than £150, and 39 per cent less than £100. Of the total of 42,884 uncertificated teachers, only 117 were paid £100 or more a year.[6] The changed arrangements for training and the continuing poor salaries led to a crisis in teacher supply. By 1913–14 the number of pupil teachers in the elementary schools had declined to 1,454 from a figure of 11,108 in 1906–07 (when the first full effort to reorganise recruitment had been carried out), while the number of new student teachers and bursars in the secondary schools was only 598 boys and 2,434 girls.[7]

Part of the problem over inadequate teacher salaries related to the financial arrangements between local education authorities and the State. Despite increased public expenditure on education, by 1910–11 the burden was falling increasingly on the local rates rather than on national taxes.

Table 1 *Public expenditure on education*

Date	*Total local education authority expenditure*	*Proportion contributed by local rates (%)*	*Proportion contributed by national tax (%)*	*Proportion of rates spent on education (%)*	*Proportion of taxes spent on education (%)*
1900–01	£16,200,000	43·6	56·4	14·2	5·9
1910–11	£27,537,000	51·5	48·5	21·8	9·8

Source: Education, 1900–1950, Report of the Ministry of Education, 1950, Cmd 8244, p. 250.

In 1909 Walter Runciman, President of the Board of Education, told his Cabinet colleagues that there was growing unrest amongst both local education authorities and teachers over the imbalance in educational financing. From 1906–07 to 1908–09 State grants actually fell by £200,000 while rates had increased by £1,300,000.[8]

The State grant system for education was complex – the product of a variety of calculations that had been introduced at different periods over the previous half-century. In particular, the grants for elementary education were calculated in respect of individual schools and bore little relation to the needs of an area or its ability to raise local rates. The result was an inequitable distribution of the financial burden throughout the country, and the poorer areas with large populations were particularly hard pressed. In 1911–12 the local rateable value of property in relation to each child ranged from £13 to £106, while local expenditure per child ranged from £2 12*s* to £7 10*s* and the local rate from under 6*d* in the £ to over 2*s*.[9] As early as 1901 the minority report of the Royal Commission on Taxation had recommended a system of fixed-percentage block grants-in-aid to support national services (such as education) at the local level. The proposal was not acted upon, but in 1911 the Treasury appointed a departmental committee under Sir John Kempe to consider the whole area of local taxation.

Many contemporaries saw other educational deficiencies which required both extra finance and legislative action. The prospects of school leavers were a major concern. The law of school attendance allowed a child to obtain full exemption from school as early as the age of twelve and partial exemption from eleven. The most common practice in this regard was the 'half-time system' existing mainly in Lancashire and Cheshire, where children divided their time between school and the cotton mill. After the age of fourteen most youths and young women had no contact at all with the educational system.

Table 2 *Adolescent education in England and Wales, 1906–07*

Age	*Population (estimate)*	*Not attending day school (estimate)*	*Not attending day school (%)*	*Attending evening school*	*Not attending day or evening school (%)*
12–14	1,377,600	210,825	15·30	40,530	12·36
14–17	2,022,300	1,754,548	86·76	256,199	74·09
17–21	2,639,900	2,592,613	98·21	198,796	90·68

Source: Consultative Committee of the Board of Education on Attendance, compulsory or otherwise, at Continuation Schools, Cd 4757, p. 29.

The problem of urban adolescents was much present in the minds of early twentieth-century educationalists. Youth organisations and settlement groups focused on the need for greater measures of control and direction. In 1907 the educationalist Michael Sadler wrote,

> In the course of every year, more than half-a-million children in England and Wales leave the public elementary schools at thirteen or fourteen years. Not more than one of every three of these children receives in point of general or technical education, any further care. Yet those who fail to receive such care, are, broadly speaking, those who need it most. And the years which follow the day school course are the central years of adolescence when stimulating discussion, technical training and well-directed guidance in matters of conduct and personal hygiene are often most helpful towards healthy living and self control. Those whose work lies among boys and girls of this age, especially in the cities, lament the spoiling of promise and the waste of power which they see caused by lack of tendance and of invigorating discipline.[10]

These conclusions were reinforced by studies of unemployment. In 1909 the social investigator William Beveridge noted the growth of 'blind-alley' occupations such as light work in factories or positions as messenger and van boy: areas of employment that offered no security or training and yet which also destroyed the 'habits of obedience and regularity' inculcated in the elementary schools.[11]

Both the majority and minority reports of the important Royal Commission on the Poor Laws devoted considerable attention to the problem of 'boy labour'. The commission found that in London, of elementary school leavers, 40 per cent became van and errand boys, 14 per cent shop boys, 8 per cent office boys and clerks, and 18 per cent entered the building, metal, woodwork, clothing and printing trades. In none of these areas was any training provided; many boys were simply dismissed when they became too old.[12] The majority report concluded that the problem of 'boy labour' was perhaps 'the most serious of the phenomena which we have encountered in our study of unemployment'.[13]

The minority report, composed by the Webbs and signed by Beatrice Webb, the socialist, Lansbury, the trade union representative, Francis Chandler, and Russell Wakefield, the Anglican Dean of Norwich, argued even more strongly on this issue:

> We regard this perpetual recruitment of the Unemployable by tens of thousands of boys who, through neglect to provide them with suitable industrial training, may almost be said to graduate into unemployment as a matter of course, as perhaps the gravest of all the grave facts which this Commission has laid bare.[14]

Among its proposals for a national minimum of efficiency, the minority report recommended that in Britain not only should the school leaving age be raised to at least fifteen but that all youths aged fifteen to eighteen should attend an institute of technical and physical training for not less than thirty hours per week.[15]

By the eve of the first world war, some form of part-time continuation school was seen by official and other educational opinion as the answer to the educational needs of the vast majority of adolescents. As in other areas, English educationalists were influenced by German examples. At Munich the celebrated Dr Georg Kerchensteiner sought to develop not merely trade or technical education but also a sense of civic and moral responsibility amongst his pupils. Many in England found his ideals appealing.[16]

In contrast, in England as in Germany, secondary education was still perceived as being reserved for the few. Developments following the 1902 Act had at least established links between what had

The Lion let loose on its Victim.

"It was not for him to say what the future held in its grasp. The Board of Education would administer the law fearlessly—(Ministerial cheers)—and with a bloodless indifference to anything except to see that the due course of the law was observed and the cause of education maintained at its proper level. The Opposition would fail, and in the day of their failure they would deeply regret the rejection of this measure."—Mr. Birrell in the House of Commons.

The political conflict over State aid to denominational schools generated much heat and occupied a large amount of the attention of pre-war Parliamentarians. The Bill introduced by the President of the Board of Education, Arthur Birrell, in 1906 was the first unsuccessful effort to change the terms of the 1902 Act. (From *Western Mail*, 22 December 1906)

previously been the generally separate spheres of elementary and secondary education. Regulations laid down in 1907 provided that up to 25 per cent of places in secondary schools receiving State grants would be reserved for former elementary school pupils. A number of local education authorities also supplemented free tuition in secondary schools with allowances for books and travel, and, in certain cases, payment of a 'maintenance grant' to help students remain at school. By 1911–12, of the 600,000 children leaving the elementary schools each year, one in twenty-two went on to a grant-aided secondary school and one in forty-six received free education there.[17] Yet not only were the majority of secondary schools in middle-class districts, but middle-class children also tended to win most of the free places at the local school. As one delegate told the 1913 Trades Union Congress, of the twenty-three elementary schools in his area, the two in middle-class districts won 70 per cent of free places at the local secondary school.[18]

Those working-class adolescents who proceeded to a secondary school had an even slighter opportunity to go beyond. In 1908–09 less than 3 per cent of secondary school pupils went on to university, while almost two-thirds of the boys and half the girls left before turning sixteen.[19] While about one-third of local education authorities did provide university scholarships, they were unevenly distributed. Overall, in 1911 only 187 boys and 149 girls in secondary schools maintained by a local council went on to a university.[20]

Still predominantly upper-class in composition, the universities of Oxford and Cambridge in particular remained impervious to the demands of a modern industrial society. The 'playground for the sons of the wealthier classes' the Anglo-Catholic bishop, Charles Gore, described them as in 1907.[21] A more serious attack came from the proponents of science and technology. 'Our position as a nation, our success as merchants, are in peril chiefly – dealing with preventable causes – because of our lack of completely efficient universities and our neglect of research,' declared the scientific propagandist Norman Lockyer in 1903.[22]

Despite numerous inquiries and Royal Commissions in the nineteenth century, calling for more attention to scientific studies, classics still held a dominant position, particularly at Oxford. As one example, over the years 1906–15, of the 1,777 Oxford scholarships and exhibitions, 1,062 were in classics.[23] Science and technology were better represented at a number of the civic universities, established in industrial centres in the Midlands and North during the late nineteenth century. Many of these new institutions received maintenance grants from the State. From 1900 to 1914 the number of students at English university institutions receiving State aid rose from 4,500 to 9,000, while State grants increased from £40,000 in 1902–03 to £170,000 in 1913–14.[24] Nevertheless there were only 1,487 students of engineering and technology at English universities and colleges in 1912–13, and a further 1,199 advanced students in technical institutes. The comparable total in Germany was 11,000.[25]

Many critics believed that lack of attention to science and

technology was the result of lack of understanding by those in government. Most politicians remained attuned to the 'religious question' in education, with its continuing sectarian rivalries. The Liberal government elected in 1906 tried unsuccessfully on three occasions in 1906–08 to redeem an electoral pledge to change the financial arrangements for denominational schools contained in the 1902 Act. A hostile House of Lords frustrated these efforts, but the commitment remained. Opening the Liberal campaign for the 1910 election, Prime Minister Asquith indicated that his government maintained its stand of four years previously.

> The anomalies and injustices created by the Act of 1902 have still to [be] set right. We have to secure by statute the access of every child to a school under the complete control of a popularly elected authority and in which the office of teacher is not forced about by any sectarian test.[26]

This concern with past disputes continued to dominate political discussion. Where candidates from the Conservative and Liberal parties discussed education during the 1910 election they did so overwhelmingly in terms of the religious question.

Table 3 *Education as an issue at the January 1910 general election*

Electorate	*Unionist candidates (%)*	*Liberal candidates (%)*
London		
(*a*) Education as an issue in electoral manifestoes	81·2	79·4
(*b*) Education discussed solely in terms of the 'religious question' as % of (*a*)	79·9	66·7
English counties and boroughs		
(*a*) Education as an issue in electoral manifestoes	68·4	55·1
(*b*) Education discussed solely in terms of the 'religious question' as % of (*a*)	90·0	74·5

Source: The manifestoes of 511 Unionist candidates and 412 Liberal candidates held at the National Liberal Club, London.

By 1910, however, new political concerns were emerging. The 'opportunity of opportunities' was the way J. A. Hobson, one of the major ideologues of the 'New Liberalism', described education.

Challenging the selective nature of the secondary schools, Hobson argued that there should be

> not an educational ladder, narrowing as it rises, to be climbed with difficulty by a chosen energetic few, who, as they rise, enter a new social stratum, breathe the atmosphere of another class, and are absorbed in official and professional occupations which dissociate them from the common life of the people. It is a broad, easy stair, and not a narrow ladder, that is wanted, one which will entice everyone to rise, will make for general and not for selected culture.[27]

This view found some sympathy in the organised trade union movement and the newly formed Labour Party. At the 1906 Trades Union Congress a resolution was carried calling for a school leaving age of sixteen and provision of secondary and technical education secured by maintenance grants.[28] More consistent support came from the Workers' Educational Association. Formed in 1903 to promote education among the working class, the W.E.A. soon included among its supporters the young historian Richard Tawney and an Anglican bishop, William Temple, although its links with the organised labour movement before 1914 remained tenuous.

Some observers believed that there remained active working-class hostility to State compulsion in education. 'All the poor want,' wrote the junior Liberal Minister and social analyst Charles Masterman in 1909, was to be 'left alone . . . They don't want compulsory thrift, elevation to remote standards of virtue and comfort, irritation into intellectual or moral progress.'[29] In particular, the cotton operatives of Lancashire opposed the abolition of the half-time system and attempts to raise the school leaving age. The leaders of the cotton unions informed the 1911 Trades Union Congress that they were attempting to reform the views of their members;[30] but even in 1912 Labour Party members from Lancashire made it clear in the Commons that they would be bound to oppose the abolition of the half-time system.[31]

Rather than Liberal humanitarianism or working-class egalitarianism, the main drive for educational change came from within the movement which has been described as the 'campaign for national efficiency'. Spurred on by the industrial challenge from Germany and the disasters in the Boer war, the campaign united apparently diverse political interests. At its heart were the Fabian socialists, Sidney and Beatrice Webb, with their emphasis on a 'national minimum' of education for all and the need for leadership from 'an elite of unassuming experts who would make no claim to superior status'.[32]

The claims of 'national efficiency' found some allies in government. One was the Liberal imperialist R. B. Haldane, Secretary of State for War from 1905 to 1912. Partly educated in Germany, Haldane was influenced by Hegelian idealism. His political philosophy was founded on a view of social integration which would unite the nation through imperialism and maintain the loyalty of the working class by promising them measures of social reform. Education was the social issue on which he laid most emphasis. Much of his early interest was in higher education. During the 1890s he had worked with Sidney Webb to help reform the University of London as a teaching institution.[33] Impressed by German technical institutes, in 1901 Haldane delivered a series of addresses calling attention to the relation between higher education, research in science and technology and industrial growth.[34] He later chaired a Treasury committee which brought about a continuing advisory body on State grants to universities and also promoted the plan which helped found the Imperial College of Science and Technology in 1909. After 1905 much of his attention was focused on army reform, but he remained committed to general educational reform.[35]

The other major figure in government actively promoting education was Robert Morant, permanent secretary of the Board of Education from 1903 to 1911. Morant had helped frame and develop much of the administrative structure of the 1902 Act. Educated at Winchester and Oxford, he had spent a considerable period as adviser to the king of Siam – an experience which appears to have strengthened his mandarin-like attitudes. His outlook was elitist, calling for the 'guidance of brains' in a democracy.[36] Suspicious of the efforts to develop popular 'higher' elementary schools as a form of secondary education during the 1890s, after 1902 he set out to ensure that the main aim of elementary education should be to create 'followership' within the masses.[37]

Unique among government departments for having retained patronage as the means of appointment for its top posts, the Board under Morant became an initiator of policy. Those whom Morant gathered around him were of similar educational background and social outlook. The main qualification for appointment to the Board was not teaching experience but rather the traditional education of the upper classes. As Gillian Sutherland has written, most recruits before 1914 were 'amiable young gentlemen who had achieved a reasonable degree of academic success'.[38] Of the ninety-three central office staff, one-third had been educated at the three public schools, Winchester, Eton and Marlborough; fifty-five had been to Oxford and twenty-three to Cambridge. Of the nineteen assistant secretaries and related top posts, six came from Winchester, Morant's old school.[39] At university the overwhelming majority had studied classics rather more modern subjects. Of the fifty-five Oxford graduates thirty-six had taken 'greats', while only three had studied science. Of the twenty-three Cambridge graduates, twelve had studied classics and only two were scientists.[40]

The background in classics had implications for the development of early twentieth-century education. The 1904 secondary school regulations of the Board stipulated that, in those schools receiving State grants, instruction should be academic and general and not vocational and specialist in nature. The curriculum was to include English language and literature, geography and history, one language – and where there was a second language it should be Latin – mathematics and science. It has been suggested that these regulations did receive general support and did not necessarily count against the interests of science.[41] Nevertheless their overall aim was to re-create in the newly emerging secondary schools a pattern of education similar to that of the English public schools.

The interest of Morant in 'higher education' carried over into attempts to formulate a policy for the universities. In 1910 he established a university branch in the administration at the Board of Education. He also tried to win control of the administration of Treasury grants to the universities but met resistance not only from the universities but from Lloyd George, Chancellor of the Exchequer. In 1911 the administration of the grants did pass to the Board, although responsibility for expenditure still remained with the Treasury.[42]

The most notable changes in policy under Morant after 1904 related to the social welfare aspect of educational services. Following concern over the poor physical state of many army recruits in the Boer war, an Interdepartmental Committee on Physical Deterioration had recommended various measures, including the strengthening of regulations governing the employment of children, the need for physical exercises in the schools, restrictions on exemption from school attendance below the age of fourteen, school medical inspection, school meals, nursery schools and compulsory attendance at continuation classes for school leavers.[43] In 1906, under pressure from the newly elected Labour Party, the Liberal government passed the Education (Provision of Meals) Act allowing local education authorities to provide school meals.[44] A year later Morant himself created a medical branch at the Board, placing in charge George Newman, a doctor whom he had met through Beatrice Webb. The 1907 (Administrative Provisions) Act, passed partly through the efforts of Morant, required local education authorities to establish medical inspection of all elementary school pupils and allowed them to provide treatment.[45]

The concern with social welfare was related to Morant's role in the national efficiency campaign. By 1910 he was responding to the plight of the unemployed school leaver. The Choice of Employment Act of 1910, drawn up under his guidance, allowed local education authorities to create bureaux to advise juveniles on future careers. By 1913 forty-one schemes had been established under the joint auspices of the Boards of Education and Trade.[46] Of more importance, Morant began to show greater interest in curriculum changes and the need for part-time continuation schools. While not disturbing existing regulations for secondary school grants, the Board started to encourage new forms of 'higher' elementary schools, particularly 'central' schools in London which provided instruction in vocational subjects for older pupils preparing for industrial and commercial vocations, and also in London and the north of England 'junior technical schools' designed for former elementary pupils and offering preparation for a trade.[47]

In 1910 Morant entrusted one of his high officials, E. K. Chambers, with the whole task of reformulating technical education. An English scholar who later produced a study of Shakespearean drama, Chambers had earlier carried through the reorganisation of the elementary and secondary branches at the Board. He was now assisted in his new task by Frank Pullinger, chief inspector of the technological branch. One of the few Board officials with a scientific background, Pullinger himself had an interest in expanding and developing the whole scope of further and technical education.[48]

In 1909 Pullinger had produced a report analysing existing weaknesses in further education. The grant regulations failed to define the aims of technical education, while the central authority had only an examining role for science and art, leaving uncovered the vast fields of literary, commercial, technical and domestic instruction. Further, there were no building grants for technical education or aid for research.[49] The overall result was that 'insufficient attention is focussed upon trades and industries and their related educational needs, that individual schools are dealt with while systems of schools are more or less neglected, and that educational considerations as distinguished from grant considerations are kept in the background'.[50]

In the north of England, particularly in Yorkshire, Cheshire and Lancashire, there had grown up after 1902 a system of grouped courses in technical education.[51] This helped to stimulate the expansion of the junior technical schools described above. In 1911 the Board itself issued a circular indicating its intention to revise the grant regulations in technical and further education. In place of the existing examinations in single school subjects, the legacy of the system under the now defunct Department of Science and Art, there was to be a system of course work[52] (thereby somewhat emulating the earlier reform carried through by the secondary school regulations of 1904). This step was to help lay the basis for what Morant, Chambers and Pullinger hoped would eventually be a new, balanced culture for the masses, combining both technical and literary studies. Continuation classes would form an integral part of this plan. According to John Dover Wilson, the Shakespearean scholar who, as a junior inspector in the technological branch of the Board, worked under Frank Pullinger from 1912 to 1920, it was the aim of Morant that the continuation schools 'would ultimately bridge the fatal gap between education and industry, since its pupils would be at factory, workshop or mine for half the working day and for the other half would be learning what their working life meant'.[53]

Prospects for change in this and other areas had to overcome opposition. Interested parties such as local education authorities, teachers and such bodies as the London City and Guilds Institutes believed that the Board was not consulting them enough.[54] Further legislative change was difficult. In 1911 Walter Runciman introduced into Parliament a Bill aimed at abolishing the half-time system (by raising the school leaving age to thirteen) and enabling local education authorities to establish continuation classes up to the age of sixteen (to a maximum of 150 hours a year); where compulsion to attend continuation classes was not enforced, fourteen was to be the normal school leaving age.[55] The measure was later withdrawn. Runciman told J. A. Pease, his ministerial successor, that the Board had been deeply at work for two years on the question of raising the school leaving age and providing for continuation classes. 'There are numerous pitfalls and members from Lancashire implore me to go slow but I am not without hope of making progress some time.'[56] Some at least of his hopes were soon to be realised.

Notes

1 *Hansard*, Commons, 4th ser.; CVII, 8 May 1902, col. 1102.

2 From 1902 to 1911 the number of children in voluntary schools declined from 3,790,000 to 2,826,000 while those in council schools rose from 2,888,000 to 3,980,000. W. H. G. Armytage, *Four Hundred Years of English Education*, Cambridge, 1964, p. 202.

3 Report of the Board of Education, 1911–12, *Parlt. Pprs*. 1913, XX, Cd 6707, p. 68. By 1918, of the 119 schools on the Headmasters' Conference, thirty-three were receiving grants from the Board and a further thirty-eight were inspected. Report of the Committee Appointed to Enquire into the Position of Natural Science in the educational system of Great Britain, *Parlt. Pprs*. 1918, XI, Cd 9036, p. 8.

4 Education 1900–1950, Report of the Ministry of Education, 1950, *Parlt. Pprs*. 1950–51, XI, Cmd 8244, p. 85.

5 *Ibid.*

6 Donna F. Thompson, *Professional Solidarity among the Teachers of England*, New York, 1927, p. 23. For analysis of the problems of status faced by teachers as part of the lower middle class see Geoffrey Crossick (ed.), *The Lower Middle Class in Britain*, London, 1977, pp. 31–2.

7 Report of the Board of Education, 1912–13, *Parlt. Pprs*. 1914, XXV, Cd 7341, p. 149. In contrast, the number of clerks increased by over 37 per cent in the decade 1901–10. Gerald Bernbaum, *Social Change and the Schools, 1918–1940*, London, 1971, p. 4.

8 P.R.O., Ed 24/270; The Need for an Increase of Exchequer Grants in Aid of Education, 12 December 1909.

9 There were fifty-seven separate grants; seventeen for elementary and forty for higher education. Grants were calculated on ten different bases and were related to seven different periods. L. A. Selby-Bigge, *The Board of Education*, London, 1927, p. 85.

10 Michael Sadler (ed.), *Continuation Schools in England and Elsewhere*, Manchester, 1907, introduction.

11 W. H. Beveridge, *Unemployment. A Problem of Industry*, London, 1909, pp. 125–6.

12 *Report of the Royal Commission on the Poor Laws and Relief of Distress*, 1909, VI, ii, p. 168.

13 *Ibid.*, VI, i, p. 418.

14 *Ibid.*, VI, iii, p. 618.

15 *Ibid.*, VI, iii, p. 653.

16 J. Scobell Armstrong, *The Trade Continuation Schools of Germany*,

London, 1913, and E. H. Best and C. K. Ogden, *The Problem of the Continuation School and its Successful Solution in Germany*, London, 1914. See also Dr Georg Kerchensteiner, *The Schools and the Nation*, translated by C. K. Ogden, London, 1914.

17 Report of the Board of Education, 1911–12, Cd 6707, p. 13.

18 *Trades Union Congress Report*, 1913, p. 325. See also Flan Campbell, *Eleven Plus and all That*, London, 1956, pp. 44–5.

19 Report of the Consultative Committee of the Board of Education on Examinations in Secondary Schools, *Parlt. Pprs.* 1911, XVI, Cd 6004, pp. 67 and 108.

20 G. S. M. Ellis, *The Poor Student and the University*, London, 1925, p. 10.

21 *Hansard*, Lords, 4th. ser.; CLXXVII, 24 July 1907, col. 1527.

22 Sir Norman Lockyer, 'The influence of brain power on history', in *Education and National Progress*, London, 1906, p. 187.

23 *Classics in Education*, London, 1921, p. 50.

24 D. S. L. Cardwell, *The Organisation of Science in England*, London, 1957, p. 155.

25 M. Argles, *South Kensington to Robbins*, London, 1964, p. 74. Michael Sanderson, however, has pointed out that Cambridge physics and Sheffield and Birmingham metallurgy were still superior to anything in Germany. Michael Sanderson, *The Universities and British Industry, 1850–1970*, London, 1972, p. 23.

26 *The Times*, 11 December 1909, p. 8. See also the address of Lloyd George to a large Nonconformist gathering. *The Times*, 17 December 1909, p. 6.

27 J. A. Hobson, *The Crisis of Liberalism*, London, 1909, p. 94.

28 Olive Banks, *Parity and Prestige in English Secondary Education*, London, 1955, p. 117.

29 C. F. G. Masterman, *The Condition of England*, London, 1970, p. 92. See also Henry Pelling, 'The working classes and the origin of the welfare State' in *Popular Politics and Society*, London, 1968, pp. 4–5.

30 *Trades Union Congress Report*, 1911, pp. 160–3. See also Edmund and Ruth Frow, *A Survey of the Half Time System in Education*, Manchester, 1970.

31 *Hansard*, Commons, 5th ser.; XXXVII, 26 April 1912, cols 1417–25.

32 Beatrice Webb, *Our Partnership*, London, 1948, p. 48. See also G. R. Searle, *The Quest for National Efficiency. A Study in British Politics and Political Thought, 1899–1914*, Berkeley and Los Angeles, 1971.

33 Eric Ashby and Mary Anderson, *Portrait of Haldane at Work on Education*, London, 1974, pp. 32–40.

34 R. B. Haldane, *Education and Empire*, London, 1902.

35 Ashby and Anderson, *Portrait of Haldane*, pp. 41–85.

36 B. M. Allen, *Sir Robert Morant*, London, 1934, p. 126.

37 E. J. R. Eaglesham, *The Foundations of Twentieth Century Education in England*, London, 1967, pp. 51–4.

38 Gillian Sutherland, 'Administrators in education after 1870. Patronage, professionalism and expertise', in Gillian Sutherland (ed.), *Studies in*

Nineteenth Century Government, London, 1972, p. 269.

39 P.R.O., Ed 23/216 (D); 'A Patronage Office', p. 34–5.

40 *Ibid.*, pp. 38–9.

41 E. W. Jenkins, *From Armstrong to Nuffield*, Studies in Twentieth Century Science Education in England and Wales, London, 1979, pp. 1–28.

42 Ashby and Anderson, *Portrait of Haldane*, pp. 93–101. See also Eric Eaglesham, 'The centenary of Sir Robert Morant', *British Journal of Educational Studies*, XII, 1963, pp. 14–5.

43 Report of the Inter-departmental Committee on Physical Deterioration, *Parlt. Pprs.* 1904, XXXII, Cd 2175, pp. 90–2.

44 Brian Simon, *Education and the Labour Movement*, London, 1965, pp. 278–85.

45 Bentley Gilbert, *The Evolution of National Insurance in Great Britain*, London, 1966, pp. 105–58.

46 *The Government's Record*, London, 1913, p. 67.

47 S. Maclure, *One Hundred Years of London Education, 1870–1970*, London, 1970, pp. 94–5, and Banks, *Parity and Prestige in English Secondary Education*, pp. 105–6.

48 J. Dover Wilson, *Milestones on the Dover Road*, London, 1969, pp. 67–73. See also F. P. Wilson and J. Dover Wilson, *Sir Edmund Kerchever Chambers*, from Proceedings of the British Academy, XLII, London, n.d., and J. Leese, *Personalities and Powers in English Education*, Leeds, 1950, pp. 309–19. According to Stephen Hobhouse, nephew to Beatrice Webb and young official at the Board, there was an office riddle about Madame Tussaud's – 'it has a Chamber of Horrors but our Board has a horror of Chambers', Stephen Hobhouse, *Forty Years and an Epilogue*, London, 1951, p. 87.

49 Library of Department of Education and Science; Memorandum of 7 July 1909; Revision of T. Regulations No. 1, p. 2 in *T. Revision Memoranda.* (This bound volume contains memoranda and minutes of discussion on the reform of technical and further education as carried on at the Board from 1909 to 1914.)

50 *Ibid.*, p. 3.

51 Argles, *South Kensington to Robbins*, p. 64.

52 Board of Education, Circular 776, 20 June 1911.

53 Dover Wilson, *Milestones on the Dover Road*, p. 88. See also Eaglesham, *The Foundations of Twentieth Century English Education*, pp. 68–72.

54 F. E. Foden, *Sir Philip Magnus*, London, 1970, pp. 264–72.

55 Bill No. 229, *Parlt. Pprs.* 1911, I, p. 983.

56 N.C.L., G.P., 49 (b); Runciman to Pease, 3 January 1912.

II

Plans for educational development, 1911–14

In October 1911 Sir Robert Morant was removed from office as permanent secretary of the Board of Education. He had been dismissed mainly as a result of the storm raised by the publication of the 'Holmes circular', a document, drawn up by the chief inspector of elementary education, which criticised the local authority inspectors, most of whom were drawn from the ranks of the elementary teachers. The circular was intended merely for the Board and its own inspectors but a copy reached outside sources, leading to questions in the Commons and providing ammunition for Morant's opponents, of whom there were many, particularly among the teachers.[1]

The shadow of Morant was so great that the period following his removal from office has often been seen as one of quietude.

> The period of Morant's administration from 1902 to 1911 was fully occupied with the work of carrying out the 1902 Act, and it is not surprising that after such a legislative meal a period of digestion was needed. In fact, the next five years, beginning with the Agadir crisis and ending with the Lloyd George coalition, were not marked by any new big educational development.[2]

This view needs to be somewhat revised. Indeed, much of the origin of wartime developments in education must be sought in the years 1911 to 1914.

At the outset it must be admitted that the change in the administrative head of English education seemed to indicate a less controversial approach in the formulation of educational policy. The successor to Morant was Lewis Amherst Selby-Bigge, principal assistant secretary of the Board's elementary branch since 1903.[3] Like Morant, Selby-Bigge had been educated at Winchester and Oxford. In the 1880s he had been a lecturer in philosophy at University College, Oxford. Yet, whereas Morant had been dynamic, Selby-Bigge was cautious and anxious to avoid controversy. In April 1912 he wrote to Pease, the Minister who had now replaced Runciman as President of the Board of Education, outlining what he saw as the proper role for the permanent secretary of the Board:

> The Secretary however always has to keep his eyes open to the 'political' aspects of proposals – not so much their effect on *party* politics as their effect on public opinion, vested interests, the interests of the teaching profession, the susceptibilities of LEA's, the divisions of opinion among educational experts, the rival claims of different branches of the office work for additional Treasury aid and additional staff and all the *general* considerations of policy which it is not the business of any particular Officer to balance against each other.[3]

The new Minister, J. A. Pease, was also a man of caution. A former Liberal chief whip, he seemed to be aware of the need to appease interested parties and establish good relations both between the central authority and local administration and between the central authority and the teaching profession. Pease told a gathering of teachers in March 1912 that he would rely entirely on the staff of the Board of Education, but his 'great ambition' was to bring about administrative reforms and co-ordination in the educational system so that all sections might work harmoniously together and avoid misunderstandings.[4]

The departure of Morant thus seemed to inaugurate a new era in the central administration of English education. Professor Armytage has described the period from 1911 to 1944 as one of 'change through consultation', whereby the focus of 'liberal consultation' became the Consultative Committee of the Board of Education.[5] (The committee was composed of representatives of universities and other educational bodies). Some indication of this new approach was seen in the publication of two reports designed to influence the development of the secondary schools. The first, issued in 1911, called for an end to the multiplicity of external examinations. Instead, the committee proposed a general leaving certificate at sixteen, a second examination for those intending to enter the universities and the higher levels of the professions and commerce, and the creation of a central Examination Council which would be representative of the various examining bodies.[6] The second, issued in 1912, urged the introduction of more practical subjects into the curriculum.[7] As will be shown, both reports were to have a significant impact on Board policy.

Structure of the pre-1914 Board of Education
(not including clerical and lower grades)

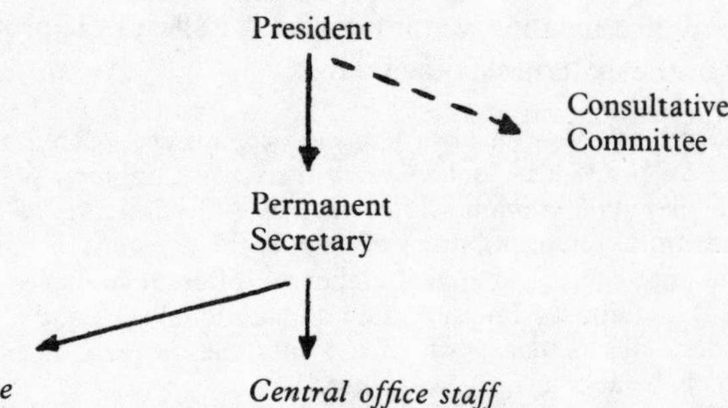

Inspectorate

A chief inspector controlling the respective areas: elementary, secondary and technological education.

Central office staff

A principal assistant secretary controlling the respective branches of elementary, secondary, technological and university education. A chief medical officer in charge of the medical branch. A pattern of organisation in the elementary, secondary and technological branches as below:

Principal assistant secretary

↓

Three divisions, corresponding to divisions created in the inspectorate. Each division under an assistant secretary.

↓

Senior examiners

↓

Junior examiners

Despite the new approach to the problems of administration, the break with past policy was not decisive. As Dover Wilson has pointed out, 'Selby-Bigge, though an official of far less force of character, had agreed with his [Morant's] ideas and was prepared to develop them on lines he might have approved.'[8] Early in 1912 Selby-Bigge himself told Pease that the major task before the Board was the reform of technical and further education, upon which E. K. Chambers had been working since 1909. However, he would not move until he was sure of what was to be done, particularly since he believed that Chambers was 'constitutionally incapable of realising how his methods will strike the ordinary man or the ordinary L.E.A. or of estimating the opposition they will give him'.[9]

If the Board retained its aim of improving technical and further education, then the Nonconformists remembered Asquith's 1910 election pledge to press for a new settlement of the religious question. One historian has seen the failure of the 1906 education Bill as marking the decline of political Nonconformity.[10] Another has stated that after 1908 'the Liberal Government made no major effort to meet the needs of the Nonconformists'.[11] Such views are misleading. Nonconformity did not hold the same political weight in the Liberal Party after 1906 as before, but its influence remained strong. With a virtual deadlock between the two major parties, the Liberals were dependent not only upon Labour, but also upon the Irish nationalists. To maintain the support of the latter group, the government introduced the 1911 Home Rule Bill that was to occupy so much of the time of Parliament over the next three years. Commitment to Home Rule having been one condition of support from the Irish nationalists, this led to blackmail from sectarian interests within the Liberal Party itself.

On 24 October 1911, the day after Pease was appointed President of the Board of Education, the Baptist leader John Clifford wrote to the new Minister requesting that the government carry out its promise to rectify Nonconformist grievances by introducing an education Bill in the next session of Parliament. Clifford claimed that such action was necessary in the interests of the Liberal Party, for 'many of our friends feel that they cannot work enthusiastically for Home Rule in Ireland unless they can be sure of being free from Rome Rule in English education'.[12] Three weeks later G. Hay Morgan, the secretary of the parliamentary committee of Nonconformists, also pointed out to Pease, himself a Nonconformist, the need to take together the Home

Rule Bill and a further attempt to remove Nonconformist grievances. Such strategy was necessary, Morgan claimed, because home-rulers believed that Home Rule might be prejudiced at by-elections unless the government dealt with education at the same time. Similarly the Nonconformists feared that Irish members, once sure of Home Rule, would refrain from voting to remove the religious grievances in England.[13]

General Nonconformist dissatisfaction came at the March 1912 meeting of the Free Church Council, the body representing united Nonconformist opinion. The secretary of the council read out a letter from Prime Minister Asquith indicating the government's intention to introduce, in the next parliamentary session, an education Bill that might 'prove satisfactory' to the Nonconformists. The council unanimously passed a resolution, proposed by John Clifford, calling on the government to give this question immediate priority.[14]

This Nonconformist concern was now to provide the initial pressure to a new direction in educational policy. To carry out Asquith's pledge, in late 1912 Pease presented to Cabinet two memoranda setting out the policy and main features of an education Bill for 1913. Pease argued that any direct attack on the dual system in elementary education would be impossible: a view which he believed most Nonconformist members of Parliament also accepted. The Irish Roman Catholics, upon whose support the government had to rely, would certainly not accept any measure which would destroy Roman Catholic schools or prohibit their creation. They would also insist upon their teachers being Roman Catholics and their schools being maintained out of public funds.[15] Thus Pease suggested a short Bill with three main aims. First, to amend the 1902 Act to secure the maximum public control over denominational schools and thus abolish religious tests for teachers in its most objectionable form. Secondly, to facilitate the establishment of new council schools and thereby deal with the single-school areas' grievance. Thirdly, to establish a new system of grants and hence secure support for the Bill from the local education authorities.[16]

The Cabinet considered these proposals on 5 December 1912 and decided to set up a committee which included the Lord President of the Council, Crewe, the Chancellor of the Exchequer, Lloyd George, Pease and Runciman, the former President of the Board of Education. Other members co-opted included Selby-Bigge, the permanent secretary of the Scottish Education Department, Sir John Struthers, the chairman of the Consultative Committee of the Board of Education, Arthur Acland and A. E. Hutton, who was chairman of the Northern Counties Education League, a body which supported the building of new council schools rather than direct take-over of existing denominational institutions. The chairman of the committee was to be Haldane, now Lord Chancellor.[17]

It has been implied that Haldane, long anxious for a 'large policy' in education, had been responsible for the establishment of the committee. 'This time he did stimulate support from his colleagues. Early in December 1913, it was agreed that Haldane should become chairman of a hybrid committee of ministers, officials, and educational experts, to work out a comprehensive scheme of reform.'[18] This view ignores the pressure of the Nonconformists and the initiative of Pease in bringing the matter before the Cabinet. Once the committee was established, however, Haldane soon influenced its deliberations. The time was opportune. His appointment as Lord Chancellor in the summer of 1912 had released him from departmental duties. For over four years he had also been chairman of a Royal Commission set up to consider the government of the University of London.[19] The report was published in early 1913, allowing more opportunity to consider general government policy.

Political circumstances favoured such a course. By 1912 the first phase of Liberal social reform was over. The school meals Act, the provision for the medical inspection of children, the old age pensions Act and, most important of all, the principle of insurance for health and unemployment were all on the statute book. There were now pressures to move into other areas of social and economic policy. Lloyd George, with whom the cause of Liberal social policy was now closely identified, was planning a great campaign for land reform.[20] The future direction of government policy was open and Haldane now sought to direct it.

On 6 December 1912, a day after the Cabinet established the committee on educational policy, Selby-Bigge wrote to Pease that he had had a 'lovely' conversation with Haldane. Haldane had told Selby-Bigge that he had undertaken lengthy discussions with the Chancellor of the Exchequer, Lloyd George, who, Haldane claimed, was very reluctant to provide any sums for an educational scheme unless it had an educational background which could 'strike the imagination' and be 'fairly represented as a step towards the establishment of a national system of education regardless of denominational squabbles'.

Haldane, however, admitted that no government member would touch an education Bill unless it satisfied the demands of the Nonconformists. Therefore the problem was to 'apply any new money in such a way that it might appear to be available and intended for the mitigation of denominational grievances, while it was really intended for the more fruitful purpose of stimulating the provision of good education'. In response Selby-Bigge had pointed out that this was a 'pretty intractable problem' and the 'double game' would be very difficult. Selby-Bigge had suggested that the best way would be to start with the idea of remedying grievances and then get as much educational advantage out of the Bill as possible. Thus Haldane starting from one end and Pease from the other might find a good deal of common ground. The measure could be concentrated on administrative reforms to meet Nonconformist grievances, but the reforms would be steps forward, as they would give local education authorities greater control over education. The proposed new grant system would encourage higher elementary and central schools. Further, there would be an attempt to overcome the difficulties arising out of the 1902 administrative arrangements whereby a distinction had been drawn between Part II and Part III local education authorities. Haldane himself, Selby-Bigge informed Pease, also wanted the proposed Bill to include provision for improving the relations between the Board of Education and the universities. Finally, Selby-Bigge had urged that the Cabinet committee decide on a line of advance to frame a Bill to tackle the Nonconformist grievances, and then proceed to the other spadework.[21]

Two weeks after this conversation the Cabinet committee itself met. At the outset the committee decided that, whatever the 'ultimate scope' of the education Bill, the 'immediate occasion' was to be the denominational grievance Asquith had pledged to remove, and the best way to carry out this aim was to amend the Act of 1902 in order to facilitate and stimulate the provision of local education authority schools. The committee believed that parents should have the right to petition a local education authority for a council school, and that the State should provide extra finance for such a programme.[22]

The dissenting view again came from Haldane. He told the committee that the government would raise money only for a much larger scheme of education.[23] This view he repeated at another meeting with Selby-Bigge, where he suggested that there should now be a tinkering Bill to rectify denominational grievances and embody such non-controversial measures as the abolition of the provision in the 1902 Act restricting county authorities to the expenditure of a 2*d* rate on higher education, as well as provide for the consolidation of existing grants as a step towards a scheme for educational development involving expenditure of £4 million to £5 million. Haldane wished to see a provision for the registration and inspection of all schools, and some foreshadowing of the examination reform as proposed by the Consultative Committee in 1911. There would be a need also to create larger administrative areas as a condition of establishing a national system of education. Finally Haldane urged the Board to push on with its tinkering Bill, for although he doubted whether the government would be able to proceed with the measures (because of probable opposition from the Lords), he also believed that some administrative reforms might be preserved out of the wreck.[24]

Whilst urging Selby-Bigge to work behind the scenes, Haldane himself now took a more definite step to commit the government to action. On 9 January 1913 he wrote to Pease informing that he had spoken to the Prime Minister about 'our plans'. Haldane continued:

> He is keen, & thought it would be a good thing if I said something at Manchester tomorrow night about the decision of the Liberal Govt. to take up, in succession to Old Age Pensions & Insurance, a great Education policy as a foremost item in its policy for the future.[25]

Acting upon this apparent commitment from Asquith, Haldane spoke to the Manchester Reform Club on 10 January 1913, inaugurating what he hoped would be a major campaign for educational reform. The speech was important in two respects. First, Haldane suggested that the government had already decided that education would be the 'next and most urgent of the great social problems we have to take up'.[26] Secondly, he outlined an actual programme of reform. Much of the substance reflected his conversations with Selby-Bigge. Arguing that equality of educational opportunity would stabilise democracy and break down class barriers, he proposed that any national system would need co-ordination so as to create 'one entire whole'.[27] There would have to be opportunities for the able to reach university and, for the rest, advanced work in elementary or continuation schools. It might also be necessary to create larger administrative areas through the establishment of provincial councils and to take general action to improve the secondary schools. Finally, the teachers needed greater aid and support. On the question of religious grievances, he stressed that if education was put first the nation could take this issue in its stride.[28]

Peter Rowland has suggested that Haldane's aim at Manchester was to divert attention from Lloyd George's more radical proposals for land reform.[29] This is to ignore Haldane's positive and long-standing commitment to what he himself regarded an important field of social policy. On the other hand, there does seem some doubt regarding his own assertion that the government had decided upon education as the next and most important area of social policy. After talking to Lloyd George, who was very angry that his own campaign for land reform might now be obscured, C. P. Scott noted that the Chancellor of the Exchequer

> was very severe on Haldane who he said had indeed consulted himself and Pease and the Prime Minister, but had spoken quite vaguely to each, representing to each in turn that he had fully consulted the other two and had their sanction for his proposals thus obtaining an easy assent from the third, whereas in fact not one of the three had more than the vaguest and most perfunctory explanation and the Cabinet had of course not been consulted at all. The Prime Minister had merely cautioned him not to be precise – an injunction which the Prime Minister sarcastically added he had amply observed. Interminable verbiage was George's description of the speech, and he added something more scathing about 'a barrel of tallow', a picturesque description of Haldane's physical peculiarities – which when set fire to could indeed produce 'any amount of smoke but not flame – no sort of illumination'.[30]

Lloyd George made it clear that, whatever Haldane's understanding of the government's views on education, he himself regarded the religious question as the most important issue. At the meeting of the Cabinet committee on education on 13 January 1913 he urged a direct approach to the single-school grievance in order to satisfy the Nonconformists and redeem the government's pledge.[31] However, Haldane's ploy had worked in part. Committed to action by his speech, the government programme for the new parliamentary session foreshadowed proposals for a 'national system of education'.[32]

Preparation for such a programme had begun even before the Manchester speech. By early January 1913 the Board had produced memoranda setting out lines of educational development. The major paper, entitled 'Notes on the Main Lines and Conditions of Organising Education on a National Basis', was signed by Selby-Bigge, although it reflected the points of discussion raised earlier with Haldane and drew upon other views, particularly those of H. F. Heath, in charge of the university branch at the Board, and W. N. Bruce, head of the secondary branch.[33] As an outline reflecting a Board view on the need for change it is worth noting in some detail.

The memorandum attempted to set down the 'constituents of a policy, gradually developing a national system of education': objectives that would take years to realise, and would depend on increased State finance and a change of attitude at the local level. As an initial step, the memorandum argued, the State should have the right to require 'a sufficient supply of educational institutions of all grades and of educational facilities properly related to each other and to the occupations of the people and to preparation for the duties of citizenship'.[34] Simultaneously the powers of the Board of Education should be strengthened in regard to other government departments and examining and professional bodies. It might be necessary also to establish a larger unit of local administration by providing for provincial councils to aid the co-operation between local education authorities, organise teacher training, assist the creation of a national examination system, control endowments and co-operate with the universities.[35] In general, the Board believed that a national system would mean organisation from above in order to co-ordinate the various parts of English education and provide for a national plan. This implied a closer relation between the State and the universities, including Oxford and Cambridge, and insistence on their greater accessibility to the best and most promising pupils of the whole system. For the full development of university work, building grants were required and also State scholarships for postgraduate industrial research. In regard to teacher training, the Board urged that a proportion of free places in training colleges for elementary teacher trainees might be required, while it would be necessary to overcome problems of training secondary teachers and establish the whole system on a wider geographical and financial basis.

In secondary education the Board wanted a register of all schools, including boarding and private institutions. The memorandum suggested that present State secondary schools were defective because most pupils left early and teachers were poorly paid and ill-qualified. On the other hand, some work done in the secondary schools would be better undertaken in other types of institutions such as advanced elementary or junior technical schools. In the areas of technological and technical education the Board recommended the growth of central colleges to assist both full and part-time instruction. In elementary education, despite changes since 1902, there was still a need for nursery schools and new forms of higher elementary schools such as the London central schools experiment. Even after all due provision was made for full-time education there remained the problem of providing for the vast majority of adolescents. A universal leaving age beyond fourteen was likely to be unattainable for many years, and all Western European countries were aiming at compulsory continuation schools. The difficulties of such a system were enormous and its introduction could be affected only on a local option basis, but voluntary part-time day work should be encouraged, and evening continuation classes improved. Finally the Board stressed that finance was at present the State's only lever to bring about change. The existing grant system should be increased and improved. Extra finance was also related to the question of the single-school areas. Rather than specifically compelling local education authorities to build in single-school areas, increased grants should stimulate the general provision of new council schools.[36]

Drawn up in the main without much outside consultation, the memorandum reflected ideas and a strategy which seemed appropriate to the new central administration in English education. The Board was not setting out to restructure English education, as Morant had in 1902. The emphasis was on co-operation and co-ordination to create a 'national system'. Anxious to allay any suspicions that the plans of the government involved an attempt to reorganise from above, Pease told an audience of teachers in March 1912:

> They were not going to revolutionise the present system or impose a new bureaucratic product on the country. What they did intend to do was stimulate the existing product, and induce all agencies to co-operate, and to fill up the various gaps in our educational system and expand the share of educational effort.[37]

After the committee had discussed a number of detailed Board proposals, Pease presented to the Cabinet another Board memorandum on a draft education Bill. He pointed out in this paper that the committee had acted on the assumption, first, that it would not be possible to enact the measure until the next session of Parliament and, secondly, that they should try to produce a Bill which would not only pass the Commons but would prove acceptable to the Lords. Thus:

> We contemplated a large measure of educational development which would

> interest the country, enlist the support of Local Education Authorities, both from an administrative point of view, and a financial point of view, and would present our treatment of the denominational difficulty as an integral part of educational reform.[38]

The paper on the draft Bill posed three questions for the Cabinet. First, should an attempt be made during the existing parliamentary session to pass a Bill to satisfy the Nonconformists (in accord with the wishes of Lloyd George, who wished to withdraw State and rate aid from denominational schools in single-school areas and allow such schools the alternatives of leasing or selling their premises to the local education authority or closing down) or should proposals be merely introduced with a view to enacting them in the next session of Parliament; secondly, was the Cabinet prepared to provide for a national scheme of education which would provide for an initial sum of £2 million in 1914–15, rising to £7 million in all by 1920; thirdly, would the Cabinet be prepared to accept a compulsory attendance age of fourteen and face the unpopularity of the proposal in Lancashire and portions of the West Riding of Yorkshire?[39]

The draft education Bill itself contained five major sections. It was a detailed effort to give effect to many of the general aims set out in the earlier Board memorandum. First, the Bill imposed new duties on local education authorities, which were to be required to make provisions for education higher than elementary and to both systematise their provision by co-ordinating it with other local authorities and extend elementary education to as late an age as practicable. The Bill therefore recognised the right to free education a long way beyond the 'three Rs', and abolished such limitations as were imposed on that right by the Cockerton judgement of 1900 (which had confined elementary education to being only the instruction of children). It also deliberately created a debatable land between Part II and Part III authorities by recognising that advanced elementary or 'intermediate' education might be given under either part or by either authority. The draft Bill raised the compulsory school leaving age to fourteen (a local education authority could grant exemption to children aged thirteen to fourteen if they attended continuation classes) and empowered authorities to raise the school leaving age to fifteen and require attendance at continuation classes until sixteen. The 'systematisation' of education would be assisted by changes in the grant system to make each authority, and not individual schools, the unit for which grants would be paid. Secondly, the Bill attempted to rearrange the powers of local education authorities. The general organisational framework of the 1902 Act would remain, but the Board would be able to convert an urban area into an autonomous Part II authority responsible for all purposes of education, deprive a Part III authority of its powers over elementary education, and authorise an urban authority to raise more than a penny rate for higher education in cases where it was not prejudicial to the organisation of education by the county. There would also be provision for advisory provincial councils which would aid the training of teachers, control exams and co-ordinate the secondary schools with technical institutes and universities. Thirdly, the Bill provided for the Board of Education to have power to define the meaning of 'education', and thus to allow local education authorities to extend the provision of physical and medical education, and in particular to establish nursery schools for children under the age of five. The general aim here was to ensure the medical fitness of the child and so link up the school medical service with the public health system. Fourthly, the Bill provided for the Board to have powers of inspection and registration of all private educational institutions in order to obtain information and require some compliance with a minimum of efficiency and healthiness. Finally, the Bill sought to tackle the grievances of the Nonconformists, not along the lines of the measures of 1906–08 but by stimulating the establishment of new council schools throughout the country so that more and more children would be educated in schools under popular control. The Bill also allowed for further powers over secular instruction in voluntary schools and prohibited religious tests for head teachers in single-school areas.[40]

The Bill attracted little comment from the Ministry. The Cabinet merely decided that in the current session of Parliament there should be a Bill increasing grants to local education authorities, but that the more comprehensive reforms should be brought forward in 1914.[41] As a result, on 22 July 1913, Pease presented to Parliament a Bill to give further aid of £150,000 to local education authorities.[42] At the same time he outlined the basis of the more comprehensive Bill to be introduced in 1914. Stressing the relation between educational development and national efficiency, he argued that the problems of denominationalism, class feelings and lack of administrative co-ordination must be tackled if Britain were to create a national education system and engage in 'healthy rivalry' with European powers.

> A well organised system of education is the most powerful means we have of developing the social life of the nation. If the present generation can attend to the physical condition of their children, enlarge their occupations, widen their sympathies, increase their intellectual freedom, and encourage them to use their gifts in mutual service, it will have done the best thing it can do to ensure the peace, the prosperity and the independence of our country.[43]

Thus the 'principal object' of legislation would be the organisation of intermediate education (meaning all forms of education between the elementary schools and the universities) by extending the powers, duties and resources of local education authorities.[44] Pease argued that since 1902 there had been many advances in elementary education, particularly the development of medical services and physical education, while there had also been an expansion of university education.[45] But there were 'a large number of broken arches' between the elementary schools and the universities and a general administrative confusion in organising education.[46] He went on to give a general outline of the proposed education Bill as presented to Cabinet. Finally, turning to the religious question, he admitted the need to 'redress that balance between the parties' so heavily weighted on one side by the Act of 1902. The government would therefore deal with the single-school grievance.[47]

Such, then, was the educational programme and the government commitment that had emerged from the pressure of the Nonconformists, the initiative of Haldane, the contributions of Selby-Bigge, Pease and the Board of Education, and the deliberations of the Cabinet committee. What had originally been a move by the government to satisfy the Nonconformists had become a commitment to a much wider programme of reform. Such activity now helped to stimulate other groups.

In July 1913, at the same time that Pease presented the outline of the proposed education Bill to Parliament, the Unionist Social Reform Committee appointed its own sub-committee on education. Its report was published early in 1914. In the introduction F. E. Smith stressed the importance of post-primary education, particularly continuation classes. 'The Conservative party, and indeed, I think, all schools of educational reformers, are of the opinion that a boy, within certain limits, ought to be brought up in the way which will make him the most efficient in the sphere of work he will occupy as man.'[48] The report of the committee also had as one of its major themes the need to improve the efficiency of the administrative machinery, and to end the waste of bad health, misdirected teaching and child labour. However, the notion of selectivity remained strong. Secondary education should be provided only for those of 'exceptional merit', while for the ordinary child part-time continuation classes would suffice.[49] On the other hand it was urged that the scholarship system would have to be developed to encourage the able, for 'The nation cannot afford to lose their brains.'[50]

In 1912 the Labour Party conference had appointed a special committee to report on educational reform. The report published in 1914 went little beyond the programme that Pease had announced to Parliament. The report recommended the immediate raising of the school age to fourteen, the growth of advanced elementary education, and, concurrent with the provision of more free places and the establishment of maintenance grants in the secondary schools, the founding of continuation schools for the vast majority of adolescents. In regard to university education, the committee called for more popular control and a Royal Commission to enquire into the administration and finances at Oxford and Cambridge.[51] Judged in these terms, there does seem justification for the claim of Rodney Barker that 'the last year of peace found Labour, whatever its framework of political ethics, firmly tied to the policy of gradual improvement of existing services, and gradual implementation of Liberal reforms'.[52] Within Parliament, Labour also failed to show much interest in even the reform programme of the government. According to Selby-Bigge, Philip Snowden had told Lloyd George that while his party would support the proposals of the government, most Labour members were 'rather wooden on the subject'.[53]

In contrast the National Union of Teachers, the other major representative of organised popular opinion on education, had a more active interest in the proposed education Bill. At its annual conference in 1913 the N.U.T. had passed an educational programme which included support for the abolition of the half-time system, a school leaving age of fourteen, compulsory continuation classes for fourteen-eighteen-year-olds, juvenile employment bureaux, the principle of free secondary education, maintenance allowances and State university scholarships.[54] The N.U.T. also drew up a standard salary scale to be applied generally throughout the country.[55] The prospect of another education Bill and the reopening of the religious question raised other issues. In early January 1914 J. H. Yoxall, president of the N.U.T., wrote to Pease insisting that the proposed Bill exclude any 'contracting out' for denominational schools or the right of denominational entry into council schools. Yoxall pointed out that the N.U.T. wished to see the Bill include abolition of half-time, grants paid to areas rather than individual schools, special financial aid for rural schools, class sizes of forty, a school leaving age of fourteen allowing local education authorities to raise it to fifteen, and ample provision of secondary education for those fit to receive it. Other points included support for the development of playing fields and school meals, the co-opting of elementary teachers to local education committees, extension of medical treatment, and powers for local education authorities to require attendance at continuation classes.[56]

Despite some differences in emphasis, there was little in the programmes of the Unionist Reform Committee, the Labour Party or the N.U.T. that conflicted with the terms of the education Bill announced by Pease. A far more radical critique of English education arose from within the ranks of the Liberal Party itself. During 1913 a Liberal Education Group was formed under the chairmanship of J. H. Whitehouse. A Scottish member, first elected in 1910, he had been secretary of Toynbee Hall, the university settlement in east London. Upon his election in 1910 he had initiated a debate in the Commons calling for the establishment of continuation classes as a matter of national urgency.[57]

In late 1913, under the auspices of the Liberal Education Group, Whitehouse published his own statement, *A National System of Education*. This suggested that the real weakness in English education was the lack of any relationship between primary and later education. What should be done was to 'cease to regard as normal or necessary the education of different social classes under different systems, unrelated save for an occasional scholarship ladder', and instead institute the elementary school as a preparatory stage to the age of twelve, with secondary education then provided for all classes.[58]

For the vast majority of Liberal members such appeals had little impact. The religious question was still of prime interest. In particular, the Nonconformist Parliamentary Committee was concerned about the proceedings of the Cabinet committee and particularly disturbed by Whitehouse's Liberal Education Group, who, it was argued, should have no say in Nonconformist grievances.[59]

Haldane and others tried hard to overcome sectarian interests. In April 1913 three members of the Cabinet committee, Haldane, Pease and Crewe, addressed the Eighty Club, the Liberal imperialist group that Haldane himself had helped to found in the 1880s. All laid stress on the need to develop education so as to widen social opportunities and combat foreign competition.[60] Yet, after presiding over a meeting of forty to fifty Liberals at the club, Charles Trevelyan, Parliamentary Secretary at the Board of Education, concluded that there would be no support for educational reform unless the Nonconformists felt the proposed Bill was worth a fight.[61] Even the National Education Association, the representative of radical Nonconformist opinion, showed equal concern for religious grievances as for reform. The N.E.A. report for 1914 called for not only more school places and the securing of State grants by statute, but also public control of all public money, so that local education authorities should have powers to appoint and dismiss all teachers and organise and co-ordinate all the schools maintained from public funds.[62]

Nonconformists also found support in the Cabinet. Although Lloyd George had come to be regarded as the apostle of reform in the Liberal Ministry, he was still well aware of the need to retain the support of Nonconformity, upon which he had drawn for much of his earlier political career. Susceptible to the influence of those who held some sway over political opinion, he was a particular intimate of both the newspaper proprietor Sir George Riddell and Robertson Nicoll, the editor of the Nonconformist *British Weekly*.

After talking to Robertson Nicoll, Riddell informed Lloyd George that the leading Nonconformists were bitter about the government's handling of their educational grievances. They were particularly upset by reports of a proposal of Pease to bus Dissenting children in single-school areas to the nearest council school. Nicoll himself had compared such a plan to 'conveying little lepers in Tumbrils'.[63] At Riddell's invitation, Lloyd George met Nicoll, who made it clear that the leading Dissenters were so upset that they intended to issue a manifesto condemning government policy; they specifically 'distrusted' Haldane handling educational policy. On the suggestion of Lloyd George, Nicoll agreed to write to Asquith stating the case of the Nonconformists.[64]

As a result, and after a conference with other Nonconformist representatives, Robertson Nicoll wrote to Asquith that there was 'widespread dissatisfaction' that might be easily 'kindled into revolt'. The Nonconformists did not expect the government to present to the Lords any measure that would meet the fate of the previous Bills of

1906–08. On the other hand, it should take up the problem of the single-school grievance and either buy or rent existing Church schools or build new council ones. A 'bold' measure would revive the Nonconformist enthusiasm so necessary for the government, whereas 'mere tinkering' would do nothing but 'dishearten, alienate and estrange'.[65]

The confrontation over this issue came to a head at a Cabinet meeting in December 1913. Pease had produced a further memorandum on the clauses in the proposed education Bill affecting the denominational schools. It was now suggested that, in single-school areas, the local education authority would appoint and dismiss all teachers, while no teacher would be allowed to give denominational instruction. Outside single-school areas there would be provision to place a council school within the reach of every child whose parents desired it, and to facilitate the erection of new council schools. An alternative plan of purchasing denominational schools in single-school areas was rejected as not only involving the difficult question of compensation but also raising the possibility of a future Conservative government establishing a system of universal facilities for denominational instruction in all elementary schools.[66] Despite these objections to a direct attempt to settle the single-school grievance, the pressure of the Nonconformists was too great for the Cabinet to ignore. After talking to Lloyd George, Riddell recorded:

> The Dissenters have been appeased in regard to the education question. The Prime Minister has determined to abandon any attempt at compromise in regard to single-school areas. He is going straight ahead to carry out the Dissenters' policy. It seems that Haldane and Pease were beaten to a frazzle in the cabinet.[67]

The issue was not quite that cut-and-dried. At first Pease attempted to find a solution. The draft education Bill he submitted to the Cabinet in May 1914 still contained not only proposals for educational development, as had been decided upon by the Cabinet committee in 1913, but also provision to tackle the single-school grievance through such means as local education authority appointment of all teachers in single-school areas, rather than a direct attempt to purchase or rent denominational schools.[68] It was only after a conference on 30 June 1914 between the Cabinet representatives, Lloyd George, Pease and the Attorney General, Sir John Simon, and the leading spokesmen for Nonconformity, that the government's position became clear. It was thence decided to frame a Bill containing the principle that from 1 September 1914 all grant-aided elementary schools in single-school areas would be council schools.[69]

The need to satisfy the Nonconformists helped to hold up any more immediate progress on the general proposals for educational development as contained in the draft education Bill. Some signs of other change resided elsewhere. In February 1914 the Liberal Richard Denman, who was associated with a social reform group known as the Committee on Wage-earning Children, had introduced a private members' Bill that included certain clauses similar to those in the proposed government Bill, particularly in its provisions for raising the school leaving age to at least thirteen and allowing local education authorities to introduce continuation classes to the age of sixteen.[70] The measure also allowed for local education authorities to regulate the employment of children – a proposal being considered by the Board of Education itself.[71] The Bill received the sanction of the Board and was backed by members from all parties, including the Conservative Samuel Hoare, who had been the chairman of the education sub-committee of the Unionist Social Reform Committee, and Goldstone, the Labour educationalist and representative of the N.U.T.[72] Despite opposition from the Lancashire Labour members, who still opposed the abolition of half-time, and also the representatives of industrial and agricultural interests,[73] the Bill survived both second reading and committee stage in the Commons. Its further progress was delayed by other concerns, particularly the deteriorating international situation during July 1914. The outbreak of war put an end to what hope there was of its passage.[74]

The government did at least now commit itself to an increase in grants for education. In December 1913 Pease reminded his Cabinet colleagues of the demands of the local education authorities for financial relief and of the promises of the government to overcome the problem. He saw the situation as desperate and believed public pressure could not be long resisted.[75] Three months later the Kempe committee on local taxation issued its long-awaited final report. The committee recommended that, instead of the existing complicated State grant system for elementary education, there should be a single percentage grant related to both the needs of an area and its ability to raise finance through the rates.[76] This proposal involved a greatly increased financial commitment from the State. In late April, Haldane told Selby-Bigge that he had talked to Asquith and thought that the

Prime Minister would also agree to a general increase in the educational budget, involving £500,000 for 1914–15, £3,500,000 for 1915–16, and £4,250,000 for 1916–17.[77] As a result of both these developments, in May 1914 Lloyd George informed the Commons that the government would implement the recommendations of the Kempe committee, increasing elementary education grants by £2,750,000 in 1915–16. Also in 1914–15 there was to be an immediate £500,000 both for school meals and for extra grants for poor and populous areas. A further £1 million would be provided for new educational services in 1915–16.[78] According to a later Commons statement by Pease, this latter sum would provide for the development of secondary education, technical education, teacher training, universities, health work and special schools.[79] In line with the increased grants for secondary education, the Board of Education also issued a circular indicating its intention of reforming the secondary school exam system in accord with the report of the Consultative Committee in 1911.[80]

Here, then, despite the delay of the education Bill, was at least some promise for educational development. Viewed from mid-1914, the future seemed to hold out some hope for those interested in education.

Commenting on the last years of peace, H. V Emy has written:

> Enough evidence is available to suggest that far from the Liberal concern for social policies slackening after 1914 through their pre-occupation with Home Rule and Welsh Disestablishment, the opposite may have been the case i.e. the traditional issues were simply debts which had to be honoured while social and industrial reform remained the major theme.[81]

The planning for educational change in 1911–14 supports that judgement, with certain qualifications. In the first place, there was the question of the priority of the reforms themselves. Education was in competition for attention with other areas, particularly the land campaign of Lloyd George. The 'debts' of the past also intruded into the moves towards reform. Significantly, it was the pressure of the Nonconformists that not only provided the initial impetus but also remained the major factor in Cabinet decisions on the question of education. Looking back on the period just prior to the war, Haldane wrote in his autobiography:

> Over the reform of Education the Liberals were pretty bad. Crewe and I were anxious to begin the work of founding a national system but from the first it was clear that the Nonconformist insistence of getting rid of the Church school system blocked the way. The Church Schools were indeed

> very deficient. But they could not be abolished at once, and although we were working through first-rate administrators, such as Sir Robert Morant, we could not get the public or Parliament to agree on any plan or reform. The truth was that, despite the vast importance of the question, too few people were keenly interested in Education to afford us the requisite breeze for our sails. I sat on Cabinet Committees on the subject, and interviewed earnest men like Dr. Clifford. But their prejudices I could not break down single-handed, and I had no keen allies. In this region I failed.[82]

Accepting that this view attributes too much to Crewe and not enough to Pease and the Board, it is still a fairly accurate assessment of the pre-war situation. For the vast majority of the Liberal Party, and for most of the Cabinet, the sectarian grievances of the Nonconformists had to be faced before other proposals for educational development could be accepted. In contrast, Haldane and the Board officials, and to some degree Pease, were united on the national importance of education. As Haldane told his mother in May 1914, reforms in the areas of education and health were 'badly needed, for if our generation does not make an effort the nation will fall behind all others'.[83] Related to national needs was at least some recognition of social pressures. Neither Haldane nor the Board of Education were reformers in the sense of wishing to reshape society or even the educational system. They were prepared to accept that some extension of educational opportunities was not only a necessary condition of national progress but also a means of responding slowly to the changing nature of society, and thus offsetting more radical claims for restructuring social and economic relations.

Yet, overall, there was little recognition of the claims of education. In 1914 there still appeared to be many other issues of far greater importance. Problems in Ireland, labour unrest, the claims of the suffragettes, international tension – these were the main concerns of the politicians in 1913–14. As Sir Philip Magnus, the Conservative member of Parliament and propagandist for technical education, was to claim in 1915, 'The Commons is, I am sorry to say the last place in which any speaker urging educational reform receives a sympathetic hearing. There are other matters, he is told, of far greater interest and importance.'[84]

Such lack of interest was merely a reflection of the general situation in the country at large. Even Haldane, trying valiantly to raise public interest, admitted in 1913, 'Things are difficult just now and it is not easy to raise enthusiasm about Education or anything else.'[85] Perhaps the best comment came from *The Times Educational Supplement*, itself a firm supporter of educational reform. In an editorial devoted to Haldane's public campaign, it noted:

> Education, it must be admitted, is not popular in England. Expenditure upon it is productive expenditure from a national point of view, yet to demand any serious addition to local rates might quench altogether the slight flicker of interest in education that is beginning to show itself. When the public understands its own educational needs it will establish an efficient educational system.[86]

The test of that view had yet to come.

Notes

1 For a fuller account of the storm raised over the 'Holmes circular' see Allen, *Sir Robert Morant*, pp. 254–62. Morant did not disappear from public life. He became secretary to the newly formed National Health Insurance Commission. In his new post he helped support those working for a Ministry of Health.

2 Education 1900–1950, Report of the Ministry of Education 1950, Cmd 8244, p. 6.

3 N.C.L., G.P., 49(b); Selby-Bigge to Pease, 14 April 1912. Morant had been so much the embodiment of English educational administration that the leader of a north country deputation who was hard of hearing could even refer to the new secretary as 'Sir Amorous Selby-Bigge'. Lowndes, *The Silent Social Revolution*, p. 111.

4 *The Times*, 23 March 1912, p. 8.

5 Armytage, *Four Hundred Years of English Education*, p. 204.

6 Report of the Consultative Committee of the Board of Education on Examinations in Secondary Schools, *Parlt. Pprs.* 1911, XVI, Cd 6004, pp. 106–7, 126–37, and 141.

7 Report of the Consultative Committee of the Board of Education on Practical Work in Secondary Schools. *Parlt. Pprs.* 1913, XX, Cd 6894, *passim*.

8 Dover Wilson, *Milestones on the Dover Road*, pp. 87–8.

9 N.C.L., G.P., 49(b); Selby-Bigge to Pease, 14 April 1912. For his part E. K. Chambers seems to have had his own view of Selby-Bigge. In 1958 Dover Wilson told Eric Eaglesham that among some of Chambers's papers was the following poem written on Selby-Bigge's retirement: 'Adieu, farewell, goodbye, dear Selby B, The faithful servant of the N.U.T., For years of blameless assiduity, Fitly created Bart, and K.C.B.' N.L.S., Dover Wilson papers, MS. 14315, f. 126; Dover Wilson to Eric Eaglesham, 27 October 1958.

10 Noel Richards, 'The Education Bill of 1906 and the decline of political Nonconformity', *Journal of Ecclesiastical History*, XXIII, 1972, pp. 49–63.

11 Benjamin Sacks, *The Religious Issue in the State Schools of England and Wales, 1902–1914*, Alberquerque, N.M., 1961, p. 65.
12 P.R.O., Ed 24/624; J. A. Clifford to Pease, 24 October 1911.
13 *Ibid.*; G. Hay Morgan to Pease, 14 November 1911.
14 *The Times*, 6 March 1912, p. 4.
15 P.R.O., Cab 27/212/117; Memorandum on the Policy and Main Features of an Education Bill for 1913, 24 October 1913. Much of the material on the draft education Bill of 1913–14 discussed in this chapter is also contained in both P.R.O., Ed 24/629, and the Gainford papers (items 72 and 109) at Nuffield College Library.
16 P.R.O., Cab 37/113/31; Proposals for Education Bill, 2 December 1912.
17 A list of members is contained in P.R.O., Ed 24/628.
18 Ashby and Anderson, *Portrait of Haldane*, p. 114. Ashby and Anderson are apparently unaware of the Nonconformist concerns and therefore present a one-sided view of educational developments in 1912–14.
19 *Ibid.*, pp. 102–11.
20 H. V. Emy, 'The land campaign. Lloyd George as a social reformer', in A. J. P. Taylor (ed.), *Lloyd George*, London, 1971, pp. 35–68.
21 P.R.O., Ed 24/628; Selby-Bigge to Pease, 6 December 1912.
22 *Ibid.*; Cabinet Committee, Minutes, 19 December 1912.
23 *Ibid.*
24 *Ibid.*; L. A. Selby-Bigge, Memorandum, 19 December 1912.
25 N.C.L., G.P., 49(c); Haldane to Pease, 9 January 1913.
26 Viscount Haldane, *National Education*, Speech delivered by Viscount Haldane, Manchester, 10 January 1913, London, 1913, p. 9.
27 *Ibid.*, p. 12.
28 *Ibid.*, pp. 13–4.
29 Peter Rowland, *The Last Liberal Governments. Unfinished Business, 1911–1914*, London, 1971, pp. 192–3.
30 Diary entry, 16 January 1913, in Trevor Wilson (ed.), *The Political Diaries of C. P. Scott, 1911–1926*, London, 1970, pp. 68–9. This description bears a somewhat similar tone and analogy to Asquith's later comment on Haldane trying to explain Einstein's theory of relativity, 'Gradually, a cloud descended until, at last, even the candles lost their lighting power in the complexities of his explanations.' Dudley Sommer, *Haldane of Cloan*, London, 1960, p. 381.
31 P.R.O., Ed 24/628; Notes of Cabinet Committee Meeting, 13 January 1913.
32 Hansard, Commons, 5th ser; L, 10 March 1913, col. 11.
33 N.C.L., G.P., 72/1 Education Bill – Cabinet Committee, Notes on the Main Lines and Conditions of a Policy of Organising Education on a National Basis, 10 January 1913. An unsigned version appears in a bound volume contained in the Gainford papers, 109 (A), and also in P.R.O., Ed 24/629. Both these latter sources contain, in two bound volumes, further memoranda prepared by the Board over the period 1913–14 as preparation for the proposed education Bill. There are also other memoranda in Ed 24/625. For the related memoranda see N.C.L., G.P., 72/1; H. F. Heath, Suggestions for a National System of

Education, Bill Memo. No. 6(1), 2 January 1913; W. N. Bruce, Suggestions for a System of more extended Inspection and Registration of Secondary Schools, Bill Memo No. 6(2), December 1912; W. N. Bruce, Suggestions for more complete organisation of Secondary Education in England, 28 December 1912; W. N. Bruce, Free Secondary Schools, Bill Memo. No. 6(4), 2 January 1913. These memoranda are also contained in N.C.L. G.P., 109 (A) and Ed 24/629. There is another memorandum on proposals for educational reform, dated 6 January 1913, signed by Frank Pullinger, and contained in P.R.O., Ed 24/625.

34 *Ibid.*, p. 1.

35 *Ibid.*, pp. 2–4.

36 *Ibid.*, pp. 4–12.

37 *The Times*, 17 March 1913, p. 40.

38 P.R.O., Cab 37/115/32; Education Bill – 1913, 23 May 1913, p. 1. For details of the Board proposals on which the draft Bill was based see P.R.O., Ed 24/629 and N.C.L., G.P.. 72/1.

39 *Ibid.*, pp. 2–3.

40 *Ibid.*, pp. 3–8.

41 Rowland, *The Last Liberal Governments. Unfinished Business, 1911–1914*, p. 211.

42 *Hansard*, Commons, 5th ser., IV, 22 July 1913, cols. 1907–09.

43 *Ibid.*, col. 1910.

44 *Ibid.*, col. 1911.

45 *Ibid.*, cols., 1913–16.

46 *Ibid.*, col. 1916.

47 *Ibid.*, col. 1923.

48 *The Schools and Social Reform*, London, 1914, p. xii.

49 *Ibid.*, p. 31.

50 *Ibid.*, p. 33.

51 *Labour Party Report*, 1914, pp. 40–2.

52 Rodney Barker, *Education and Politics*, Oxford, 1972, p. 25.

53 P.R.O., Ed 24/628; Selby Bigge to Pease, 24 February 1913.

54 *National Union of Teachers Annual Report*, 1913, pp. xcvii–iii.

55 The scales were:

	Men	*Women*
Provincial head teachers	£150 (minimum)	£120 (minimum)
Provincial class teachers	£ 90 (minimum) £200 (maximum)	£ 80 (minimum) – £160 (maximum)
Metropolitan class teachers	£100 (minimum) £250 (maximum)	£ 90 (minimum) – £200 (maximum)

National Union of Teachers Annual Report, 1913, p. xcv.

56 J. H. Yoxall to Pease, 3 January 1914, in *National Union of Teachers Annual Report*, 1914, p. cxxii.

57 *Hansard*, Commons, 5th ser., XVI, 20 April 1910, col. 2200.

58 J. H. Whitehouse, *A National System of Education*, Cambridge, 1913,

pp. 1–3. For a critical analysis of this scheme see *The Times Educational Supplement*, 2 December 1913, p. 201.

59 *The Times*, 25 April 1913, p. 8.

60 *National Education*, Speeches delivered by Marquess of Crewe, Viscount Haldane and J. A. Pease, at the Eighty Club, 4 April 1913, London, 1913.

61 P.R.O., Ed 24/631; Minute by Charles Trevelyan, 31 July 1913.

62 National Education Association, *First Principles and other Matters*, 17 February 1914. (Pamphlet located in Dr Williams Library, 207.8.)

63 Diary entry, 12 November 1913, in Lord Riddell, *More Pages from my Diary, 1908–1914*, London, 1934, pp. 184–5.

64 Diary entry, 15 November 1913; *ibid.*, pp. 185–6.

65 P.R.O., Ed 24/630; Robertson Nicoll to Asquith, 17 November 1913.

66 P.R.O., Ed 24/629; Education Bill, 1914, 16 December 1913.

67 Diary entry, 14 December 1914 in Riddell, *More Pages from my Diary, 1908–1914*, p. 190.

68 P.R.O., Ed 24/629; Education Bill, 1914, 5 May 1914.

69 P.R.O., Cab 37/120/79; Memorandum on the Education, Single School Areas, Bill, 30 June 1914.

70 *Hansard*, Commons, 5th ser., LVIII, 20 February 1914, cols. 1295–304. See also R. Denman, *Political Sketches*, Carlisle, 1948, pp. 82–3.

71 P.R.O., Ed 24/629; Board of Education, Regulation of the Employment of Children and Young Persons, 18 November 1913. See also *ibid.*, Education Bill, 1914.

72 *Hansard*, Commons, 5th ser., LVIII, 20 February 1914, cols. 1326–30, 1304–9, and 1339–46.

73 *Ibid.*, cols. 1310–19, 1319–23 and 1357–60.

74 *Ibid.*, col. 1366; *Hansard*, Commons, LXII, 19 June 1914, cols. 1434–514; and Denman, *Political Sketches*, pp. 84–5.

75 P.R.O., Ed 24/629; Note on the Necessity for Increased Financial Aid to Local Education Authorities in 1914–1915, 13 December 1913.

76 The formula suggested was £1 16*s* per child in average attendance plus two-fifths of the total expenditure of a local authority less the product of a 7*d* in the £ rate. To prevent parsimonious authorities benefiting, no authority was to receive more than two-thirds of its expenditure so long as the amount falling on the rates was less than 1*s* in the £. Final Report of the Departmental Committee on Local Taxation. *Parlt. Pprs.* 1914, XL, Cd 7315, p. 33.

77 P.R.O., Ed 24/628; Haldane to Selby-Bigge, 20 April 1914. Haldane also wanted to offer £20,000 a year to Oxford and Cambridge for science.

78 *Hansard*, Commons, 5th Ser., LXII, 4 May 1914, cols. 79–82.

79 *Ibid.*, 28 July 1914, cols. 1782–3.

80 Board of Education, Circular 849, July 1914.

81 H. V. Emy, *Liberals, Radicals and Social Politics, 1890–1914*, Cambridge, 1973, pp. 274–5.

82 R. B. Haldane, *An Autobiography*, London 1929, pp. 218–19.

83 N.L.S., H.P., 5991, fol. 151; Haldane to his mother, 1 May 1914.

84 F. E. Foden, *Philip Magnus*, London, 1970, p. 235.
85 N.L.S. H.P., 5989, fol. 118; Haldane to his mother, 2 April 1913.
86 *The Times Educational Supplement*, 1 April 1913, p. 61.

III

War and its impact

War affected English education in a number of different but related ways. In the long months from August 1914 to December 1916 three phases can be perceived. The initial shock of war led to a brief flirtation with proposals for educational change. Such concern was followed by a run-down in normal educational services as teachers, students and children were caught up in the war effort. The third and final phase might be regarded as a culmination of the first two. With the war still not over after two and a half years of fighting, and with continuing damage to the social and economic fabric of the nation, many had come to believe by December 1916 that post-war reconstruction must mean a new order of things.

Hints of what was to come were there from the outset. Calling upon teachers to maintain the educational system, J. A. Pease stressed that, as war involved destruction of both capital and skilled manpower, 'when the conflict is over we shall not only have to reconstruct the material fabric of civilisation but reaffirm its spiritual purpose'.[1] Even as he wrote, however, more material concerns were being highlighted. In particular, war revealed dramatically deficiencies in English scientific and technical education.

Specific focus came over industrial supply.

> The outbreak of war found us unable to produce at home essential materials and articles. We were making less than a couple of dozen kinds of optical glass out of over a hundred made by our enemies. We could hardly make a tithe of the various dyestuffs needed for our textile industries with an output worth over £250,000,000 a year. We were dependent on Germany for magnetoes, even for the smelted tungsten used by our great steel-makers and for the zinc smelted from the ores which our own Empire produced.[2]

The most important of these deficiencies was the artificial dye industry, which produced a number of crucial by-products, including drugs, explosives and lethal gas.[3] To overcome the problem here, the government founded the British Dyestuffs Company with a capital of £3 million.[4] Yet the question was one not merely of organisation and finance, but of the relation between applied science and industrial processes. This raised afresh the issue of scientific and technical training.

Against this background, Pease met his officials in December 1914 to discuss the programme of the Board of Education in view of the war, particularly in relation to the fate of the pre-war plans for educational development and the former government promises of extra educational grants in the budget of 1915–16. They were joined by Christopher Addison, who had replaced Charles Trevelyan as Parliamentary Secretary (Trevelyan having resigned in protest at Britain entering the war). A medical doctor, social reformer and supporter of Lloyd George, Addison realised the opportunity the circumstances of war had presented. Despite the reluctance of Selby-Bigge – apparently prepared to 'fold his hands, resign himself to fate and surrender without a struggle all the advances promised by the budget'[5] – both Pease and Addison agreed that the war had underlined the claims for much more and not less higher technical and secondary education. Pease was prepared to give Addison full authority to work out a comprehensive programme.[6]

Addison soon sought support from within the Cabinet. Early in January 1915 he met Lloyd George and two others – E. S. Montagu, Financial Secretary at the Treasury, and Lord Reading, both of whom had helped Lloyd George overcome the financial crisis of the early days of war.[7] It was indicative of the impact of war that Lloyd George, the man who a few months previously had been prepared to block educational reform in the interests of Nonconformity, now told Addison that he was impressed by the handicap the country was under owing to lack of scientific training,[8] and was apparently even speaking of the development of university and secondary education as the first plank of his post-war reconstruction platform.[9] Although he gave no promise of financial aid, he was prepared to listen to Addison, who urged that the government take advantage of the circumstances to establish for the future a sound system that would command confidence by its success. The aim would be not to open the elementary school question, and so become 'embroiled with the wranglings of parsons', but rather to develop the secondary schools through bursaries and grants and provide scholarships to the universities and technical institutes.[10]

While the war brought Addison and even Lloyd George as new allies to the cause of education, equally significant was the influence of those who had been involved in the pre-war plans. Addison later wrote that his original submission to Lloyd George was timid and governed by financial considerations. It was Haldane who at a meeting on 29 January 1915 urged him to be bold and prepare a large scheme.[11] Similarly, the committee Addison chaired to decide a programme to present to the Cabinet was itself composed of Board officials who had played a leading role in pre-war discussions and plans. Prominent among them was E. K. Chambers, who had been working on the development of technical education since 1909.[12] Not unexpectedly, the Board's pre-war views played a significant part in the scheme for expanding scientific and technical education.

By May 1915 Addison and the Board officials had prepared a Cabinet memorandum, which related education, research and industrial growth as all part of the national interest. The paper argued that the war had shown up not only deficiencies in British industry but also Germany's superior skill and energy in scientific research. The present crisis was seen as a prelude to post-war trade rivalry and a 'grave danger, possibly amounting to economic ruin, which will be incurred by our industries if they have to face fresh and embittered competition without enlarged scientific resources'. In the United Kingdom there were only 1,500 chemists, whereas four German dye firms alone employed 1,000. If Britain was to maintain its industrial position it would have to develop scientific, technological and commercial education and research.[13]

The problem was identified as twofold: to make best use of existing scientific talent through postgraduate research, and to ensure a fuller supply in the future by providing 'an educational ladder by which the ablest boys in the country may climb through the secondary schools or technical colleges to the Universities.' The proposed scheme thus concentrated on the upper reaches of the educational system. It consisted of two parts. The first half provided for extra finance for technical training, secondary schools, scholarships for universities, and extra university grants. It thereby demonstrated a continuity with the pre-war plans of the Board of Education, particularly in its proposals for the growth of advanced courses in the secondary schools, examination reform and the development of technical education, all of which had been included as part of the new grants for education that Lloyd George had originally promised would take effect from 1915–16. What was new was the proposal to establish a national scholarship scheme to the universities, although even this had been discussed by Selby-Bigge in the January 1913 Cabinet paper.[14]

The second half of the scheme was concerned not so much with educational development as with the relation between the State and industrial and scientific research. Its proposals and recommendations were a new departure related more directly to the deficiencies revealed by the war. It provided for the expansion of industrial research through postgraduate scholarships and fellowships in science, technology, commerce and economics, aid to research projects and finance to encourage the formation of specialised departments. As a further development, the administration of this half of the scheme was to be initially under a council responsible to the Board of Education.[15] Considered together, both halves of the scheme were intended as a consistent attempt to develop scientific and technical education in the near future. However, as a whole scheme it simply failed to develop.

Political circumstances provide part of the explanation. On 30 April 1915 Lloyd George gave his unreserved approval to the proposals.[16] At a meeting on 3 May between Lloyd George, Montagu, Pease and Asquith it was agreed to sanction grants.[17] Ten days later, Pease announced provision for the formation of an Advisory Council on Industrial Research, so giving partial effect to the second half of the scheme.[18] The council was later transformed into the Department of Scientific and Industrial Research, which gave some financial support to industrial research projects while the war lasted.[19] Pease also told the Commons that in order to retain its industrial position after the war Britain would have to keep its ablest pupils longer at school.[20] But on 24 May, Asquith reshuffled his Cabinet to form the first coalition government of the war. Those who had shown an interest in the educational proposals were either no longer in positions of power or had other tasks before them.

Both Pease and Haldane were dismissed from office. The former returned in 1916 in the junior position of Postmaster General, later being elevated to the upper House as Baron Gainford. The latter was confined to the political wilderness as a sacrifice to those who criticised his alleged pro-German leanings. The new President of the Board of Education was Arthur Henderson, who had been brought into the

Cabinet as the representative of Labour and was therefore to be mainly concerned with negotiating wartime arrangements with the trade unions.[21] Rather than providing extra grants for education, the new government supported measures of wartime economy. A report of the Retrenchment Committee (appointed by the Treasury) even urged the exclusion of all under-fives from school and the implementation of administrative reforms by the Board.[22]

The result was that not only did the first half of the Board's schemes involving the development of secondary, technical and university education progress no further but educational policy in general was no longer prominent in the high offices of power. On the other hand, the point had been made. War had helped to demonstrate the importance of education. Even though the impetus had been temporarily lost, the significance for future policy remained.

If the early months of war had emphasised scientific and technical education, the period following was one of marked neglect of educational questions. In general the education system suffered throughout 1915 and early 1916. Arthur Marwick's suggestion that war is destructive is enlightening for this period at least.

One issue here was the fate of those whose studies the Board had just sought to encourage. The army showed little concern for the talents of students drawn into its ranks. In November 1915 Arthur Acland, the president of the Imperial College of Science and Technology, pointed out to Selby-Bigge that his institution would be hindered in its research work unless it retained sufficient students and staff. Imperial College normally had 1,000 students and 280 staff, and it now asked to retain ninety-four students and seventy-seven staff of military age.[23] After the introduction of conscription in early 1916 the Board of Education eventually reached an agreement with the War Office whereby it was established that up to 500 scientific and technical students throughout England could be exempted from the call-up if they enlisted in the Army Reserve.[24] By early 1917, however, only ninety-two students had been reserved under this arrangement.[25]

Casualty rates among young officers highlighted the problem. The Headmasters' Conference in December 1915 expressed grave concern at the employment of exceptional mathematical and scientific students in line battalions. Francis of Blundell's said that the present war would be child's play compared to the 'industrial Armageddon' which Britain might have to face with the loss of the brains of half a generation.[26]

Conscription also affected teachers. The Board of Education had pointed out in December 1914 that the Army Council regarded teaching as a public service and therefore grounds for not enlisting.[27] After the introduction of conscription the army did agree that certain teachers and education officials might be reserved from service.[28] But by mid-1916 over 20,000 male elementary teachers, approximately half the pre-war numbers, had joined up.[29] Similarly, the number of male students in the teacher training colleges declined from 4,242 in 1913–14 to only 700 in the autumn of 1916.[30]

The problem of staffing was temporarily overcome by the further employment of women. By July 1916 approximately 17,500 were replacing male teachers on military service.[31] Problems remained. Increasingly during the war women found other opportunities in commerce and the civil service as inflation undermined the already low salaries of many teachers. (By July 1916 the price of food had risen 60 per cent since the outbreak of war and the general price index 45–50 per cent).[32] Conscription, inflation and new areas of employment – all emphasised the problem of teacher supply evident before the war. Despite a temporary rise from 6,368 in 1914 to 7,047 in 1915, attributed to extra assistance granted to secondary school bursars from 1913 and to increases in rural pupil teachers, the numbers of new intending teachers again declined to 6,291 in 1916.[33]

Of most concern, however, was the effect of the war on children. As early as August 1914 both Asquith and Pease had sanctioned the temporary employment of schoolchildren in agriculture provided no other labour was available at harvest and sowing time.[34] Within six months a deputation from the Workers' War Emergency Committee, the organisation set up to protect the interests of trade unions during the war, was protesting to the Board of Education that the whole law of school attendance had collapsed and children were being employed full-time in agriculture.[35] Despite further regulations the problem continued. Unwilling to employ women or to increase adult wages, farmers found children a cheap source of labour. By 1916 15,753 children, mostly boys, had been exempted from school to become agricultural labourers. Of this number, 546 were aged between eleven and twelve.[36]

Agricultural employment was only part of the picture. A post-war report indicated that in one town as many as 40 per cent of elementary school boys were working out of school hours by October 1917.[37] The numbers of children exempted from school continued to increase. Overall, those leaving elementary schools between the ages of twelve and fourteen rose from 196,943 in 1915 to 240,556 by 1917.[38]

Even more significant was the alteration in the pattern of employment among school leavers. There was a rapid shift away from peacetime industries into those associated with the war. By October 1916 approximately 205,000 boys and girls were employed in the manufacture of munitions.[39] At Woolwich Arsenal alone there were 10,000 boys in early 1916, of whom 3,000 were aged fourteen to sixteen, working shifts as long as twelve hours.[40]

In February 1916 Sir James Yoxall of the N.U.T. reflected generally on what he saw as the damage wrought by eighteen months of hostilities. Up to 200,000 children aged eleven to thirteen had been let out of school, and 250,000 juveniles aged twelve to fourteen were working for wages either full or half-time. Many evening schools and even secondary schools had been closed. The nation was spending £5 million a day on the war and yet at the same time neglecting the educational system that could help to double its future earning capacity. The universities were three-quarters empty, and the supply of teacher trainees was being drained off by conscription and the attractions of more lucrative employment in other areas. At a time when there was flourishing wealth and prosperity, particularly in areas where demands for a lower school rate had been loudest, education, the encouragement of which was the only way in which the national debt could be liquidated, was being neglected and despised by municipal authorities.[41]

By early 1916 a number of groups were pressing the Board to take action to repair the damage. Many stressed the need for long-term planning. W. B. Walker, a member of a T.U.C. delegation, argued that the war had already shown that 'if England was to maintain her legitimate place among the nations and fulfill her Imperial duties' she would have to 'create equality of educational opportunity'.[42] Equally significant were the views of the National Education Association, which wanted a full inquiry into the whole area of juvenile employment. As a member of the N.E.A. delegation, R. A. Bray, chairman of the London Juvenile Advisory Committee, claimed that the war had brought about three related evils. First, in London, there had been a decline from the pre-war figure of 33 per cent of ex-elementary boys entering skilled trades to a mere 13 per cent. Secondly, the long shifts of work in such places as Woolwich Arsenal were injurious to health, while munition wages of up to £3 per week had a harmful moral effect on adolescents. On the other hand agriculturists were exploiting children for pay as low as 4*s* a week. Finally, if present trends continued it would be difficult to obtain boys for apprenticeship after the war.[43]

As President of the Board of Education, Arthur Henderson was put in an obviously embarassing situation by these requests. He knew little of educational matters, but as a labour leader he could be expected to have some sympathy for the plight of working-class children. On the other hand he was now a member of Asquith's coalition government, which was exerting a firm hand over domestic expenditure. His initial response was to tell his trade union colleagues that there could be no 'controversial' legislation or extra grants while war lasted: '. . . as far as education is generally concerned we must wait for happier times than we are living in at the moment'.[44]

Nevertheless, after further submissions from R. A. Bray,[45] he did agree to set up a departmental committee of inquiry under Herbert Lewis, the successor to Addison as Parliamentary Secretary of the Board of Education. The terms of reference were to be an investigation of the related problems of children abnormally employed, juveniles who could not find a suitable job after the war, and those who required special training. The purpose of the committee was therefore related to the immediate crisis, but Henderson informed Lewis that, while he did not want the committee to investigate the whole educational system, it should feel free to make recommendations about other areas related to juvenile employment and lay down a policy that would not only meet a post-war emergency but establish a basis for the future development of education.[46]

The formation of the Lewis committee recognised the impact of war on children and young persons. By taking some action the government helped revive plans for post-war reconstruction that had been lost when the Asquith coalition was formed. At the same time, by early 1916 a whole debate on education had opened up.

As in late 1914, the claims of national efficiency and particularly the importance of scientific and technical education were at the forefront. Despite the fate of the Addison programme, the demands of war brought change. The establishment of a Ministry of Munitions meant a new role for the universities and technical colleges. As early as August 1915 the Universities of Liverpool, Leeds, Manchester and

Birmingham were involved in testing high explosives, while research was later carried out at Oxford, Cambridge and the Scottish universities of St Andrews and Glasgow. Other institutions were involved in the manufacture of drugs and glass and the development of aircraft.[47] Universities also trained skilled men. By 1918 King's College, London, alone was to have 1,000–2,000 munition workers and 400 aeronautical instructors in training.[48] As *The Times* said in February 1916, 'when the story of the scientific side of the War comes to be told in full, it will be found that our modern Universities have woven themselves into the very fabric of our national life in a way which had never been open to them before'.[49]

Addison, moved from his post at the Board of Education, established a small section in the Ministry of Munitions to make use of the existing technical schools. By the end of 1916, when the supply position had become serious, training had been organised in three areas: technical schools, instructional centres, and places attached to particular works. By the end of the war over 50,000 workers had graduated through the training establishments. There were also 100 technical schools with first-class plant and a dozen large instructional centres each capable of handling 400–500 learners.[50]

Such reorganisation to meet immediate needs posed questions of future policy. The importance of scientific and technical education was reflected in a report of the Board's own Consultative Committee. Appointed in March 1913 to consider the question of scholarships for higher education, the committee had suspended its sittings on the outbreak of hostilities but had later been requested by the Board to meet again in 1915 to report on scientific and technical education in particular. In May 1916 the committee issued an interim report, which perceived a changed mood in the nation:

> A new national spirit has been aroused in our people by the war; if we are to recover and improve our position at the end of the war that national spirit must be maintained; for unless every man and woman comes to know and feel that industry, agriculture, commerce, shipping and credit, are national concerns, and that education is a potent means for the promotion of these objects among others, we shall fail in the great effort of national recuperation. In plainer words, our great firms will not make money, wages will fall, and wage-earners will be put out of work.[51]

The committee saw two main principles behind the idea of a scholarship system: providing useful servants of the community and creating equal opportunity. In general accord with the earlier Addison scheme, it proposed the development of advanced work in the secondary schools, the maintenance of grants, and scientific and technical scholarships to the universities and higher technical institutes.[52]

Increasing attention to scientific and technical education threw into question the whole educational background of those directing Britain's military effort. After a year and a half of struggle victory was no closer. The political and military leaders seemed incompetent and lacking in ideas. There were glaring examples of past neglect. The indecisive confrontation between the Grand Fleet and the German High Seas Fleet off Jutland revealed not only the weakness of British naval design, particularly in armour, but also the failure of tactics, leadership and training at the secondary level of command, if not directly at the top. As Corelli Barnett has claimed, Jutland 'was in fact a defeat for British technology. More than that, as with the French at Crécy and Sedan, a social system had been exposed by battle as decadent and uncreative.'[53]

Even before, some contemporaries believed they had an answer to the failings of the civilian and military leadership. On 2 February 1916 a letter appeared in *The Times* under the prominent heading 'The Neglect of Science'. Signed by thirty-six leading scientists, it argued that Britain's failures in the war were due directly and indirectly to 'a lack of knowledge on the part of our legislators and administrative officials of what is called "science" or "physical science".' What was wanted was a new attitude at the top. 'Our success now, and in the difficult time of reorganisation after the War, depends largely on the possession by our leaders and administrators of scientific method and the scientific habit of mind.' After fifty years the bias towards classics still remained: entrance examinations to the civil service and the army should be reformed so that men of science would find a place in administration and government.[54]

The letter brought about the formation of a powerful scientists' lobby known as the 'Neglect of Science Committee'. A memorial to Asquith requested a Royal Commission to consider the whole area of education, and particularly the position of science, pointing out the need for trained men in industry, commerce and research.[55] An overcrowded meeting at the Linnean Society on 3 May 1916, chaired by Lord Rayleigh and addressed by such speakers as Lord Montagu and H. G. Wells, passed resolutions calling not only for natural science to be an integral part of the public schools' curriculum and of university internal examinations but also the reform of civil service and army entrance exams.[56]

The aims of the committee focused on redirecting the education of the elite. Yet its formation emphasised the importance of all educational issues. By revealing national concerns the war had strengthened the representives of collectivist opinion. As early as October 1915 *The Times Educational Supplement*, supporter of imperial efficiency, had urged a revolution in education to create a 'universal system of secondary education' for all adolescents from the age of eleven to fifteen.[57]

This vision of educational reconstruction was part of a much wider plan for the State to organise and develop all its resources. In July and August 1916 a series of articles appeared in *The Times* calling for:

> grouping and amalgamating our industries, our food supply and our labour organisations, upon a national scale; that only upon these lines can we hope to make our industries scientific and progressive, defeat foreign competition, secure a satisfactory home food supply, and come to an understanding and keep peace with labour, and the alternative to such a reconstruction boldly and openly planned and carried through is decadence and Imperial disintegration.[58]

In the application of science to industry education was crucially important, for 'Our economic and political organisation will be futile if it does not carry with it an organisation of our present aimless and confused national intelligence'.[59] This meant not only technical training, 'necessary for the economic efficiency of the citizen', but also 'an education of the national mind in general ideas'.[60]

The Times's social imperialist views were partly mirrored in the Fabian *New Statesman*, which supported educational reconstruction both on grounds of necessity – 'Large pieces of educational machinery have been knocked to pieces by the War and others have suddenly been revealed as decrepit' – and because a unique opportunity presented itself with the universities emptied and other parts of the educational system in limbo.[61] What was needed, it argued, was a Minister to survey and co-ordinate the educational system in the light of national needs. There must be an expansion of the secondary schools, and for the mass of adolescents 'a deliberately planned four years of . . . training, physical and technological'. Among the upper classes in turn a new spirit was called for, and greater recognition of the importance of education.[62]

The call for action was not confined to educational groups or those who had supported reform before the war. The response was general throughout society. Fear and uncertainty of the future were predominant. The war now seemed part of a much wider struggle for survival. By the second year even the Board of Trade had been discussing post-war economic measures to counter trade rivalry from Germany.[63] At a gathering of mayors at the Guildhall in January 1916, called by the London Chamber of Commerce and the National Patriotic Association, the main speaker, Sir George Pagnell, said that education was the 'root of all future progress' and technical and commercial training would have to be remodelled if the country were to hold its own. Businessmen would have to insist that education be 'driven home like a wedge' until it reached from the elementary school to the university.[64] In Parliament Sir Phillips Magnus called for an inquiry by a Commons committee to advise on the need for a closer relationship after the war between education and commercial and industrial needs.[65]

Ferment did not necessarily mean agreement on policy. Strong forces of tradition resisted the emphasis on utilitarian ends. On 4 May 1916 a letter appeared in *The Times* signed by such prominent academic and public figures as Viscount Bryce, J. B. Bury, Lord Curzon, H. A. L. Fisher, Gilbert Murray and G. O. Trevelyan. It was intended as a reply to the claims of the Neglect of Science Committee:

> Under the shock and stress of the war, the aims and methods of education have to be considered anew. This reconsideration, in the special conditions of the time, brings with it a risk that we may ignore elements in education vital to the formation and maintenance of national character. A great war, in which material means and special skill are the most obvious factor in deciding the issue, inclines a nation to prize these to the exclusion of forces finally even more important; and if in our reforms we fix our eyes only on material ends, we may foster among ourselves that very spirit against which we are fighting to-day . . . . It is of the utmost importance that our higher education should not become materialistic through too narrow a regard for practical efficiency. Technical knowledge is essential to our industrial prosperity and national safety; but education should be nothing less than a preparation for the whole of life.[66]

Even more significant was the attitude of the government itself, and particularly the Board of Education.

In general terms, by early 1916 the Asquith government had recognised the need to plan for the post-war world not only in education but throughout the social and economic life of the nation.

On 18 March, Asquith established a Reconstruction Committee under his own chairmanship to consider the problems of readjustment.[67] As Paul Johnson has pointed out, however, it was Asquith's policy to work through and not against the existing departments.[68] The demand for an independent inquiry or Royal Commission on education was rejected. The Marquess of Crewe, delegated to handle the pressure for an inquiry, told Arthur Acland, acting on behalf of the Neglect of Science Committee, that the Prime Minister did not like the idea of the Board, which was responsible for scientific as well as other branches of education, being left out of the discussion.[69]

Asquith's attitude left the Board in a strong position to resist public pressure. Significantly, Arthur Henderson as Minister neither knew nor understood much about educational issues. Occupied for most of his time with labour disputes, he found himself in an increasingly embarrassing position. In August he finally persuaded Asquith to transfer him.[70] Consequently much of the decision and policy-making at the Board in mid-1916 rested with the permanent officials, particularly Selby-Bigge. To the Board officials the general agitation seemed meaningless. They had, after all, already spent a good deal of time during the pre-war period and the early months of 1915 preparing plans for educational development. Pease, the Minister who had helped to guide this work, had been removed from office, but the main permanent officials, including Selby-Bigge and E. K. Chambers, were still at their posts.

Replying to a circular from the Reconstruction Committee, they remained wedded to the scheme of 1913–14 with its 'comprehensive and systematic treatment of educational problems', which, though it might be 'modified' by the war, would still be 'practicable' in peacetime. Since the outbreak of war steps had been taken to improve scientific and technical training by the foundation of the Advisory Council on Scientific and Industrial Research, and reports had been produced or were pending on university scholarships, juvenile employment, trade education, technical education, the pensions of teachers and the reform of the University of London.[71]

This attitude was understandable. Selby-Bigge was to tell the Marquess of Crewe, 'The collapse of the 1914 scheme was as you can imagine a horrible disappointment as we had put nearly 3 years hard work into it.'[72] Yet commitment to pre-war plans meant a narrow view of the demand for action. Whilst formally agreeing with those who wanted more attention to science, Selby-Bigge pointed out that much of the criticism was directed at the older universities and public schools, over which the Board of Education had no control.[73] He rejected the idea of a Royal Commission as too cumbersome and time-consuming.[74] The answer to public pressure, he told Vaughan Nash, the secretary of the Reconstruction Committee, was for the Prime Minister to announce the formation of a reviewing committee. It would 'get rid of a good deal of the agitation'.[75]

Selby-Bigge's anxiety to protect his and the Board's position, combined with the weakness of having Henderson as education Minister, meant that the Board itself had been handicapped in pushing forward the educational plans it had already worked out. What now spurred on both the Board and the government was not only the demand for a Royal Commission but the influence of one who had played an important role in the pre-war planning – Lord Haldane of Cloan.

Excluded from office on the formation of the coalition government in May 1915, and attacked for his alleged pro-German leanings, Haldane had lain low for a number of months. The growing crisis of the war, however, both reinforced and demonstrated his own social imperialist views. By early 1916 he felt free to speak out. Delivering an address at the University of London in March, he stressed that the nation would face a 'new world' after the war, a world in which there would be intense economic competition.[76] To meet the challenge it was particularly necessary to develop technical education 'based on a mental training which is not merely special but general'.[77] This not only meant the development of the universities but that even the working classes should be 'infused with the reflective habit which is born of knowledge'.[78] Whereas in Manchester in 1913 Haldane had spoken of the need for equality of educational opportunity, the war had introduced new priorities. The answer to mass education was to be found not in extending the principle of egalitarianism but in developing vocational continuation classes to train adolescents, combining trade skills and general knowledge in the manner of Dr George Kerchensteiner at Munich.[79]

Haldane did more than urge action. He took steps to see that something was done. In a memorandum to the government he proposed a reviewing committee of Cabinet and former Ministers to consider problems of English and Scottish education. Under it there should be a committee of experts, with Haldane himself as chairman.[80] Selby-Bigge baulked at the idea, telling Crewe that not only was he afraid of the scheme for a secret committee of experts, particularly if it leaked out that Haldane was chairman,[81] but that he also believed it would be a 'waste of time' and would 'add little' to what the pre-war Cabinet committee had achieved.[82] Yet Haldane now had a powerful ally. At the Ministry of Munitions Lloyd George had developed an interest in the welfare and training of juvenile workers.[83] Early in April Haldane arranged a meeting at his London home so that he could meet Sir William McCormick, president of the Advisory Council on Scientific and Industrial Research, Sir John Struthers, secretary of the Scottish Education Department, Sir Robert Blair, the chief education officer of the London County Council, and Frank Heath, a Board of Education official, later secretary of the Department of Scientific and Industrial Research. This group apparently drew up plans, and Haldane and Lloyd George formed an 'alliance' to put them through.[84]

In formal terms the course of action now adopted by the Asquith government was a compromise. First, it was agreed to ask Haldane to act as adviser on education.[85] Secondly, at its meeting on 23 June the Reconstruction Committee decided to follow the proposals of Selby-Bigge and allow both the Board of Education and the Scottish Education Department to conduct inquiries into particular questions such as the neglect of science and the teaching of modern languages, while at the same time establishing a sub-committee to review proposals for developing the public system of education.[86]

These decisions had twin implications. They were designed in the first place to appease public opinion, the scientific lobby in particular. Meeting in the rooms of the Board of Education, the science and modern languages committees were to remain little more than departmental inquiries.[87] On the other hand, it is not the case that the general reviewing committee 'achieved nothing other than a convenient facade with which to confront those who persistently demanded an overall and independent investigation'.[88] Its establishment was not merely an attempt to appease public opinion but was also, in official circles at least, a step forward. As Crewe told Asquith, the committee was to be the 'body to set in motion any immediate action to be taken . . . and to extract money from the Treasury'.[89] As such, its formation was a response to Haldane's call for action. The reviewing committee, consisting of Crewe (shortly to become President of the Board of Education), Christopher Addison, Austen Chamberlain, Lord Curzon, J. A. Pease (now Postmaster

General), the Conservative Under-secretary of State at the Colonial Office, A. Steel-Maitland, the Liberal Secretary of State for Scotland, H. H. Tennant, and the Conservative Chief Secretary for Ireland, H. E. Duke,[90] met on 11 August and put Haldane in what he considered a 'position of great responsibility for plans and powers to mould them'. The committee also decided on 'secrecy' so that it would be difficult for *The Times* to hear anything definite.[91]

The formal terms of reference were that the committee should consider the education system as a whole and formulate developments from experience gained during the war. There was, however, to be special reference to the proposals prepared before the war, memoranda already submitted by the Board of Education and Scottish Education Department, and any other proposals submitted by other departments, special committees or 'responsible organisations'.[92]

The programmes of the Board of Education and particularly the pre-war schemes were thus a prime consideration. What gave them added focus was the make-up of the sub-committee of educationalists chaired by Haldane. It was essentially a small, select official group, including Selby-Bigge and Frank Heath of the Board, and Sir William McCormick, and Sir John Struthers, both of whom had been meeting Haldane. The only outsider was Sir Robert Blair of the London County Council. Blair, however, had earlier told Selby-Bigge that 'What is wanted is not knowledge of things to be done, but, after some sifting, knowledge of how to accomplish what in an afternoon could be written down as the few things necessary'.[93] Even Haldane himself, while differing with Selby-Bigge over strategy, still agreed that much of the formal groundwork had already been laid. Addressing the Lords on 12 July in an important debate he had initiated on national training, Haldane had used the language of change – 'The old order is passing away, and we are face to face with a new order. Our old methods will not avail us any longer'[94] – but he had also stressed that 'the plans are worked out well. All that is wanted is the decision of the Government to give effect to them.'[95]

Thus he apparently agreed with Selby-Bigge that the pre-war plans should form the substance of an educational programme. Despite this consensus, Selby-Bigge, still anxious to protect his own position, at first refused to co-operate, complaining to Crewe that the ex-Minister was raiding the Board of Education by attempting to secure the services of Frank Heath as secretary for the reviewing committee.[96] In response Haldane sent Crewe, now President of the Board, a double-edged ultimatum offering to abandon the idea of the reviewing committee and devote himself to 'organising, by discussion inside and outside Parliament, that driving force of public opinion which is requisite for your success'.[97] Aware that this could mean trouble for the government, Crewe and Asquith gave Haldane full authority to proceed with the reviewing committee.[98]

The sub-committee of experts met at Haldane's London residence during October and November. Over six meetings it reviewed the whole structure of English education. Discussion centred essentially on a revision of the pre-war schemes, although educational aims had risen. In line with Haldane's earlier speech in March, the sub-committee agreed that a school leaving age of fourteen and the creation of at least six hours a week of compulsory continuation classes were essential.[99] Such provision would be an important advance on the terms of the 1913–14 Bill, which had allowed for a school leaving age of at least thirteen and the establishment of voluntary continuation classes until sixteen. Other points discussed and agreed upon were long familiar. The provision for a percentage grant system in elementary education had been proposed by the Kempe committee in 1914 and been included in the government's pre-war plans for extra education grants.[100] The formulation of educational schemes by local education authorities, provision for advanced elementary education and greater supervision over child welfare were all part of the 1913–14 Bill, while improved salaries and conditions for teachers had been part of the extra grants announced in 1914.[101] The establishment of a scholarship system had been discussed in 1913 and had been put forward as part of the plans of the Addison committee in 1915, and was the subject of the report of the Consultative Committee early in 1916. Similarly, the development of the secondary schools through advanced courses and examination reform had been part of the 1913–14 plans, and financial provisions had been included in the extra grants announced in 1914. Extra finance for the universities had also been discussed in 1913–14 and was part of both the extra grants announced in 1914 and the recommendations of the Addison committee in 1915.[102] Finally, the development of provincial councils to assist educational development had been strongly supported by Haldane in 1913 and had been included in the 1913–14 draft Bill.[103]

There was thus strong continuity between the programme and education Bill that had emerged from the Cabinet committee of 1913–14 and the decisions and aims of the 1916 reviewing committee under Haldane. Yet the war had at least emphasised educational priorities. A report of Haldane's sub-committee stressed that the two 'main lines of advance' should be the establishment of daytime compulsory continuation classes and the provision of an adequate supply of well trained teachers.[104]

The importance of both these issues was underlined by other developments in late 1916. In July the executive of the National Union of Teachers approved local action to improve stipends. Four months later it was decided to reopen the national salary campaign that had been suspended on the outbreak of war.[105] Support for compulsory continuation classes also received further impetus from the departmental committee on Juvenile Employment and War chaired by Herbert Lewis. Although the Lewis committee did not publish its final report until April 1917, its proposals were well known to the Board before the end of 1916. In the main, the committee did not challenge existing policy. Rather, it set out a new national ideal for education.

> We have to perfect the civilisation for which our men have shed their blood and our women their tears; to establish new standards of value in our judgment of what makes life worth living, more wholesome and more restrained ideals of behaviour and recreation, finer traditions of co-operation and kindly fellowship between class and between man and man.[106]

Despite its appeal to idealism the Lewis committee argued that the problems it had identified were not new but rather the 'standing problem of the adolescent wage-earner aggravated by the effect of war-time conditions'.[107] The solution it proposed drew upon pre-war suggestions. Finding no evidence that public opinion was yet ready for universal full-time education after fourteen, the committee recommended a uniform leaving age of fourteen and, for fourteen-to-eighteen-year-olds, attendance at day continuation classes for eight hours a week or 320 hours a year.[108]

The recommendations of the Lewis committee did not differ substantially from the proposals put forward by Haldane's sub-committee. Its report was another example of how far those associated with official educational circles were agreed on the main aims and lines of advance. What official opinion did not recognise, however, was the changed political and social climate after more than two years of war. There was now a new openness to reform throughout the structures of government. Unlike 1913–14, education now drew strength from other areas of social policy. As Paul Johnson has shown, the

Reconstruction Committee itself soon formed a wide vision of post-war reconstruction. Other government departments had added their own programmes and the initial emphasis on 'making existing economic institutions stronger' had by the end of 1916 become an agenda that included such areas as health and housing.[109] More significantly, the war had raised new demands for and expectations of change that had not been present in 1914. Not only the Neglect of Science Committee but also other groups in the educational world and other sections of society were organising to formulate educational programmes.

The influences upon government had changed since the days of educational debate in 1913–14. Sectarian disputes still had some claim. Lord Sheffield, president of the National Education Association, had said in May 1916 that 'my ideals for education are what they were before the war'.[110] He wanted not only reform but also the re-establishment of school boards and an end to all sectarian influences in education.[111] Similarly, the Archbishop of Canterbury reminded Crewe of the claims of the Church in reconstruction, particularly in regard to reinforcing religious instruction in elementary education.[112]

But there were now other groups with educational demands quite unrelated to denominational issues. An Education Reform Council, composed generally of liberal educationalists associated with the universities, published a report in November 1916 reflecting a view of education that was grounded as much in humanitarian ends as in the need for national training.[113] Its programme was in general accord with the declarations of the Haldane reviewing committee, supporting the idea of provincial councils, continuation schools and higher elementary education. Its main new idea was a proposal to transfer able children through scholarships from the elementary schools to the secondary schools at the age of eleven, so foreshadowing the eleven-plus exam.[114]

More drastic proposals came from the National Union of Teachers. The report of an N.U.T. sub-committee, published in December 1916, urged the principle of free education throughout the system and compulsory school attendance from the age of five to eighteen. Yet in detail the N.U.T. proposals for immediate reform were not very different from those of Haldane's sub-committee or the Lewis committee. It suggested full-time education at least to fourteen, with power for local education authorities to extend the leaving age to either fifteen or sixteen. School leavers should have eight hours of continued education each week until eighteen. As a corollary the N.U.T. programme urged the development of higher elementary education of a general rather than vocational nature. Other proposals included local development of the curricula, a percentage grant system in financing, encouragement of physical training and restrictions on the employment of children, and finally, improvements in the salaries, training and qualifications of teachers.[115]

Support for education from educationalists was to be expected. What was new was the interest being shown by the organised labour movement. At the forefront was the Workers' Educational Association. The war helped to strengthen the position of the W.E.A. in Labour circles. In the first place, it played a leading part in the campaign to resist education cuts during late 1915 and early 1916, particularly in London, where it organised trade unions and teachers to protest.[116] Secondly, the links between the W.E.A. and organised labour, never close before the war, were strengthened when the shipwright J. M. Mactavish replaced Albert Mansbridge as secretary of the organisation in 1916.[117] More than anything else, however, Labour's own lack of commitment to and knowledge of education provided the impetus for the W.E.A. As A. J. Corfield has argued, 'The W.E.A. seized the initiative because at this time there was virtually no other organisation which could . . . The Labour party as yet had no effective research department and was certainly unable to specialise in education.'[118]

The W.E.A. thus emerged as the leading spokesman and interpreter of an independent Labour policy on education. In April 1916 it adopted a new constitution to include not only support for adult education but the promotion and growth of a national system of education providing for the complete development of all as individuals and citizens.[119] Four months later its pamphlet *What Labour wants from Education* stressed the need to guard against reform merely for the sake of industrial efficiency. Rather, the aim of Labour in education was:

> health and full development for the body, knowledge and truth for the mind, firmness for the feelings, good-will towards its kind, and coupled with this liberal education, such a training as will make members [of society] efficient, self-supporting citizens of a free self-governing community.[120]

In late 1916 the W.E.A. produced its own policy statement. Its programme had two aims. The first was to present a scheme of educational reform appropriate to the interests of the working classes. On most issues it therefore went beyond – certainly in degree and partly in kind – what was being proposed and discussed at the Board of Education. This was particularly so in regard to the school leaving age and the provision for continuation classes. The principle of free education throughout the system was adopted as a major point. The programme also supported the establishment of nursery schools for two-to-six-year-olds, and a school leaving age of fifteen with provision for local education authorities to raise it to sixteen. For most adolescents there should be continuation classes of twenty hours a week to the age of eighteen (with hours of labour limited to twenty). The programme also stressed a greater expansion of educational opportunity so that secondary education would be open not to a particular class of society but to the intellectually able. This aim would be achieved through entry standards, maintenance allowances, provision of a variety of schools and facilities to transfer from continuation schools to full-time secondary schools. For capable students there should be adequate maintenance in universities, the governing bodies of which should represent working-class people and other sections of the community.[121]

The W.E.A. programme was not merely framed to represent the educational needs and interests of the working classes; it was also designed to rouse the labour movement itself. The strategy was partly successful. At the 1916 Trades Union Congress a number of speakers laid the blame for lack of popular interest in education squarely on the shoulders of labour. R. Farrah of the National Union of General Workers said that working-class parents had been too anxious to get their children into the workshops,[122] while a delegate from Durham claimed that in his county the miners and the railwaymen had acted against the cause of education.[123] A month later another meeting of trade unionists was held at Bradford in Yorkshire. Councillor A. J. Sutton of Bradford, who presided over a gathering that represented 60,000 workers,[124] said that the whole question of an educational programme had arisen out of a W.E.A. conference at Oxford. In the past workers had shown little interest in education, nor had there been any opportunity for them to express their views. The time had come to discuss the question generally.[125]

The Bradford conference drew up a comprehensive programme that was to be adopted as official Labour Party policy at the conference in January 1917. The majority of its points had been covered in the

W.E.A. platform, but the most important principle of the 'Bradford Charter' was that of universal free and compulsory education to the age of sixteen.[126] In formal terms at least, and in contrast to the immediate pre-war position, Labour was now committed to a restructuring of English education.

Labour's new awakening to the importance of education was merely a reflection of the undercurrents and expectations of change now moving throughout society. One indication was growing enrolments in secondary schools. With rising incomes in certain sections of the work force, some parents were apparently prepared to seek out places in secondary schools for their children and then kept them there longer than previously. By October 1916 the secondary school population had increased by 9,124 in twelve months, and 7,048 of these were pupils staying longer at school.[127] Equally significant was the new popular interest in education. As an observer of apathy before the war Haldane was well qualified to assess the new situation. After holding a number of public meetings in late 1916 he later told the Lords:

> instead of an education meeting bringing together 200 to 300 people as used to be the case before the War, the audiences packed the halls, and there were from 2,000 to 3,000 present on almost every occasion. These audiences were composed largely of representatives of the working classes.[128]

By the end of the year ideals were being realised in practical programmes and demands for change. Much had altered since 1913–14. How far it would show in terms of policy remained to be seen.

Notes

1 *The Schoolmaster*, 5 September 1914, p. 341.

2 Report of the Committee for Scientific and Industrial Research, 1915–16, *Parlt. Pprs.* 1916, VIII, Cd 8336, pp. 7–8.

3 For fuller discussion see Sanderson, *The Universities and British Industry*, p. 215, and W. H. G. Armytage, *The German Influence on English Education*, London, 1969, p. 73.

4 *The Times*, 2 September 1914, p. 5, and Report of the Committee for Scientific and Industrial Research, 1915–16, Cd 8336, p. 8.

5 Diary entry, 2 and 3 December 1914, in C. Addison, *Four and a half Years*, London, 1934, I, p. 48.

6 *Ibid.*
7 Cameron Hazlehurst, *Politicians at War*, New York, 1971, pp. 171–4.
8 Diary entry, 19 January 1915, in Addison, *Four and a half Years*, I, p. 59.
9 P.R.O., Ed 24/1315; Selby-Bigge to Pease, 15 January 1915.
10 Diary entry, 19 January 1915, in Addison, *Four and a half Years*, I, pp. 59–60.
11 C. Addison, *Politics from Within*, London, 1924, I, pp. 48–9. See also diary entry, 29 January 1915, in Addison, *Four and a half Years*, I, pp. 60–1.
12 In January 1915 E. K. Chambers prepared a memorandum urging that the promised pre-war aid for technical education should now go forward and even be increased. P.R.O., Ed 24/1315; E.K.C., Additional Assistance for Technical Education, 18 January 1915. W. N. Bruce, principal assistant secretary of the secondary branch, also prepared a memorandum on organising advanced secondary school work. P.R.O., Ed 24/1654; W.N.B., Grants to Encourage late Attendance at Secondary Schools, March 1915. See also an unsigned memorandum on industrial research possibly prepared by Addison, contained in P.R.O., Ed 24/1580.
13 P.R.O., Ed 24/1581; Proposals for a National System of Advanced Instruction and Research in Science, Technology and Commerce, 6 April 1915.
14 *Ibid.*
15 *Ibid.*
16 Diary entry, 30 April 1915, in Addison, *Four and a half Years*, I, p. 73.
17 P.R.O., Ed 24/1576; Memorandum in regard to expenditure during the year ending March 31 1916. See also diary entry, 4 May 1915, in Addison, *Four and a half Years*, I, p. 74.
18 *Hansard*, Commons, 5th ser., LXXI, 13 May 1915, col. 1907. The actual organisation was announced in a White Paper issued in July 1915. *Parlt. Pprs.* 1914–16, L, Cd 8005.
19 Harry Melville, *The Department of Scientific and Industrial Research*, London, 1962, pp. 28–32.
20 *Hansard*, Commons, 5th ser., LXXI, 13 May 1915, col. 1997.
21 Henderson informed Pease, 'When I told the P.M. there was nothing appropriate in my occupying such a post he replied there was nothing appropriate in any of the appointments.' N.C.L., G.P., 49(d), Henderson to Pease, 18 May 1915.
22 Final Report of the Committee on Retrenchment in the Public Expenditure, *Parlt. Pprs.* 1916, XV, Cd 8200, pp. 13–16.
23 P.R.O. Ed 24/1692; Arthur Acland to Selby-Bigge, 15 November 1915.
24 Board of Education, Circular 931, 26 November 1915. A secret agreement between the Board and the War Office also provided that up to 300 science teachers might be exempted. P.R.O., Ed 24/1692; Lord Derby to Selby Bigge, 22 December 1916.
25 P.R.O., Ed 24/1693; Memorandum, 23 January 1917.
26 *The Times*, 24 December 1915, p. 3. As one example, Lieutenant

Moseley, a valuable assistant to the physicist William Rutherford, took part in and was killed in the landings at Gallipoli in April 1915. Marwick, *The Deluge*, p. 228. See also J. M. Winter, 'Balliol's lost generation', *Balliol College Record*, 1975, pp. 23–6.

27 P.R.O., Ed 24/1683; Pease to Kitchener, 7 December 1914, and Board of Education, Circular 882, 16 December 1914.

28 Board of Education, Circular 952, 26 June 1916.

29 Report of the Board of Education 1914–15, *Parlt. Pprs.* 1916, XI, Cd 8274, p. 62.

30 Report of the Board of Education, 1915–16, *Parlt. Pprs.* 1917–18, XI, Cd 8594, p. 62.

31 N.U.T. [National Union of Teachers], *War Record 1914–1919*, London, 1920, p. 37.

32 A. W. Bowley, *Prices and Wages in the United Kingdom, 1914–1920*, Economic and Social History of the World War, British Series, Oxford, 1921, p. 70. From late 1915 many local education authorities paid war bonuses to offset inflation, but rates varied and were generally lower than bonuses paid in other areas such as the railways. See *The Times Educational Supplement*, 21 September 1916, p. 141; 28 September 1916, p. 155; 12 October 1916, p. 171; 14 December 1916, p. 243; and 21 December 1916, p. 251.

33 Report of the Board of Education, 1915–16, Cd 8594, pp. 47 and 51–2.

34 *Hansard*, Commons, 5th ser., LXVI, 28 and 31 August 1914, cols. 274 and 368.

35 P.R.O., Ed 24/616(a); Deputation on Child Labour in Agriculture, 11 February 1915. See also *Hansard*, Commons, 5th ser., LXX, 25 February 1915, cols. 402–84.

36 Report of the Board of Education, 1915–16, Cd 8594, p. 7. See also I. O. Andrews, *The Economic Effects of the War on Women and Children*, Carnegie Endowment for International Peace, Preliminary Economic Studies of the War, New York, 1918, pp. 63–7.

37 Ministry of Reconstruction, *Juvenile Employment during the War – and After*, London, 1918, p. 6.

38 *Ibid.*, p. 49.

39 *History of the Ministry of Munitions*, London, 1922, V, iii, p. 5. Over the period July 1914 to October 1917 the number of boys under eighteen employed in the metal trades rose by 106,000, and the number of girls under eighteen in the same trades by 62,800. In contrast, the number of boys employed in the building industry fell by 15,000, while the number of girls employed in the clothing trade fell by 16,500. Ministry of Reconstruction, *Juvenile Employment*, p. 11.

40 *The Schoolmaster*, 18 March 1916, p. 370.

41 *Manchester Guardian*, 12 February 1916, p. 5.

42 P.R.O., Ed 24/616(a); Deputation from the Parliamentary Committee of the Trades Union Congress, 17 February 1916.

43 P.R.O., Ed 24/1175; Deputation from the National Education Association, 22 February 1916.

44 P.R.O., Ed 24/616(a); Deputation from the Parliamentary Committee

of the Trades Union Congress, 17 February 1916.

45 P.RO., Ed 24/1175; R. A. Bray, 'Juvenile Employment and the War', 10 March 1916.

46 *Ibid.*; Henderson to Herbert Lewis, 10 April 1916.

47 Sanderson, *The Universities and British Industry*, pp. 221–7.

48 *Ibid.*, pp. 231–2.

49 *The Times*, 9 February 1916, cited in Sanderson, *The Universities and British Industry*, p. 239.

50 Sir James Currie, *The War and Industrial Training*, paper read before the Royal Society of Arts, 25 February 1920, p. 2. (Pamphlet located in the W.E.A. Library, London.) Selby-Bigge thought Addison at the Ministry of Munitions had become too preoccupied with munition needs in science and technology and not enough with future policy for peacetime. See P.R.O., Ed 24/1576; Addison to Selby-Bigge, 21 June 1915 and 8 July 1915, and Selby-Bigge to Addison, 22 June 1915.

51 Interim Report of the Consultative Committee on Scholarships for Higher Education. *Parlt. Pprs.* 1916, V, Cd 8291, p. 4.

52 *Ibid.*, pp. 66–7.

53 Corelli Barnett, *The Swordbearers*, London, 1963, p. 183.

54 *The Times*, 2 February 1916, p. 10.

55 P.R.O., Recon. 1/14; Neglect of Science Committee, Memorandum.

56 The Neglect of Science, Report of Proceedings at a Conference, 3 May 1916. (Pamphlet located in C.U.L., C.P., Box M/8(3).)

57 *The Times Educational Supplement*, 5 October 1915, p. 119.

58 *The Elements of Reconstruction* (London, 1916, p. 72), under which title the articles were reprinted with an introduction by Lord Milner.

59 *Ibid.*, p. 197.

60 *Ibid.*

61 *New Statesman*, 27 May 1916, p. 175.

62 *Ibid.*, p. 176. See also Sidney Webb and Arnold Freeman, *Great Britain after the War*, London 1916.

63 V. H. Rothwell, *British War Aims and Peace Diplomacy*, Oxford, 1971, p. 271.

64 *The Schoolmaster*, 5 February 1916, p. 168. See also H. B. Gray and S. Turner, *Eclipse or Empire*, London, 1916, and T. Farrow and W. W. Cotch, *The Coming Trade War*, London, 1916.

65 *Hansard*, Commons, 5th ser., LXVII, 26 January 1916, cols. 1265–6.

66 *The Times*, 4 May 1916, p. 6. After the appearance of this letter, groups forming themselves under the titles of the Council for Scientific Studies and the Council for Humanistic Studies met to try and reconcile differences and to decide on timetables for public and secondary school curricula. See W. H. G. Armytage, *Sir Richard Gregory*, London, 1957, pp. 70–2, and F. G. Kenyon (ed.), *Education, Scientific and Humane. A Report of the Proceedings of the Council for Humanistic Studies*, London, 1917.

67 Johnson, *Land fit for Heroes*, p. 10.

68 *Ibid.*, pp. 11–32.

69 C.U.L., C.P., Box M/8(3); Crewe to Acland, 4 April 1916.

70 M. A. Hamilton, *Arthur Henderson*, London, 1938, pp. 105–6.
71 L.S.E., P.P., XIII, Reconstruction Papers, A. pp. 53–4; Board of Education to Reconstruction Committee, 18 May 1916.
72 C.U.L., C.P., Box M 8(3); Selby-Bigge to Crewe, 14 August 1916.
73 P.R.O., Recon 1/14; Selby-Bigge, 'The Neglect of Science'.
74 *Ibid.*; L.A.S.B., Notes on the Proposal for a Royal Commission, 29 May 1916. This memorandum closely mirrors the views of an earlier paper dated 8 May 1918 by W. N. Bruce. See P.R.O., Ed 24/1173.
75 *Ibid.*; Selby-Bigge to Vaughan Nash, 3 May 1916.
76 Viscount Haldane, *The Student and the Nation*, address delivered at the University of London, 23 March 1916, p. 1.
77 *Ibid.*, p. 3.
78 *Ibid.*, p. 4.
79 *Ibid.*, pp. 4–9.
80 P.R.O., Recon 1/14; Memorandum. This memo is unsigned and untitled but a manuscript heading says 'From Lord H.'.
81 C.U.L., C.P., Box M/8(3); Selby-Bigge to Crewe, 11 May 1916.
82 *Ibid.*; Selby-Bigge to Crewe, 19 May 1916.
83 *History of Ministry of Munitions*, V, iii, pp. 2–12 and 38–46. In early April 1916 Sir George Newman of the Board of Education saw Lloyd George to discuss such matters as the employment of boys and girls, hours of labour and welfare work. Ministry of Social Security Library, London, Sir George Newman diary, entry 4 April 1916.
84 N.L.S., H.P., 6012, fol. 126; Haldane to Elizabeth Haldane, 5 April 1916. Beatrice Webb noted in her diary after a dinner with Haldane at this time, 'He sees something of his former colleagues, even of Lloyd George, and has been trying to persuade him to take up a great scheme of half-time education, between 14 and 18. "Though I have not been heard of," he pathetically remarked, "I have been very busy. I have now a room at the Education Office." ' B.L.P.E., P.P., i, 33, p. 42, diary entry, 4 April 1916.
85 N.L.S., H.P., 5995, fol. 163, Haldane to his mother, 24 May 1916.
86 P.R.O., Cab 37/150/14; Reconstruction Committee, Conclusions, 23 June 1916.
87 E. W. Jenkins, 'The Thompson committee and the Board of Education, 1916–1922', *British Journal of Educational Studies*, XXI, i, 1973, pp. 76–85.
88 E. W. Jenkins, 'The Board of Education and the Reconstruction Committee, 1916–1918', *Journal of Educational Administration and History*, V, 1973, p. 48.
89 C.U.L., C.P., Box M/8(3); Crewe to Asquith, 9 June 1916.
90 P.R.O., Ed 12/5; Reconstruction Committee, List of Sub-committees. Crewe told Curzon, who was apparently reluctant to serve on the reviewing committee, 'that the committee would not meet often and for a long time would only have to consider broad principles of enquiry.' C.U.L., C.P., Box M/14(3); Crewe to Curzon, 12 August 1916.
91 U. of L., B.C., Haldane–Gosse correspondence, v, Haldane to Gosse, 11 August 1916. In October 1916 Bonar Law informed the Commons

that Crewe was presiding over the reviewing committee, and he also revealed its terms of reference. *Hansard*, Commons, 5th ser., LXXXVI, 10 October 1916, cols. 16 and 22.

92 P.R.O., Ed 12/5; List of Sub-committees: Review of Education.

93 P.R.O., Ed 24/1172; Sir Robert Blair to Selby-Bigge, 24 May 1916.

94 *Hansard*, Lords, 5th ser., XXII, 12 July 1916, col. 682.

95 *Ibid.*, col. 680.

96 C.U.L., C.P., Box M/14(3); Selby-Bigge to Crewe, 20 August 1916.

97 C.U.P., C.P., Box M/14(1); Haldane to Crewe, 26 August 1916.

98 U. of L., B.C., Haldane–Gosse correspondence, v, Haldane to Gosse, 15 September 1916.

99 P.R.O., Ed 24/1473; Minutes of meetings at Queen Anne's Gate, 10, 18, and 26 October 1916, points 4 and 5.

100 *Ibid.*, point 6.

101 *Ibid.*, points 6–8, and Minutes of meeting, 10 November 1916, point 9.

102 *Ibid.*, Minutes of meeting, 10 November 1916, points 10–16.

103 *Ibid.*, Minutes of meeting, 27 November 1916, points 19–20.

104 P.R.O., Recon 1/14; Report of Lord Haldane's Sub-committee of the Reviewing Sub-committee.

105 Thompson, *Professional Solidarity*, p. 261.

106 Report of the Departmental Committee on Juvenile Education in Relation to Employment after the War, *Parlt. Pprs*. 1917–18, XI, Cd 8512, p. 2.

107 *Ibid.*

108 *Ibid.*, pp. 7–14.

109 Johnson, *Land fit for Heroes*, p. 12.

110 *Education after the War*, Report of Proceedings at the Annual Conference of the National Education Association, 11 May 1916, p. 36. (Pamphlet located in Dr Williams Library, London, 207.8.)

111 *Ibid.*, pp. 4–9.

112 P.R.O., Ed 24/1491; Archbishop of Canterbury to Crewe, 29 November 1916, outlining details of their previous discussion.

113 *The Times Educational Supplement*, 30 November 1916, p. 221. For formation of the council see *The Times Educational Supplement*, 2 May 1916, p. 2, and 6 June 1916, pp. 73–4.

114 *Ibid.*, pp. 221–2.

115 *The Times Educational Supplement*, 28 December 1916, pp. 259–60. See also the rather critical editorial comment on this scheme, *ibid.*, p. 257.

116 *The Highway*, February 1916, p. 79.

117 M. Stocks, *The Workers Educational Association*, London, 1953, p. 70.

118 A. J. Corfield, *Epoch in Workers' Education*, London, 1969, p. 169.

119 Stocks, *The Workers Educational Association*, p. 72.

120 J. M. McTavish, *What Labour wants from Education*, W.E.A., 1916, p. 5.

121 *The Times Educational Supplement*, 14 December 1916, p. 237. Other points included the need for technical education to be divorced from

commercialism and related only to public service, the development of corporate school life and the physical and medical services, restriction of class sizes to thirty, increased grants for teacher supply, a public inquiry into educational endowments and further provision for W.E.A. classes.

122 *Trades Union Congress Report*, 1916, p. 371.

123 *Ibid.*

124 *The Times Educational Supplement*, 26 October 1916, p. 187.

125 *Bradford Daily Telegraph*, 21 October 1916, p. 5.

126 See *The Times Educational Supplement*, 19 October 1916, p. 180, 26 October 1916, pp. 185 and 187, and *Labour Party Conference Report*, 1917, pp. 135–7.

127 Report of the Board of Education, 1915–16, Cd 8594, p. 29. See also B. A. Waites, 'The effect of the first world war on class and status in England', *Journal of Contemporary History*, 11, 1976, pp. 27–48.

128 *Hansard*, Lords, 5th ser.; XXV, 9 May 1917, col. 3.

IV

The new government and the new Minister

The formation of the Lloyd George coalition Ministry in December 1916 was an important turning point in the history of the British war effort. More than a change of government, it was 'a revolution British-style'.[1] The first wartime coalition under Asquith had been essentially an agreement between the two major parties, with Arthur Henderson brought in to appease Labour. Not only did Lloyd George transform the direction of the war effort by centralising power in a small War Cabinet of five, he brought Henderson and the imperialist Lord Milner into the War Cabinet and included two other members of the Labour Party in his Ministry. In appearance at least it was a truly national coalition, the origins of which may be found in the pre-war moves towards a non-party government of imperial strength, efficiency and social reform but whose purpose and meaning were also directly related to the crisis of war itself.[2]

There was now full commitment to an all-out effort. Speaking for the first time as Prime Minister, Lloyd George told Parliament that all the nation's resources would have to be mobilised towards victory, however long and exhausting the struggle might be.[3] But victory alone was not enough, and organisation for efficiency raised questions of post-war policy. In education as in other areas of national life the severe test of war had emphasised deficiencies and it seemed that there could be no return to past ways. It was not merely improvement of the old society that was sought. The United States' entry into hostilities gave a new dimension to international war aims. In answer to the threat of international socialism the Allies were fighting for the building of a new Europe founded on the principles of nationalism and self-determination.[4] The ideal of reconstruction abroad was reflected in hopes of a more just and harmonious society at home. This expectation the Prime Minister himself was prepared to encourage, for he realised the importance of associating his government with a broad programme of social reconstruction. Such a programme would have implications not only for the future but for the immediate present. As Bentley Gilbert has argued,

> The need personally to recapture and revive the Liberal party represented only one of Lloyd George's goals. A second, of perhaps more immediate importance in 1917, was the aim of sweeping away the residue of pacificism and war weariness that threatened to suffocate Britain's military effort.[5]

The advisers now surrounding Lloyd George contributed to the new mood. In August the Welsh radical Tom Jones had been brought to London to act as confidant. Jones was associated with Richard Tawney and A. E. Zimmern, both members of the W.E.A. All three were in close contact with Lloyd George just before the fall of the Asquith government.[6] Such men were committed to a better Britain. In particular, education was high among their priorities. It was related to the spiritual purpose of the nation, Tawney argued in *The Times* in February 1917

> A reconstruction of education in a generous and liberal spirit would be the noblest memorial to those who have fallen even though many of them were but little educated; it would be the formal and public recognition of the world of the spirit for which they fell. It would show that the nation was prepared to submit its life to the kind of principles for which it thought itself justified in asking them to die.[7]

If education was going to be crucial in the post-war world, then the selection of the right man to head the Board of Education would be vital. The Marquess of Crewe was ruled out by his close association with Asquith. One of the most striking features of the new Ministry was the number of figures from outside the general realm of political life. The shipping magnate Sir Joseph Maclay became Shipping Controller (and later Minister of Shipping), while the agriculturist Prothero became President of the Board of Agriculture. Similarly, the choice of President of the Board of Education fell not on a politician but on a man intimately associated with the world of education – H. A. L. Fisher, historian and Vice-chancellor of the University of Sheffield.

Aged fifty-one in December 1916, Herbert Albert Laurens Fisher was the son of a tutor to the royal family and a descendant of Antoine de l'Etang, a favourite at the court of Marie Antoinette. Cousin of

Vanessa Bell and Virginia Woolf, he had been raised in the atmosphere of Victorian upper middle-class society. His social milieu was part of the late nineteenth-century 'intellectual aristocracy'.[8] 'Eminence came to Fisher as a duty and a birthright,' says his official biographer, David Ogg.[9] Educated at Winchester, he read 'Greats' at Oxford. As an undergraduate he had formed a close and lifelong friendship with the classicist and liberal intellectual Gilbert Murray, and had been influenced by the writings of the late nineteenth-century Hegelian T. H. Green, who reinterpreted liberalism to justify State intervention in areas of social welfare, particularly education.[10] A religious sceptic, Fisher maintained a firm belief in intellectual freedom and a basic liberal faith and commitment to human progress. These views carried over into his political life. Within the Lloyd George Ministry Fisher was to be one of the few who spoke out for the rights of the conscientious objectors.[11]

He had become Vice-chancellor at Sheffield early in 1914. He quickly established a reputation for promoting links between the university and the surrounding industrial city.[12] The war had brought him more fully into the public limelight. In Sheffield itself, one of the main English munition-producing centres, Fisher encouraged the development of the department of glass technology at the university and assisted in the formation of the Sheffield munitions committee.[13] He was also caught up in government work. In 1914 he was appointed to the commission which reported on German atrocities in Belgium. Two years later he was invited to serve on the committee to enquire into the position of modern languages, and in April 1916 was sent on a mission to study French propaganda.[14]

Although his credentials were good, it is not entirely clear why Fisher, rather than anyone else associated with education, should have been chosen to become President of the Board. There were others, particularly the educationalist Michael Sadler, with equal claims.[15] Fisher himself has offered a partial explanation. In his autobiography he records a breakfast with Lloyd George a few months before.[16] The future Prime Minister had pressed him for his views on a post-war settlement in Europe – a topic in which Fisher, as a European historian, could be thought to have had some interest if not competence.[17] He later claimed, 'At that time nothing was further from my expectations than that I should be ever summoned to take a share in governing the country.'[18] It was apparently a surprise when in December he was roused from his sickbed by a telephone summons to

London, where he saw Lloyd George and Bonar Law and was formally offered the presidency.[19]

This account leaves the impression that Lloyd George himself settled on Fisher, perhaps considering him as a candidate even before he became Premier. There is, however, another version which appears in the published diaries of Christopher Addison and Tom Jones. According to them the allocation of the education portfolio was neither immediate nor easy. Thus it was Tom Jones who first put forward Fisher's name.[20] Jones himself had heard of his qualities from his old mentor, Sir Henry Jones, Professor of Moral Philosophy at Glasgow University.[21] Christopher Addison, one of the chief parties to the formation of the new government, seized upon the suggestion. After further discussions, during which Talbot, the Conservative chief whip, also spoke highly of Fisher, it was agreed that Lloyd George should invite him to accept the post.[22]

Whatever the full story, the government could at least be assured that the choice was popular. His appointment won the support of various shades of opinion. Geoffrey Dawson, editor of *The Times*, told Lloyd George that Fisher was an 'admirable selection',[23] *The Times* itself described him as an 'educationalist with ideas'.[24] Even the *Daily News*, the chief press support of the deposed Asquith, said, 'No better selection could have been made than that of H. A. L. Fisher. His appointment would be an honour to any administration.'[25]

Similar praise came from working-class opinion. *The Highway*, journal of the W.E.A., wrote of Fisher as an 'old friend' through his work at Sheffield University, and saw his appointment as breaking with tradition and being a 'good omen' for educational reconstruction.[26] As a member of the parliamentary committee deputation of the T.U.C. that waited on the new Minister, Will Thorne claimed that since Fisher was a 'practical educationalist' the trade unions were hoping for a great deal from him.[27]

The views and praise of contemporaries provide only one perspective. Just how far was Fisher committed to change? Was he one of those Paul Johnson has described as 'reconstructionists', believing that 'war served reform both objectively by the sheer momentum of trends it began, and subjectively by the creation of a new mentality and new purpose'?[28] It should be said first of all that Fisher himself was not fully behind the new government. Before 1916 he had not been actively involved in politics, but his outlook drew him to the Liberals. Although he had been an anti-imperialist during the Boer war,[29] his sympathies lay with the Asquithian side of the Liberal Party rather than with its radical wing. His faith in Asquith presented something of a dilemma in deciding whether to accept office under Lloyd George. Justifying his decision to Gilbert Murray, Fisher said that although all his sympathies were on the side of Asquith, and he had little confidence in the new government, 'it was made clear to me that I was not being invited to join as a politician but as an educationalist and in consequence of a principle which I believe to be sound and fruitful, that the President of the Board of Education should be a person versed and interested in the subject'. He had himself stressed that he could only join the government provided education were taken seriously and money spent on it, and Lloyd George had given such assurances.[30] After further reflection he again wrote to Murray that, in time of war, he felt he could not decline a 'big piece of national work' purely on ground of personal distaste. He went on:

> And Education seemed to me to lie apart (Just now particularly) from the ordinary clash of political and party interests so that there was a real chance, if I could rely upon help from Haldane and you and Sadler and Hadow and other friends to get improvements upon a large scale started which would endure long after the war and bring permanent benefit to the country. I felt that now was the time to strike, that during the war the country would be in a mood to accept schemes, which in the general lassitude succeeding the peace, it would be too weary to support, and that if on the first occasion on which the Education Office was offered to an educationalist on educational and not political grounds, the offer was declined, my profession might have cause to complain.[31]

If Fisher believed that the war served reform by providing an opportunity to introduce schemes for educational improvements, then it must also be said that his own views on war and social change were limited by his liberal philosophy and his sceptical outlook. For a Liberal such as Fisher the horror of war was as much destructive as positive. It had reinforced his scepticism and partly destroyed his Liberal faith in progress. An address he gave to the Edinburgh Philosophical Society in November 1918 reflects the philosophical position he had adopted by the end, but it also throws some light on his attitude in December 1916. Casting his eye to the future on the subject of 'Political Philosophies', Fisher reminded his audience that 'The great perturbation of human affairs which the world has just experienced during the past four years has given rise in every region of society to a vague expectation of change'.[32] This had led to the belief that change must come, ushered in by a great man who would create a new society and reform the international order.[33] Because faith in progress was so 'deep-rooted' Fisher believed that society saw the war as being merely a 'great retrogression', for 'The greater the obvious calamity, the more determined are we to read into it a message of

Herbert Fisher, President of the Board of Education 1916–22. Photographed here at his desk in 1922, even his physical features exhibit Fisher's intellectual tastes and upper middle-class background. (From David Ogg, *Herbert Fisher, 1865–1940. A Short Biography*, London, 1947. Photo: G. E. Houghton)

benefits commensurate with the unchallenged and palpable evil'.[34] Yet Fisher himself was wary of such beliefs.

> The phantom host from Archangel who marched through England on its way to Belgium during the autumn of 1914 reminds of a fact, long known to the historians of religion, that beliefs are more often proportionate to a desire than evidence, and that if we only wish for a thing to happen with sufficient intensity, we may easily persuade ourselves that the object of our desire will be, or even has been, fulfilled. It follows that, if we wish to estimate the aptitude of the present age for framing a correct forecast of the future, allowance must be made for this source of error. Sentiment obscures the judgment, passion clouds the vision. We refuse to admit that any prospect which seems to us to be odious and incompatible with a benignant scheme of the universe can in fact be possible. In the same gallant spirit of optimism, with hopes hardly more exuberant and measureless, Condorcet, the condemned prisoner of the Jacobin tyranny, composed his grand design of a perfected humanity.[35]

The future, then, was uncertain. This belief was to lead him into a cautious approach to social problems and to acceptance of what was possible rather than what was ideal. Even in December 1916 there were some associated with the new government who could detect such traits. Writing to Sir Henry Jones, Tom Jones recalled the story of Fisher's selection:

> You can tell Fisher he owes his election to *you*, for it was I who first put his name forward on Tuesday midnight to Dr. Addison who pronounced it 'an inspiration'. Of course I was acting on all I had heard you say about Fisher's quality and distinction. Some are afraid that Fisher will be too timid. Anyway you can keep him right on all main issues.[36]

It was one thing to secure him for the Board of Education. It was quite another to ensure that he would continue to accept outside advice. What Tom Jones failed to recognise was the existence of officials at the Board who were to have a much more important influence upon him than Sir Henry Jones. Their advice would help reinforce his caution.

Political change at the top was accompanied by an attempt to infuse new blood into the administrative side of government. Lloyd George created a Cabinet secretariat which was to become the nucleus of a whole corps of advisers, known as the 'garden suburb'. The Prime Minister also decided to reorganise the Reconstruction Committee. Asquith's committee had been composed of Ministers under the chairmanship of the Prime Minister. Lloyd George partly continued this form by assuming the chairmanship himself, but he created a former Minister, Montagu, as vice-chairman and decided that there should be 'persons with ideas' on the committee.[37] He dispensed with the former members and invited people outside the government to join it. Consequently, of the fifteen members on the reconstituted committee, three were Fabians (as was one of the assistant secretaries – Arthur Greenwood), two Labour men, two progressive Conservatives and one a social imperialist.[38] The general effect of the change was already being felt in Whitehall by early 1917. Beatrice Webb, one of the new recruits, noted in mid-February:

> The swollen world of Whitehall is seething – conflicting elements warring against each other. The permanent officials who in pre-war times lived demure and dignified lives, mildly excited here and there by interdepartmental jealousies, are now fighting desperately for control of their departments, against invading 'interests' and interloping amateurs, under the Lloyd George regime, each department has been handed over to this 'interest' with which it is concerned. In that way, our little Welsh attorney thinks, you combine the least political opposition with the maximum technical knowledge . . . The one shining example of this 'vested interest *cum* expert' government is the distinguished University Professor – H. A. L. Fisher – now President of the Board of Education.[39]

Remarkably, Fisher brought little change to the administrative structure of the Board. He did secure the services of Gilbert Murray, who was appointed part-time to the staff,[40] and he later brought in the former W.E.A. secretary Albert Mansbridge.[41] But he made no attempt to challenge or change the leading administrators. On the contrary, before accepting Lloyd George's offer Fisher had sought to learn the Board's opinion by consulting W. N. Bruce, principal assistant secretary of the secondary branch.[42] (Apart from brief discussion between Addison and the chief medical officer, George Newman, the Board had not been previously consulted on the new appointment.[43]) There did seem grounds for a working relationship. Herbert Lewis, the parliamentary secretary, who as a supporter of Lloyd George remained in his post, saw the appointment as marking a new era, particularly in view of the low political prestige into which the department had fallen under Henderson.[44] Fisher himself told Gilbert Murray, 'The people at the Board, whom I had time to see, appeared to want me. For ordinary times they would have preferred an expert parliamentarian *to put their measure through for them*, [emphasis inserted] but as things are, I should do better than some others. In any case I gathered that I should not be unwelcome.'[45] W. N. Bruce informed Fisher that all at the Board were agreed that 'we can think of no one by whom we should like to see the experiment tried so much as by yourself. Selby-Bigge is very happy about it and you will find yourself surrounded by old friends and acquaintances ready to give you a cordial welcome.'[46] Selby-Bigge himself wrote welcoming the new Minister but adding in reference to Fisher's lack of political experience:

> I hope you will give us your confidence without reserve.
>
> It is of course a new experiment in Government and we shall have to adjust ourselves to the conditions of the experiment, but subject to your obtaining the necessary support of the P.M. I see no reason why it should not be a success and a great success.[47]

What smoothed the way between Fisher and the officials were common backgrounds, shared experiences and past acquaintanceships. The new Minister told his predecessor, Crewe, that Selby-Bigge had been a senior boy when he first entered Winchester, and the Board was 'full of old friends'.[48] He also realised that he was more dependent on the Board officials than they were on him. He later admitted in his autobiography:

> Popular opinion pronounced me to be an 'educationalist'. That was a delusion. I had never, save for a week when I was an undergraduate, taught in a school nor addressed myself to a serious study of pedagogic literature. Though for a short time I had served as a member of two education committees, and had acted as vice-chancellor in a provincial university, compared with many experienced members of Parliament who had for many years served on such bodies I was a tiro in the problems of educational administration. My true field of study, was and had long been the history and literature of Europe, and I should have been more in place as Under-Secretary of State for Foreign Affairs, a position for which I was afterwards considered, than as President of the Board of Education.[49]

The 'experiment' of appointing a man from outside politics was therefore less dramatic than appeared on the surface. Like other new Ministers before him, Fisher listened to the advice of his permanent officials. As to be expected from such a man as Selby-Bigge, it was tempered with extreme caution. In a paper prepared early in 1917 the latter cast serious doubt on many of the plans for educational reconstruction drawn up by groups outside the Board. Thus the W.E.A. proposal of a leaving age of sixteen was written off as a 'counsel of perfection', while even the question of part-time day continuation classes was seen as 'a complex and controversial matter' which would involve the 'nicest legislative and administrative adjustment'. The cost of six hours' continued education per week would, he estimated, be £4 million, while the W.E.A. call for twenty hours of part-time education per week from fourteen to eighteen would cost £17 million. On the other hand, administrative and financial matters such as the reform of the grant system and more pay for the teachers were necessities, Selby-Bigge concluded. The controversy over the curriculum, however, was an 'endless one', and he maintained that in this area the central authority should maintain a watch rather than compel any changes. On the general question of the 'accessibility of education' Selby-Bigge admitted there was general agreement on the need to extend opportunities to 'poor talent', but the proposals of Labour groups for education to be free, compulsory and full-time to the age of sixteen, and thence part-time to eighteen, followed by free university entrance supplemented by grants, was 'so sweeping in its social, industrial and economic aspects that ordinary estimates of cost lose their meaning'.[50]

There was little doubt that the new Minister himself was in general agreement with Selby-Bigge's assessment. Whatever his views before entering office, Fisher soon revealed that he was a conservative reformer in educational matters. He reflected this outlook in a series of three articles written for an American audience in early January 1917, setting out what he considered to be the main elements of the educational needs of the nation.

In the first article, 'What England has learned from war', he made it clear that he believed there were few lessons to be gained from the experiences of the previous two and a half years. The war had merely shown that Britain had been unready for conflict. As much had been known before 1914. It was not something the nation need be ashamed of; indeed, it could be proud. To argue that unpreparedness indicated a deficiency in the educational system was almost to admit that education was to be judged by its adjustment to military ends. Its objects were civil and general, not military and particular. Education aimed at the 'elevation of character and the discipline of mind', and any practical end was valuable only if those two purposes were also served. The war had revealed the 'moral splendour' in the national character but there appeared to be no evidence of intellectual deficiencies; Britain's ability to organise for war merely proved the opposite. Nevertheless, the country was wise to seek an audit of educational aims, facilities and achievements. There was a general feeling that matters could not be left to chance. Greater efforts must be made to develop talents, and however well this was already being done more would be necessary in the future.[51]

In terms of an educational programme Fisher did not believe there was a need for drastic changes in the system. Rather, there should be an expansion of existing effort. He told his American audience that the vast expenditure involved in war had made people realise that a great deal more could and should be spent on education. The opportunity had arisen to fill in 'gaps' in the system. The main one was the lack of 'continuative education' for adolescents, a deficiency which even employers realised must be overcome if better relations were to be established between capital and labour and young workers were to become more disciplined and reasonably tempered. A second great deficiency was the continuing problem of ill health among children. The extension of the school medical service could help to overcome it. The nation also required more pupils in the secondary schools; the true proportion of adolescents fit for secondary education would depend on the 'diffusion of intelligence through the population', but the present figure of 3 per cent in secondary education compared unfavourably with Germany's 10 per cent. Finally, greater measures would have to be taken to improve the salaries and status of teachers.[52]

In higher education, however, Fisher was prepared to resist what he considered excessive utilitarian demands. Although he had played an important part in the development of applied science in Sheffield, he had also been one of the signatories of the counter-blast to the 'Neglect of Science' memorandum. In the third of his American articles he pointed out that it required no elaborate intelligence to understand that science laid the foundation for material success and national power. The expansion of science was assured by the process of war itself and by impending changes that would transform industry. The major problem would be the 'ethical spirit' of the nation. There had to be a changed outlook on the part of all sections of society. The growth of such organisations as the Workers' Educational Association was a welcome sign as evidence that the worker was becoming interested in the ethical aspects of the social system and not just higher wages. Many workers wanted more humanity and a share in the direction of industry and of their country. There was also much to look for in the spread of the 'academic spirit' among employers. It was to be hoped that what he described as the 'old rigorous autocracy' in English society would break down 'under the stress of social pressure from below and a gentler influence from above'.[53] Yet much should and would remain the same:

> The War, with its call for self-examination and energy, will bring many changes; but there are some things which will not change, whatever be the issue of the conflict. We shall not exchange our scheme of academic liberty for the state university of the Prussian system. We shall still believe in private enterprise, private endowment, local initiative. The aim of the nation will never be the attainment of mere mechanical force as an end in itself. Perhaps when the cycle of reform is complete, our enemy will declare that we are still a race of foolish gentlemen – a little less foolish than before, but still, by some silly eccentricity of nature, gentlemen in thought and act.[54]

This statement of educational and social aims reveals Fisher as a reformer, but a reformer who had no wish to remould society or even rebuild the educational system. His approach fitted in easily with the plans already worked out by the Board. The only question was how to proceed. In general terms, Selby-Bigge remained wedded to development along lines consistent with the pre-war schemes. A memorandum he had originally prepared for the Reconstruction Committee urged that the best chance of making progress was to proceed by steps. It would be 'regrettable' to postpone any specific proposals already put forward in favour of less certain radical reforms. Hence the most important task would be the reform of the grant system for elementary education as proposed in 1913–14. After that, other steps could be taken to reform and develop secondary education along the lines put forward in 1914 but since deferred; gradually expand continuation and technical education in accord with pre-war ideas and the recommendations of the Lewis committee; increase grants to universities; provide more funds for teachers' salaries, pensions and training; enlarge the provision of bursaries and scholarships; develop greater co-ordination between local education authorities, and provide for a thorough inspection of all areas of the educational system.[55]

If the programme for reform was already worked out, where did Fisher fit in? Perhaps his major contribution was a recognition of the need to move ahead quickly. His scepticism was to override the caution of Selby-Bigge. As he later wrote, 'I resolved to move forward at a hard gallop and along the whole front. If I did not strike my blow now, the opportunity might be lost never to return.'[56]

His determination drew support from another quarter. The fall of the Asquith government had worried Haldane lest things became 'more difficult' for the educational programme that the reviewing committee had drawn up.[57] After talking to Fisher, Haldane was delighted to find that he and the new Minister were entirely 'at one' and were to co-operate in constructing a programme to present to the Cabinet.[58]

Throughout January 1917 Fisher worked with Haldane and the Board officials. As a result, two papers were prepared for discussion which he was invited to present to the War Cabinet on 20 February.

The first, entitled 'Educational development – proposals for immediate action', was in two parts, both seeking extra finance. It proposed to reform the grant system in elementary education along the general lines suggested by the Kempe committee in 1914, but with an important modification. For the first time the grant system would be structured in such a way as to take account of teachers' salaries. Even before the war the declining supply of teachers had been a major problem. The war itself had accentuated it. As Fisher told the Cabinet, elementary teachers were 'miserably paid', and their discontent posed social dangers. Before the war the number of teachers leaving the profession had been 9,000 annually, and there were only 6,000 new entrants each year to replace them. With the prospect of acute shortage in the post-war period, immediate action was necessary to make teaching a more attractive occupation.[59] Thus the grant system would be restructured to provide greater State aid in such a way as to offer local education authorities direct inducements to improve salaries where they were low, and to recognise liberality where expenditure on teachers' pay was high. It was expected that the total of new money involved in the reform would be £3,780,000.[60]

The second part of the 'proposals for immediate action' was the scheme for the development of higher education, Treasury approval for which had been given before the outbreak of war. It included a superannuation plan for teachers in secondary and technical schools, reform of the examination system in secondary schools, and the issue of new regulations for technical education. The total sum incurred here would be £450,000.[61]

The second paper that Fisher presented to the Cabinet was far more extensive and wide-ranging in its proposals. It put forward twelve points for the development of English education.

1. A reformed system of elementary grants £3,900,000

2. Raising of the school age to fourteen and abolition of half-time — £500,000
3. Empowering local education authorities to provide nursery schools — £500,000
4. Additional provision for the health and physical development of children and adolescents — Cost not stated
5. Establishment of day continuation classes of not less than 320 hours a year — £3–4,000,000
6. New grants for secondary schools and a reformed exam system — £500,000
7. Promotion of university education by (*a*) an increase in and consolidation of grants, and (*b*) providing a sum to carry out the recommendations of the 1913 Royal Commission on London University — Cost not stated
8. Extension and improvement of the bursary and scholarship system to widen the highway from the elementary school to university — £100,000 rising to £300,000
9. An increase in grants for technical education — £100,000 rising to £300,000
10. A State pension scheme for secondary and technical teachers — £130,000
11. The development of teacher training — £100,000
12. Extension of 'choice of employment' work in co-operation with the Ministry of Labour, and the establishment of closer relations between schools, universities and industry, commerce and the professions. — Cost not stated.[62]

If this programme is compared with the plans of the Liberal government in 1914, and also with the first part of the recommendations of the Addison committee in 1915, it can be seen that the scale and dimensions had increased but that the major outlines remained much the same. A number of the items above had been borrowed direct from pre-war plans. Items 2–4 had been included in the 1913–14 education Bill. Items 6, 7 and 9–11 had all been included in the provision for extra education grants announced by Lloyd George in 1914. Item 8 had also been among the pre-war plans and had certainly been included in the recommendations of the Cabinet paper which had emerged from the 1915 Board of Education committee that met under the chairmanship of Christopher Addison. The item that was 'new' was the provision for a compulsory system of continuation classes of 320 hours a year for fourteen-to-eighteen-year-olds. However, this proposal was in accordance with the recommendations of the Lewis committee. The establishment of such a system of continuation classes, along with the related provision for raising the school age to fourteen and abolishing half-time schooling would, as the Cabinet paper itself claimed, be the most important and contentious of all the Board's plans. The Cabinet paper argued, though, that both reforms were necessary if the State was to undertake any effective training of adolescents. It was therefore suggested that a Bill should be introduced in the present session of Parliament providing for a school age of fourteen and requiring local education authorities, after consultation with employers and parents, to establish schemes for compulsory continuation classes.[63]

Despite the apparent breadth of the plans, Fisher and the Board were anxious to show that they were not too ambitious. In particular the hand of Selby-Bigge revealed itself in the proposal for continuation classes. At a meeting of the Board in early January 1917 both Fisher and the parliamentary secretary, Herbert Lewis, had urged that a full system of continuation classes be implemented as soon as possible. Fisher had even spoken of setting a limit of five years after the passage of the Bill for a scheme to be in operation. To Selby-Bigge, ever the voice of caution, such an aim was madness. The Permanent Secretary reminded his Minister that the administrative problems of finding up to 32,000 teachers in four years was immense and could bring disaster to the whole scheme.[64]

This advice now bore fruit. The Cabinet paper suggested that the system of continuation classes should not operate until a year after the end of the war, and, in view of the probable dislocation of the labour market once peace arrived, local education authorities should be given eighteen months to two years to prepare schemes. Once schemes were drawn up, children would come into the continuation classes in four successive batches as each batch reached the age of fourteen. Thus the system of continuation classes would not be in operation in any part of the country until four years after the Board had approved a scheme, and in view of such administrative difficulties as the shortage of teachers and the problems of accommodation the full establishment of the system over the whole country would take half a generation. It was therefore suggested that legislation be passed as soon as possible.[65]

Whilst the establishment of continuation classes was the main proposal, the final sections of the Cabinet paper noted that legislation would also be necessary to create a system of nursery schools, and to formulate a superannuation scheme for secondary and technical teachers. These were less contentious measures and would probably be opposed only by those who objected to all increased educational expenditure.[66]

Such was the programme of both short and long-term development upon which the new Minister wished to act. As Fisher himself later wrote, the pressure of war business was so great that at its meeting on 20 February 1917 the Cabinet had only half an hour to discuss educational matters.[67] In the short run this was an advantage, for both papers received formal approval. Fisher was authorised, first, to proceed with legislation to empower local education authorities to establish nursery schools and to create a State pension scheme for secondary and technical teachers; and, secondly, to consult leading businessmen on the scheme for continuation classes.[68] From Fisher's point of view at least 'the best part of the battle was already won'.[69]

On 19 April 1917, Fisher made his parliamentary debut, speaking for two and a half hours without notes.[70] The enthusiasm raised by the appointment of the new Minister was still fresh in the minds of many, and the atmosphere lent itself to rhetoric. Fisher made good use of the occasion. He began by reflecting on the changes he saw in the national attitude towards education. The impact of war had led to

> a quickened perception of the true place of education in the scheme of public welfare . . . this great calamity has directed attention to every circumstance which may bear upon strength and national welfare. It has exhibited the full range of our deficiencies, and it has invited us to take stock of all the available agencies for their improvement.[71]

There was, he claimed, a new public interest in education, demonstrated most clearly in the demands of trade unions and the support now given by enlightened employers and manufacturers. This had led to a 'remarkable consensus of opinion' on present needs and the main lines of reform. It was generally accepted that the extension of education could lay the foundation of industrial and military strength, help to end industrial strife, and restore the loss and destruction of war. There was a solemn obligation upon Parliament to provide for the future so that 'the rising generation, deprived of its natural predestined leaders, may be prepared to furnish an added measure of service to the community'.[72]

Outlining details of the proposed increases in educational grants, Fisher told the Commons that 'The first condition of educational advance is that we should learn to pay our teachers better'.[73] The new grant system would help achieve this aim. There would also be more money for secondary education, an area which he described as one of the 'weakest points' in the educational system, particularly in view of the small percentage of students who remained at school after the age of sixteen.[74] The new grants would raise the salaries of secondary teachers, increase general grants to secondary schools, and provide for advanced secondary education.[75] Yet he could not consent to the principle of free secondary education, for it would have raised 'very controversial questions'. Rather, further assistance in the form of maintenance allowances was necessary. The aim was what he described as 'social fusion', and the best way to achieve it was to have a system by which wealthy parents paid fees for their children, while those of poorer parents would be liberally assisted through free places and maintenance allowances.[76]

Turning to other areas of education and indicating the long-term plans of the Board, Fisher said the development of university education would require provision for scholarships and postgraduate research.[77] The general aim throughout the educational system was that 'We do not want to waste a single child. We desire that every child should receive the form of education most adapted to fashion its qualities to the highest use.'[78] As a result, he hoped that Parliament would soon approve legislation providing for progressive schemes of education, rural schools, higher elementary education, and continuation classes, in order that

> the foundation may be laid for a fabric of national education worthy of the genius and heroism of our people and a fitting monument of the great impulse which is animating the whole nation during the war.[79]

In the dark gloom of early 1917 even parliamentarians could be moved by visions of the future: 'I sat down amid general applause,' was Fisher's later comment.[80] On this issue at least the political parties could remain united. McKenna, opposition spokesman for education, gave his 'wholehearted support', particularly in regard to the efforts to improve the status of the teacher, introduce continuation classes and raise the school age.[81] Much of the praise was for Fisher himself rather than the actual reforms he proposed. 'We want the spirit and passion of education embodied in a man,' claimed the Labour member George Thorne, 'I believe we have it in the present President of the Board of Education.'[82] Similar views came from most sections of the press. A 'remarkable parliamentary triumph', wrote the *Daily Telegraph*. Education now had a 'competent expert in charge of it'.[83] The *Manchester Guardian* described Fisher as the first education Minister for many years who did not see his office as a stepping stone to higher politics, and who had other concerns than the delineation of elementary education between the religious sects.[84]

Despite such effusions, just how important and how new were the reforms? Provision for the development of advanced work in the secondary schools stemmed from the pre-war plans of the Board, which now issued regulations to pay grants for advanced course work in the three areas of science and mathematics, humanities and ancient studies.[85] At the same time, and as a corollary, the Board went ahead to reform the secondary school examination system in accordance with the 1911 report of the consultative committee and its own provisional regulations issued in 1914. The result was the formation of the Secondary Schools Examination Council, empowered to co-ordinate the existing examinations for secondary school students and thereby lay the basis for a school leaving certificate.[86]

The reform of the grant system for elementary education was also essentially a pre-war decision, the implementation of which had been deferred by the outbreak of hostilities. The new grant system has been described as instituting a real financial partnership between the central authority and local education authorities. 'The turning point lies in Fisher's settlement of 1917–19 and the recommendations of the Kempe committee on which that settlement was very largely founded.'[87] Relating the grant system to the financing of salaries was also a firm attempt to cope with the problem of teacher supply, although even here the disruption of war had merely accentuated and not created the problem.

While these steps were significant, they really only formed the basis for educational change. Fisher later wrote in his autobiography,

> My sympathies were democratic. I believed in the career open to talent, and was ambitious of the honour of widening the highway from the elementary school to the university.[88]

To judge by the programme presented to the War Cabinet and his Commons speech, 'democratic' was hardly the apt word to describe the Board's plans. Fisher had told the House that he specifically rejected the principle of free secondary education. The Labour member Ramsay MacDonald, one of the few in the Commons to cast a critical eye over the content of the new Minister's speech, pointed out that, although Fisher did not talk of the educational ladder, his reference to maintenance grants indicated that 'the shadow of the educational ladder still lies across the educational highway'.[89] Essentially, what the Board was aiming at was improvement of the existing system. Change would be limited and cautious.

There were some associated with the new government who thought it was not enough. Early in January 1917 A. E. Zimmern, an adviser to Lloyd George and a former official at the Board of Education, told Tom Jones that he had spoken to Fisher. Although he believed that Fisher was 'evolving his plans', Zimmern also informed Jones that it appeared the new Minister had been told that to ask for more than three hours' a week compulsory continued education would make accommodation with the employers impossible. He added,

> In the glut of labour immediately after the war half-time at any rate up to 16 ought to be practicable. I hope you can stiffen him on this point and enlist the P.M.'s imagination. We have fought this war with the very minimum of brain power and we really cannot afford to manufacture unskilled workers at the rate we are doing.[90]

Zimmern's appeal for a wide view of what was possible found a particular response from within the reconstituted Reconstruction Committee. The Prime Minister told the first meeting of the new group that 'reconstruction' would embrace not only immediate post-war problems, the most important of which would be demobilisation, but the laying of the 'foundations of a new social order'. The nation was in a 'molten condition', Lloyd George pointed out, and 'It was for the committee to advise the Government on the way to give to the nation a shape which would endure to the advantage both of the nation itself and of the whole Empire'.[91] Plans for housing, health and such issues as workers' representation in industry had all been under consideration by the Asquith Reconstruction Committee; they were now to be given further impetus.[92]

In organising for the post-war world, education was seen as being of prime importance. In a paper prepared in the early months of 1917 the historian J. L. Hammond, one of the new recruits to the Reconstruction Committee, argued that

> The Reconstruction Committee aims at something more than the mere smoothing of the path of transition. The war has thrown all the belligerent people on to their resources and every nation has to consider its future in a new and serious spirit. The war has put a new value on life and given a new clue to the sources of power. To the Reconstruction Committee is assigned the duty of finding what measures promise to develop the strength and vitality of the nation and to arrest the waste of our strength. Education is obviously of vital significance in this connection. We have learnt in the most terrible of schools that it is a crime to let our youth grow up in relative ignorance and neglect, when time trouble and money would give us a well-educated and healthy nation.[93]

The committee thus had an interest in education as part of a general programme of reconstruction. This interest raised the whole question of who held ultimate jurisdiction over educational policy. The issues here were related to the much more general question of the relationship between the Reconstruction Committee and all other government departments. Paul Johnson has argued that the change in the nature of the committee was not so much to further the cause of social reconstruction within official circles as to hamper it. He points to the Asquith Reconstruction Committee's 'cardinal virtue': being composed of Ministers and chaired by the Prime Minister himself, it directly involved government departments in the planning of reconstruction and provided a means of deciding upon action at the highest level. When Lloyd George became Premier, Johnson claims the Reconstruction Committee was to 'meet obstacles, lack of Cabinet attention, inability to speed departmental response and intolerable delays in the final decision making which under the Asquith Reconstruction Committee could almost certainly have been removed'.[94] The committee also came into conflict with the Board of Education.

Soon after assuming office Fisher had sought to clarify the relation between the committee and the Board. On 8 January 1917 he wrote to Lloyd George requesting an interview and indicating that he was anxious to hear his opinion regarding the position of the Education Reviewing Committee (which, in formal terms, had been a sub-committee of the Reconstruction Committee) and 'the procedure to be adopted in maturing the plan for educational reforms'.[95] On 23 February, just after presenting the proposed educational programme to the War Cabinet, he again wrote to the Prime Minister asking whether the Reviewing Committee would be 'kept alive' now that it had been decided to reconstitute the general Reconstruction Committee. Fisher urged that he himself should assume full responsibility for all educational proposals brought before the Cabinet, and suggested that the Reviewing Committee be dissolved. Otherwise, 'I am really rather afraid that the continued existence of the Reviewing Committee may hamper you as well as myself in working out the measures for the improvement of education in which you are so keenly interested.'[96]

The response came from the Reconstruction Committee itself. On 22 March it decided to discontinue the Reviewing Committee. However, the decision was taken without prejudice to the Reconstruction Committee's freedom to consider educational questions.[97] This was in accord with the general attitude of its members, who had decided not to be restricted by past decisions and plans. On 30 March the Reconstruction Committee decided to form, out of its own membership, four panels for the areas of education, local government, labour, and control of industry. The educational panel was directed by the full committee to consider the specific issues of juvenile employment and physical training and other special inquiries not covered by the Board of Education.[98] The panel itself was composed of a chairman, Professor W. G. S. Adams, who was a private secretary to Lloyd George over the period 1916–22 and was described by Beatrice Webb as 'a high browed idealist, who wants to change the world spirit rather than alter social machinery – about which he knows little',[99] Tom Jones, by then a member of the newly formed Cabinet secretariat, the social philanthropist and industrialist Seebohm Rowntree, and Dr Marion Phillips, a leading member of the Independent Labour Party. The secretary of the educational panel was Arthur Greenwood, a Fabian and a member of the Yorkshire W.E.A.

According to Beatrice Webb, who, as a member of the other three panels of the Reconstruction Committee was an intimate observer of events,

> The educational panel started off on idealist schemes – their special enthusiasm being adult education (W.E.A.). The Committee is, in fact, planning to do the work of the Consultative Committee of the Board of Education This panel was, at first, favoured by the R.C. [Reconstruction Committee] and the secretariat – the subjects selected for consideration being "safe subjects" – warranted not to excite criticism. But it presently

launched out into a detailed criticism of the Education Bill as a most imperfect measure, which brought it into disfavour with the Board of Education.[100]

The outcome of this dispute would help decide much of the future planning for post-war education.

Notes

1 A. J. P. Taylor, *English History, 1914–1945*, Oxford, 1965, p. 73.
2 R. J. Scully, *The Origins of the Lloyd George Coalition. The Politics of Social Imperialism, 1900–1918*, Princeton, N.J., 1975.
3 *Hansard*, Commons, 5th ser; LXXXVIII, 19 December 1916, col. 1338.
4 Arno J. Mayer, *Political Origins of the New Diplomacy, 1917–1918*, New Haven, Coun., 1959, pp. 34–6.
5 Gilbert, *British Social Policy, 1914–1939*, p. 9. The rise to power of the Prime Minister himself seemed to signal a new era. Lloyd George later wrote proudly in his memoirs, 'there had never before been a "ranker" raised to the Premiership – certainly no one except Disraeli who had not passed through the Staff College of the old Universities'. D. Lloyd George, *War Memoirs*, London, 1933, I, p. 621. However, A. J. P. Taylor points out that, like many of his best claims, this one of Lloyd George's was slightly inaccurate. The Duke of Wellington had not been to Oxford or Cambridge, either. A. J. P. Taylor, *Lloyd George. Rise and Fall*, London, 1961, p. 123.
6 K. Middlemas (ed.), *Thomas Jones Whitehall Diary*, I, *1916–1925*, London, 1969, pp. 3–4.
7 *The Times*, 22 February 1917, p. 3. This article is partly reprinted in R. H. Tawney, *The Attack and other Papers*, London, 1953, pp. 29–34.
8 The term has been applied to the closely knit pattern of intermarriage among certain sections of upper middle-class English intellectuals. Noel Annan, 'The intellectual aristocracy', in J. H. Plumb (ed.), *Studies in Social History*, London, 1955, pp. 243–87. Annan suggests that the influence of this 'intellectual aristocracy' explains the paradox of an English intelligentsia which conformed to rather than rebelled against society.
9 David Ogg, *Herbert Fisher*, London, 1947, p. 16.
10 H. A. L. Fisher, *An Unfinished Autobiography*, London, 1940, p. 50. For an outline of Green's philosophy on education see Melvin Richter, *The Politics of Conscience*, London, 1964, pp. 350–61.
11 Be.L., L.G.P., F16/7/13; Fisher to Lloyd George, 20 December 1917. See also John Rae, *Conscience and Politics*, London, 1970, pp. 199–200.
12 In April 1914 Fisher appealed to the Sheffield business community,

'Use us, use our lectures, use our courses, understand that we exist to help you. And not only do we exist to help the education of young men and young women in Sheffield; we exist also very largely for the study of problems which are connected with the local industries'. *Sheffield Daily Independent*, 25 April 1914; cutting in University of Sheffield Archives, Newspaper Cuttings, vol. 23. W. N. Gibbons, former Registrar at Sheffield, said that Fisher visualised the university as 'as a sort of central power station of the intellectual life of the diocese'. Gilbert Murray, *Herbert Albert Laurens Fisher*, London, 1940, p. 6.

13 A. W. Chapman, *The Story of a Modern University*, London, 1955, pp. 260–74.

14 Ogg, *Herbert Fisher*, pp. 57–9. Despite his war work in Sheffield, Fisher had been anxious for some form of more active government service. See B.L., F.P., Box 7; Fisher to Gilbert Murray, 2 and 27 September; and B.L., G.M., 19; Gilbert Murray to Fisher, 25 September 1915.

15 As early as July and August 1916 there had been rumours that either Sadler or Fisher might become President of the Board of Education. Sadler was most upset when he was not called upon, and he considered his chances had been ruined by the opposition of Haldane and Arthur Acland, the chairman of the Board's Consultative Committee. See M. Sadler, *Michael Ernest Sadler*, London, 1940, pp. 273–6. Fisher later wrote that, when interviewed by Lloyd George, he himself had suggested Sadler as a better choice. Fisher, *An Unfinished Autobiography*, p. 91. Yet Lloyd George agreed with Tom Jones that Sadler was 'too viewy and wordy'. Diary entry, 8 December 1916, in Middlemas (ed.), *Thomas Jones Whitehall Diary*, I, *1916–1925*, p. 10. If Fisher had refused his offer, Lloyd George would have preferred Henry Hadow, the Vice-chancellor of Newcastle University College. Diary entry, 10 December 1916, *ibid.*, p. 12.

16 Fisher says that the meeting took place in late autumn. Fisher, *An Unfinished Autobiography*, p. 89. But, according to a record in his own papers, the actual date was 27 August 1916. B.L., F.P., Box 24; Memorandum of an interview with Lloyd George, 27 August 1916. Fisher also took the opportunity here to press for exceptional young men to be reserved from the battlefront, a request upon which Lloyd George promised to take some action. *Ibid.*, Box 1, David Davies to Fisher, 2 September 1916.

17 The interview also revealed Lloyd George's ignorance of Eastern Europe. In discussing the possible post-war settlement he urged that the Austro-Hungarian Empire be broken up. The following then took place. *L.G.:* 'I admit Bohemia is a difficulty.' *Fisher:* 'The Slovaks are also a difficulty.' *L.G.:* 'Who are the Slovaks?' *Fisher:* 'Well, they are Slavs, peasants and about 2 million strong.' *L.G.:* 'Where are they? I don't seem to place them.' *Fisher:* 'On the West of Hungary.' *L.G.:* 'And where are the Ruthenes?; *Fisher:* 'On the North.' B.L., F.P., Box 24; Memorandum of an interview with Lloyd George, 27 August 1916.

18 Fisher, *An Unfinished Autobiography*, p. 90.

19 *Ibid.*, pp. 90–1. Dover Wilson, a man full of anecdotes, offers a story behind the appointment of Fisher which is fascinating but hard to verify. According to his account Fisher, Michael Sadler, E. K. Chambers and himself were all present at a dinner at Sheffield University just after the fall of the Asquith government. Sadler was apparently expounding on what he would do if he was chosen as President of the Board of Education, calling for research and the setting aside of a county to carry out experiments in teaching and organisation – suggestions which brought forth Chambers's contemptuous cry, 'What would the parents say?' Wilson continues, 'Fisher kept his silence, smiling his Chinese smile, and a few days later we read in the newspapers that it was he whom Lloyd George had chosen as President of the Board – as he must have known when we sat there.' Dover Wilson, *Milestones on the Dover Road*, p. 84. If this dinner took place after 8 December (the date when, according to an entry in the Jones diary, Lloyd George offered the education post to Fisher: Diary entry, 8 December 1916, in Middlemas (ed.), *Thomas Jones Whitehall Diary*, I, *1916–1925*, p. 10), then Fisher's response is not surprising. If the dinner took place before 8 December, then it would suggest that Fisher realised he was destined for the education post.

20 Diary entry, 7 December 1916, in Middlemas (ed.), *Thomas Jones Whitehall Diary*, I, *1916–1925*, p. 8; diary entries, 10 and 11 December 1916, in Addison, *Four and a half Years*, I, pp. 275–6.

21 T. J. to Sir Henry Jones, 10 December 1916, in Middlemas (ed.), *Thomas Jones Whitehall Diary*, I, *1916–1925*, p. 14. In October to November 1916 Sir Henry Jones had presented a series of lectures on 'citizenship' at the University of Sheffield, where Fisher was then Vice-chancellor. *Sheffield Daily Telegraph*, 2 October and 6 November 1916, cuttings in University of Sheffield Archives, Newspaper Cuttings, vol. 26. Sir Henry Jones, himself a Welshman by birth, was a firm supporter of educational reform. Like Tom Jones he was also an intimate of Lloyd George and was actually present with the latter in early December 1916 just before the fall of the Asquith government. See H. J. W. Hetherington, *The Life and Letters of Sir Henry Jones*, London, 1924, p. 126.

22 Diary entries, 10 and 11 December 1916, in Addison, *Four and a half Years*, I, p. 276. His account of Fisher's appointment is substantiated by an entry in the unpublished diary of Sir George Newman, Chief Medical Officer of the Board of Education and a confidant of Addison. Diary entry, 1–14 January 1917. (This is a joint entry recording, in part, the political events of December 1916.) Sir George Newman diary, located in Department of Health and Social Security Library, London.

23 Evelyn Wrench, *Geoffrey Dawson and our Times*, London, 1955, p. 144.

24 *The Times*, 11 December 1916, p. 9.

25 *Daily News*, 11 December 1916, p. 5.

26 *Highway*, January 1917, p. 70.
27 P.R.O., Ed 24/1384; Deputation from the Parliamentary Committee of the Trades Union Congress, 15 February 1917.
28 Johnson, *Land fit For Heroes*, p. 221.
29 It was apparently during the Boer war that Fisher had first met Lloyd George, Ogg, *Herbert Fisher*, p. 45.
30 B.L., F.P., Box 7; Fisher to Gilbert Murray, 9 December [1916].
31 *Ibid.*, Fisher to Gilbert Murray, 12 December 1916.
32 H. A. L. Fisher, *Political Prophecies*, Oxford, 1919, p. A2 [*sic*].
33 *Ibid.*
34 *Ibid.*, pp. A2 [*sic*] –4.
35 *Ibid.*, p. 4.
36 T.J. to Sir Henry Jones, 10 December 1916, in Middlemas (ed.), *Thomas Jones Whitehall Diary*, I, *1916–1925*, p. 14.
37 Such was the story recounted to Beatrice Webb by Tom Jones. See diary entry, 22 February 1917, in M. I. Cole (ed.), *Beatrice Webb's Diaries*, I, *1912–1914*, London, 1952, p. 82.
38 Diary entry, 19 February 1917, *ibid.*, p. 81.
39 Diary entry, 22 February 1917, *ibid.*, p. 83.
40 B.L., F.P., Box 7; Fisher to Gilbert Murray, 17 January 1917. Murray was appointed on a half-time basis to fill the post of Principal Assistant Secretary of the Board's university branch. B.L., G.M., 115 (a); R. S. Wood [Chief Clerk, Board of Education] to Gilbert Murray, 27 January 1917.
41 Mansbridge, *The Trodden Road*, pp. 84–5.
42 Fisher, *An Unfinished Autobiography*, p. 98.
43 Newman discussed with Addison possible appointments which would strengthen both the Local Government Board and the Board of Education. Diary entry, 9 December 1916, in George Newman diary, located in the Department of Health and Social Security Library, London.
44 N.L.W., H.L.P., Group I, Part 11 of No. 231; Diary note, 14 December 1916.
45 B.L., F.P., Box 7; Fisher to Gilbert Murray, 9 December [1916].
46 B.L., F.P., Box 3; W. N. Bruce to Fisher, 11 December 1916.
47 *Ibid.*; Selby-Bigge to Fisher, n.d. Among the letters of congratulation that came to Fisher on his appointment, one was from E. G. A. Holmes (whose circularised report on local inspectors had helped create the storm leading to Morant's downfall in 1911). Holmes had now left the Board and was a leading apostle of 'progressive education'. He warned, 'A friend of mine who is in the closest touch with the B. of E. tells me that it is secretly hostile to reform and that its policy is quietly obstructive.' B.L., F.P., Box 3; E. G. A. Holmes to Fisher, 11 December 1916.
48 C.U.L., C.P., Box C/15; Fisher to Crewe, 15 December 1916.
49 Fisher, *An Unfinished Autobiography*, p. 97.
50 P.R.O., Ed 24/1476; Review of Schemes for Reform, n.d., January 1917. The paper is unsigned but it bears the unmistakable cautious

style of Selby-Bigge.

51 H. A. L. Fisher, 'What England has learned from war', *The Outlook*, 3 January 1917, pp. 22–3.

52 H. A. L. Fisher, 'Ten millions for schools', *The Outlook*, 10 January 1917, pp. 64–5.

53 H. A. L. Fisher, 'The universities and civic patriotism', *The Outlook*, 17 January 1917, p. 113.

54 *Ibid.*

55 P.R.O., Ed 24/1461; Board of Education, R.P. No. 6, Development of the National System of Education, December 1916.

56 Fisher, *An Unfinished Autobiography*, p. 103.

57 N.L.S., H.P., 5996, fol. 158; Haldane to his mother, 4 December 1916.

58 *Ibid.*, fol. 188; Haldane to his mother, 23 December 1916.

59 P.R.O., Cab 23/1; War Cabinet Minute, 75 (10) of 20 February 1917.

60 N.L.W., T.J.C., D, i, No. 19; Educational Development – Proposals for Immediate Action, 2 February 1917. Despite an extensive search this paper cannot be located at the P.R.O. The formula suggested for the reform of the grant system was the 1914 Kempe committee proposals of £1 16*s* per child in average attendance plus an additional provision of 60 per cent of salary expenditure plus 20 per cent of other expenditure.

61 *Ibid.*

62 P.R.O., Ed 24/847 (a); Educational Reform, General Proposals, 5 February 1917. (At the time of research this document was misfiled; the P.R.O. has been informed of the fact.) A summary list of these twelve points appears in Lloyd George, *War Memoirs*, II, p. 1990.

63 *Ibid.*

64 P.R.O., Ed 24/1422; Conference on Education Bill and Continuation Classes, 9 January 1917.

65 P.R.O., Ed 24/847 (a); Educational Reform, General Proposals, 5 February 1917.

66 *Ibid.*

67 Fisher, *An Unfinished Autobiography*, p. 103.

68 P.R.O., Cab 23/1; War Cabinet Minute, 75 (10) of 20 February 1917.

69 Fisher, *An Unfinished Autobiography*, p. 104.

70 *Ibid.*, p. 105.

71 *Hansard*, Commons, 5th ser., XCII, 19 April 1917, col. 1888.

72 *Ibid.*, col. 1889.

73 *Ibid.*, col. 1897.

74 *Ibid.*, col. 1904.

75 *Ibid.*, cols. 1905–6.

76 *Ibid.*, col. 1908.

77 *Ibid.*, cols. 1909–10.

78 *Ibid.*, col. 1910.

79 *Ibid.*, cols. 1914–15.

80 Fisher, *An Unfinished Autobiography*, p. 105.

81 *Hansard*, Commons, 5th ser., XCII, 19 April 1917, col. 1915.

82 *Ibid.*, col. 1963.

83 *Daily Telegraph*, 20 April 1917, p. 5.

84 *Manchester Guardian*, 20 April 1917, p. 4.
85 The Board made it clear that grants would be paid for such courses only and not for advanced work in single subjects. Board of Education Circular 1023, 5 December 1917. This provision led to strong opposition as expressed by deputations from the Incorporated Association of Assistant Masters, the body representing secondary school masters. See P.R.O., Ed 12/196.
86 However, the strong representation of the university examining bodies on the Secondary Schools Examining Council was to bring criticism from both the teachers and the local authorities. See P.R.O., Ed 12/246. See also Banks, *Parity and Prestige in English Secondary Education*, pp. 83–6.
87 Education, 1900–1950, Cmd 8244, p. 32.
88 Fisher, *An Unfinished Autobiography*, pp. 97–8.
89 *Hansard*, Commons, 5th ser., XCII, 19 April 1917, col. 1974.
90 A. E. Zimmern to T.J., 7 January 1917, in Middlemas (ed.), *Thomas Jones Whitehall Diary*, I, *1916–1925*, pp. 19–20.
91 Johnson, *Land fit for Heroes*, pp. 37–8.
92 *Ibid.*, pp. 59–68.
93 J. L. Hammond, 'Reconstruction', cited in Johnson, *Land fit for Heroes*, pp. 57–8.
94 Johnson, *Land fit for Heroes*, pp. 31–2.
95 Be.L., L.G.P., F16/7/4; Fisher to Lloyd George, 8 January 1917.
96 *Ibid.*, F16/7/5; Fisher to Lloyd George, 23 February 1917.
97 P.R.O., Recon. 1/14; Reconstruction Committee, Minutes, 22 March 1917.
98 P.R.O., Recon. 1/40; Part I, Reconstruction Committee, Appointment of Panels, 30 March 1917.
99 Diary entry, 3 June 1917, in Cole (ed.), *Beatrice Webb's Diaries*, I, *1912–1924*, p. 85.
100 *Ibid.*, p. 87.

V

The 1918 Education Act

The educational programme Fisher had presented to the War Cabinet and Parliament had indicated the outlines of an education Bill. He claimed later that, although the war had provided the impetus for legislative change, the political circumstances of 1917–18 limited the scope of his proposals. Belonging to a coalition government, he did not feel that he could alter the religious settlement of 1902. Any effort to reopen the question would have endangered the cohesion of the government and wrecked his chance of contributing to educational change. Nor did he personally wish to do so:

> The general framework of the Balfour Act seemed to me to be sound. If the system was not ideal, it was very far from being the kind of system which it would have occurred to any statesman to construct on a *tabula rasa*, it possessed two great advantages. First, it was in actual working. Second, it was clearly compatible with great improvements and developments.[1]

While this view reflects Fisher's essentially conservative attitude, there is at least some substance to his assessment of the continuing importance of differences over the religious question. Both Nonconformist and Anglican opinion had not forgotten past disputes. The Liberal *Daily News* could still point out that the extra grants for education would go to all elementary schools alike, leading to 'a further endowment of privately controlled schools'. What was needed was the 'extension of the principle of complete public control over all publicly maintained schools'.[2] For his part, soon after Fisher became President of the Board of Education the Archbishop of Canterbury sought an interview with the new Minister to impress upon him, as he had earlier impressed upon Crewe, that the Anglican Church had an active interest in reconstruction, particularly in regard to reinforcing religious instruction in elementary education.[3]

Aware that beneath the national consensus supporting educational reform there lay sectarian differences, Fisher decided to leave the religious settlement of 1902 intact.[4] As a result the aims of the proposed education Bill were limited from the outset. His stated object of improving and developing the existing system was essentially the same as that earlier adopted in 1913 by the Board, Haldane and the pre-war Cabinet committee. Indeed, it is obvious that with one notable exception – the omission of all clauses pertaining to the single-school area grievance – the Bill prepared by Fisher and the Board in 1917 was built upon the earlier draft measure of 1913–14.

The 1917 Bill contained eight sections.[5] The first, concerned with developing a 'National System of Education', was almost exactly the replica of provisions in the 1913–14 measures. Each county and county borough was to draw up an educational scheme to provide for the progressive and comprehensive organisation of education in its area. In so doing it was to consult any Part III authorities in its area. Each educational scheme was to make provision for central and advanced elementary schools, further education, the supply and training of teachers, and also continuation schools. In order to provide for the better co-ordination of education and for general advice and assistance to both the central and the local authorities, the Board could require, as had also been proposed in the 1913–14 Bill, the establishment of provincial associations. Finally, the limits on State aid for higher education, as imposed by the 1902 Act, were removed.[6]

The second section of the Bill related to school attendance. These provisions went beyond the measure of 1913–14. Both abolished 'half-time' and allowed local education authorities to raise the school leaving age to fifteen, but whereas the 1913–14 Bill had contained a provision allowing a child exemption from school at the age of thirteen (on condition of attending part-time continuation classes until sixteen), the 1917 one imposed a universal school leaving age of fourteen years. Of more importance, it provided that, excepting those in secondary schools, all young persons between the ages of fourteen and eighteen were to attend a continuation school for not less than 320 hours a year. The Bill also provided, partly in accord with Denman's private member's Bill of 1914 and with the position to which the Board had then been moving, that no child under the age of twelve was to be employed, and no juvenile over twelve could be employed before 6 a.m. or after 8 p.m. on any school day. The administration of such employment laws was to pass to the local education authority.[7]

The third section extended the powers and duties of local education authorities. In accordance with similar provisions in 1913–14, they were empowered to establish social and physical training facilities, provide for medical inspection in secondary and continuation schools, supply nursery schools, cater for children in remote areas, and aid research.[8]

The last five sections of the Bill were primarily financial and administrative. The most important provided for the abolition of elementary school fees, a national education survey, allowing the Board to transfer the powers of a Part III authority to a county, consolidation of elementary grants, and the establishment of educational trusts.[9]

Overall the 1917 draft Bill was essentially an expansion and development of the measures of 1913–14. This is not to say that the new Minister had played no part in deciding its terms. His influence had obviously counted for much in the main advance over the earlier plans – the embodiment of the principle of compulsory continuation classes for adolescents. The 'greatest defect' in the existing educational system, Fisher had written in mid-1916, was the lack of compulsory day continuation classes for adolescents aged fourteen to eighteen. There were other blemishes but they were unimportant compared to the 'grand object' of 'securing to every citizen, male or female, some scheme of moral, intellectual and technical discipline till the eighteenth year'.[10] On the other hand, the detailed proposals did not come from Fisher. The actual terms of the scheme for compulsory continuation classes – the provision of 320 hours a year for fourteen-to-eighteen-year-olds – was drawn directly from the report of the Board of Education departmental committee under Herbert Lewis.

Such, then, was the Board's proposed education Bill. Did it go far enough? Did it meet the ideal of 'reconstruction' with which the Lloyd George government now seemed associated? The expectation of wide-ranging change stimulated those who sought to represent popular needs in education. The knowledge that the Board were preparing a Bill, as Fisher had indicated in his maiden Commons speech, provided a further impetus. In particular, the Workers' Educational Association carried forward the campaign it had begun in 1916 and made it clear what it considered both an education Bill and a general educational programme should contain.

In early May 1917 the W.E.A. convened a conference in London that was attended by over 733 delegates, representing trade unions, universities, co-operative societies, local education authorities, and W.E.A. districts.[11] The conference was addressed not only by the organisation's president, William Temple, but also by Dr Marion Phillips and Arthur Greenwood, both members of the educational panel of the Reconstruction Committee, and such trade unionists as George Dallas of the Workers' Union and Charter of the National Union of Railwaymen. Opening the conference, Temple spoke of the opportunity the war presented for educational advance:

> It is quite plain that the opportunity before us will not recur. When War is over there is bound to be a vast amount of reconstruction. If lines have been laid for our educational development before that time, along which we are to proceed when the time has come, then the process of reconstruction in industry and elsewhere will have to adapt itself to what is thus laid down.[12]

Throughout the conference it was made clear that the delegates were seeking not merely improvements in the existing educational structure but a major overhaul that would create equality of opportunity for all classes. Marion Phillips spoke of the need to establish in the elementary schools a corporate ideal similar to that of the great public schools, so that there would be real equality of educational opportunity.[13] There was also suspicion that working-class education was being confined merely to technical studies designed to improve economic efficiency. One trade union delegate said that what was wanted was good general education: there was already enough technical and manual instruction.[14] As William Temple pointed out, 'The W.E.A. has no affection whatsoever for manual training.'[15]

To formulate its demands the conference passed four major resolutions. The first called for nursery schools, a compulsory leaving age of fourteen, to be raised to fifteen within five years and to sixteen within eight years, maintenance allowances for schoolchildren over fourteen, the abolition of all child labour, class sizes of forty to be reduced ultimately to thirty, development of the school medical service, school meals and physical training, and buses for rural districts. The second affirmed the principle of the 'broad highway' from elementary school to university, which meant compulsory daytime continued education of twenty hours a week (with the hours of labour for under-eighteen-year-olds restricted to twenty-five a week). The direction of education in the continuation schools was to be towards the full development of body, mind and character, with no military drill, and teachers in such schools should also have equal status with those in the secondary schools. There should also be provision for transfering pupils in continuation schools to full-time secondary education, and a further allocation of scholarships to the universities. Finally, the last two resolutions called for adequate teacher salaries and a State grant of 75 per cent of local education costs which would be reduced if local education authorities failed to do their duty in such matters as class sizes, teacher pay, providing a variety of institutions and medical services.[16]

This programme went far beyond the plans of the Board, particularly on the question of the school leaving age and the provision of continuation classes. The W.E.A. criticised the Lewis committee both for failing to provide for juveniles affected by the war – 'those children whose interests the committee was specifically appointed to consider' – and for suggesting a leaving age of fourteen and 320 hours-a-year continuation classes for fourteen-to-eighteen-year-olds – proposals which were 'seriously inadequate'. Overall:

> Our great cause of difference with the Report is that though it confesses a sympathy with the ultimate educational and social ideals upon which our own and similar proposals are based, it is hampered by the belief that such proposals would not receive such a measure of support from public opinion as to admit of effective legislation.[17]

Some Board officials considered that the W.E.A. itself could hardly be said to reflect public opinion. E. K. Chambers believed that the 'Association can not claim to be in any way representative of the great mass of working-class sentiment', for it had a 'vast amount of missionary work still to accomplish before it will persuade any substantial proportion of parents to believe that full time education up to 16 is a good thing in itself, quite apart from any advantage which it gives to a child obtaining employment.'[18] Nevertheless the Board did recognise the W.E.A. as an important influence in working-class circles, and sought to win the organisation to its own viewpoint. Gilbert Murray interviewed R. H. Tawney, the W.E.A. secretary, J. M. Mactavish, and George Dallas of the Workers' Union. He tried to impress upon them that the proposed legislation would be a great step forward even if it did not meet all their demands. Mactavish promised support but pointed out that working-class enthusiasm would only be raised by a 'large clear programme' and 'not one with compromises in it'.[19]

As noted, the W.E.A. itself had some voice in government circles, particularly through the Reconstruction Committee's educational panel. Of the four members of the panel, Tom Jones was an intimate of the W.E.A. organiser Richard Tawney, and Marion Phillips and Arthur Greenwood had addressed the W.E.A. convention in May 1917. It was not merely a question of affiliations. Most members of the committee represented a spectrum of left-wing and progressive opinion that paid little attention to the views of the bureaucrats. The housing panel went beyond previous aims and set a target of 300,000 houses to be built.[20] Similarly, the committee as a whole was taking a much larger view than the Board of Education of what could be achieved in planning for the post-war world. It now submitted a memorandum to the Cabinet, putting forward its own educational proposals as part of a general programme of post-war reconstruction.

The committee argued that what was needed was not the mild reforms proposed by the Lewis committee but a comprehensive programme covering the next ten years, including the raising of the leaving age to sixteen and thence the establishment of half-time secondary schools to eighteen. The war provided the opportunity to lay down such a programme, and, as education was the 'foundation of true national progress', educational reconstruction would have to be placed in the 'forefront of schemes to be adopted at the end of the War'.[21]

Fisher and the Board responded in a Cabinet memorandum on their proposed Bill. Agreeing that their proposals for continuation classes fell a long way short of the demands urged by such groups as the W.E.A., they suggested that because of the problems of securing the necessary teachers and accommodation, and of 'adapting the system to the conditions of industrial employment', 'to aim at more in the measure would be to accomplish less'. It would be futile to pass an ambitious Bill that would either 'remain inoperative as a measure of Turkish reform' or fail and thus discredit the whole educational system. In any case, it would take years to organise a really effective system of continuation schools for the whole population between the ages of fourteen and eighteen. Any Bill could do little more than provide conditions favourable to development, although the government should itself adopt the policy of 'going in advance of the immediate needs of the moment' so that 'it will receive the support and even the applause of public opinion'.[22]

The War Cabinet did not see fit to discuss the Board's proposed Bill, merely instructing Fisher and the Chancellor of the Exchequer, Bonar

Law, to consider any further points before the measure was laid before Parliament.[23] The Reconstruction Committee, however, did not let the matter rest there. In a further memorandum it urged that half-time instruction for fourteen-to-sixteen-year-olds should be made compulsory at the close of the war. In line with W.E.A. policy a majority also recommended that, as a further step, within five years the universal leaving age should be raised from fourteen to fifteen and half-time attendance should be made compulsory to eighteen. Economic objections would dissolve if education were considered part of a general programme of reconstruction that would deal with low wages and the working hours of adolescents. Nor would the introduction of half-time education and a leaving age of fifteen interfere with industrial training and apprenticeship; it could check the entry of juveniles into 'blind alley' employment. More continued education would also provide for physical training and help prevent the physical deterioration so evident among army recruits. Finally, the committee pointed out, not only did the new interest in education and the probable dislocation of industry after the war provide a unique opportunity, its ambitious proposals could generate 'enormous impetus to the advancement of public opinion in this country'. Britain should begin the new era with a measure that would demonstrate its 'leadership in work which is essential to the realisation of an educated democracy'.[24]

If implemented, the scheme would have had a considerable impact upon the shape and direction of English education. Although the Reconstruction Committee had not directly supported the principle of universal secondary education for all, as others had before – including J. H. Whitehouse in 1913, *The Times Educational Supplement* in 1915 and the Labour Party conference of January 1917 – the effect of a leaving age of at least fifteen would have transformed the upper reaches of the elementary schools and brought about a radical rethinking of the whole purpose of secondary education. Half-time attendance to eighteen would also have given adolescents much more education than the mere eight hours a week allowed for in the Bill. Its provisions might have been an advance on pre-war standards, Arthur Greenwood told a W.E.A. conference in Yorkshire, but, in view of all the country had undergone since, they were a 'mockery'. The mass of working-class children would be attending 'sham schools' for eight hours a week while those of the well-to-do would be in full-time secondary education.[25]

The dispute between the Reconstruction Committee and Fisher and the Board of Education seems to have centred on what was considered possible. Fisher found Vaughan Nash, the secretary of the committee, 'very visionary'.[26] Yet the differences went deeper. Most of those on the Reconstruction Committee were seeking to transform the basis of the social structure. To their way of thinking, educational advance, industrial change and social reform were all part of a whole. The educational panel later set up a sub-committee on adult education. Chaired by A. L. Smith, an organiser of W.E.A. classes in Oxford, it had a membership of twenty, of whom eleven, including R. H. Tawney and Albert Mansbridge, were members of the W.E.A.[27] In its first interim report on social and industrial conditions the sub-committee claimed:

> In the course of our inquiries it has been forced upon our attention that education is hampered in many directions by economic obstacles, that industrial and social reform are indispensable, if the just claims of education are to be met, and that the full results of these reforms will be reaped only as education becomes more widespread.[28]

Hence, it argued, the State must take action to reduce the hours of employment, guarantee the right to work, provide holidays, humanise industrial relations and plan for housing development.[29] Only then could the nation hope to order its life 'in accordance with those principles of freedom and justice, which led so many of its best sons to the field of battle'.[30]

This vision of a new society was founded on a collectivist and egalitarian ethic. In contrast, Fisher remained committed to his Liberal and upper middle-class background. Although he supported such measures as the Ministry of Health Bill, he maintained his faith in free trade, distrusting too much State intervention and, at the end of the war, urging that economic controls be released as soon as possible.[31] As an upper middle-class intellectual he accepted the existing basis of society, arguing that the extension of education for the masses should not transform but alleviate the harsher aspects of industrialisation. He believed that many people valued education not as a means of rising out of the working class, a 'vulgar ambition', but because they knew that in the 'treasures of the mind' they could find an 'aid to good citizenship, a source of pure enjoyment and a refuge from the necessary hardships of a life spent in the midst of machinery in our cities of toil'.[32] Extended education could serve as a force against social change and an antidote to industrial unrest. In 1917's climate of worsening labour troubles the argument seemed particularly apt. He had been struck by an 'alarming growth of indiscipline in the working class population whose minds were full of nothing but industrial grievances', he informed a deputation from the Federation of British Industries in February 1918. The 'secret' of social control of young workers was to 'fill their minds with something like humane letters, or elements of science'; then 'you get a humane outlook throughout all the country and you get industrial relations more intelligently discussed'.[33]

On the specific issue of the education Bill, the views of Fisher and the Board prevailed. E. K. Chambers observed that, in contrast to the situation in 1916 when Asquith established the Reconstruction Committee to weigh reform proposals against each other, Lloyd George's committee had become 'entrusted with the functions of stimulus rather than of balance'.[34] But this did not mean its voice would be heard in Cabinet. Although the committee was responsible to the Prime Minister, Lloyd George was either too busy or not prepared to argue its case against Fisher and the Board of Education. It was not until mid-July 1917 that the Reconstruction Committee was transformed into a Ministry and placed under Christopher Addison.[35] From then on, the Ministry of Reconstruction had a stronger voice in Cabinet than its predecessor. In other areas, particularly housing, it fought and partly won disputes with the Local Government Board.[36] Vaughan Nash was to also press Addison for a further inquiry into physical training which, he suggested, could investigate the possibility of inaugurating half-time education for fourteen-to-eighteen-year-olds.[37] By then, however, the battle with the Board of Education had been fought and lost. Not only was the Board uninterested in co-operating in such an inquiry[38] but, by its silence, the War Cabinet had already indicated who would determine the nature of educational policy. The education Bill to be presented to Parliament would be that drawn up by Fisher and the Board.

Fisher presented the Bill to the Commons on 10 August 1917. As in April, he used the rhetoric of the relationship between war and reform. The measure was prompted by the 'deficiencies' revealed by the war and framed to 'repair the intellectual wastage' of conflict. If enacted before the peace it would end the evil of industrial pressure upon children, which had grown alarmingly during the past three years, and aid the transition to peace.[39] Yet he stressed that the measure was not all-embracing. 'I am not proposing to supersede or to revolutionize the educational settlement of 1902.'[40] The Bill did not cover such things as the universities, scholarships, the secondary system and pensions for teachers, or the urgent problem of catering for children directly affected by the war.[41] It was, however, related to the movement of public opinion, emphasising the need for educational advance. First, the country had come to recognise the close relation between physical and educational efficiency. Secondly, there was a growing consciousness of the lack of correlation between parts of the educational system which hampered provision for children's varying aptitudes. Thirdly, there was a growing feeling of 'social solidarity': the 'same logic' which was leading to the extension of the franchise pointed to an extension of education.[42] After outlining the main provisions of the Bill, he concluded that the improvement and extension of education was not only a national necessity but a fundamental human right:

> But we argue that the compulsion proposed in this Bill will be no sterilising restriction of wholesome liberty, but an essential condition of a larger and more enlightened freedom, which will tend to stimulate civic spirit, to promote general culture and technical knowledge, and to diffuse a steadier judgment and a better-informed opinion through the whole body of the community.[43]

As in April, press reaction was generally favourable. *The Times* called the Bill the 'Children's Charter' and described Fisher's speech as a 'historic document worthy of a great occasion'.[44] The *Manchester Guardian* said the Bill was neither great nor 'bold' but it started from the important principle of the 'sacred right of individuality, of personality'.[45] Even the Tory *Daily Mail* could find grounds for approving it, for the war had shown the importance of education, and in a 'neck-and-neck' race with Germany after it Britain could not neglect the 'high road to efficiency'.[46]

Parliament was less enthusiastic. This time there had been few in the Commons to listen. Some expressed opposition. The Conservative Sir J. D. Rees felt that it was too ambitious a measure to debate in a Parliament which was then seven years old and thus without proper electoral mandate,[47] while the radical Josiah Wedgwood condemned the scheme for continuation classes as designed merely to improve technical efficiency so that the country could compete with Germany.[48]

Fisher later claimed that the Bill had been introduced more as 'a *ballon d'essai*, or expedient for testing public opinion, than with the idea of placing it on the Statute Book as it stood'.[49] Even before presenting it, he and the Board had sought the opinion of vested interests, particularly the Churches. Selby-Bigge had reassured the Archbishop of Canterbury that any clauses affecting denominational schools were designed only to increase educational efficiency.[50] A meeting of the Anglican episcopacy in October 1917 passed a unanimous resolution supporting the Bill; a degree of consensus, the archbishop pointed out to Fisher, that was 'a rare thing when 29 Bishops are concerned'.[51] Similar support came from the Nonconformists. The Free Church Council expressed unanimous approval,[52] although the Methodist leader J. Scott Lidgett later told Fisher that he had impressed upon his Nonconformist friends the need to support the measure and reserve denominational points for subsequent consideration.[53] Other denominational opinion was less favourable. The Catholic Education Council, representing the views of both the episcopate and the laity, not only rejected full-time education past the age of fourteen as too costly for poor parents, but also insisted upon State financial support for denominational continuation classes.[54]

Apart from the religious denominations, the Board was aware that there would be certain opposition to the Bill from industrial interests, particularly in the north of England. After the Cabinet decision of February directing Fisher to consult businessmen concerning the establishment of continuation classes, F. H. Spencer, a Board inspector, had carried out a lengthy survey of industry. Having investigated 300 firms, he concluded that most employers would either welcome or acquiesce in a scheme of continuation classes. The main opposition would come from the cotton trade, particularly in Lancashire, where most workers were women and children and the conditions of employment had over a century of tradition behind them.[55]

The cotton industry revealed its hand soon after Fisher had presented the Bill to Parliament. McConnel, vice-chairman of the Fine Cotton Spinners' and Doublers' Association, claimed that the proposals would deplete the cotton trade of up to eight per cent of its labour and disrupt mill organisation. He suggested that, as an alternative, education should be improved for twelve-to-fourteen-year-olds and a few adolescents could then enter effective industrial training.[56] To counter such opposition Fisher decided to undertake a propaganda campaign through Lancashire, Wales and southern England. The tour was to reveal a remarkable degree of popular support for the Bill.

The tour began in Manchester on 25 September, with the Free Trade Hall almost packed to capacity.[57] Intense interest followed Fisher throughout Lancashire.[58] The people there, he told Gilbert Murray, had given him 'splendid meetings', and although he realised the cotton trade was organising its forces he thought the tour had enabled them to see the other side of the question.[59]

Public enthusiasm continued into the south and Wales. At the invitation of Ernest Bevin, Fisher addressed a meeting of nearly 4,000 dockers in Bristol.[60] In Swansea, in a district where there had been considerable industrial unrest and opposition to government policy, over 2,000 came to listen.[61] Herbert Lewis, who went along for part of the tour, told Lloyd George that Fisher and his Bill were a 'very powerful and popular asset to the Govt.'. In over thirty-five years' experience of public meetings he had never seen a better attended one than the gathering at Swansea,

> The Albert Hall was packed to the roof and they could have filled it twice over, had there been room. He has had similar meetings wherever he has gone. At Manchester the Free Trade Hall was packed, at Plymouth there was an audience of 4,000, at Bristol last Sunday afternoon there were 3,000 dockers. Fisher is not an exciting speaker and never plays to the gallery, but the audience jumped to its feet frequently and cheered him enthusiastically.[62]

There was clearly a groundswell of opinion that had not existed before the war. The general popularity of the Bill was even more significant in the context of the general political and military situation in the autumn of 1917. The German submarine campaign was a continuing menace; there was stagnation on the western front after the disastrous campaign in the mud of Passchendaele; defeat for the Allies in Italy; at home, labour unrest, food shortages, and the decision of the Labour Party to adopt an independent war aims policy and pursue its own course in domestic affairs. As Lloyd George later wrote, Fisher and the education Bill were one of the few bright spots for the country and the government. 'When the War was reaching its deafening crisis, he stumped the country addressing numerous meetings in every centre, expounding his proposals and secured for them a very large and rapidly consolidating opinion.'[63]

Support was matched by opposition from an unexpected source. In mid-October the Association of Education Committees, the body representing many smaller local education authorities, published a memorandum objecting to certain of the administrative clauses of the Bill, taking particular exception to the creation of provincial councils, the provision for transferring power from smaller authorities to county councils, and the establishment of the right of the Board of Education to determine the powers of an authority. The memorandum pointed out that the Bill gave no promise of financial aid, which it claimed should be 75 per cent of local education budgets.[64]

These objections stemmed from the fears of urban boroughs and district councils that the Board was seeking both to increase its own powers and to centralise educational administration. Fisher thought that the authorities had 'got into a panic quite unnecessarily',[65] and he pointed out to Sir Cyril Cobb of the London County Council that the government sought local co-operation but powers were required to compel a laggard authority to fulfil its duty. The provincial councils were a matter for discussion, yet their creation was not meant to override the powers of local authorities.[66] He also promised in a speech at Bradford that the government would provide at least 50 per cent of a local education authority's budget.[67]

Objections to the administrative clauses were significant, but what was more important was the extent of public support and expectation. Fisher informed the War Cabinet that the Bill had aroused greater enthusiasm than he had expected. He could see no opposition from the major religious bodies and expected to overcome difficulties with the Roman Catholics. He believed that the apprehensions of local education authorities could be met, while the supporters of the half-time system seemed afraid to come out into the open. The 'widespread unanimity' was unlikely to recur, and he urged the government to seize the opportunity to push the measure through at the earliest possible moment.[68]

The War Cabinet itself agreed with this assessment, the representative of labour, G. N. Barnes, emphasising the Bill's importance to the trade unions. It was decided that the Prime Minister should make an early announcement that, subject to the exigencies of the war, the Bill would be given precedence in the next session of Parliament.[69] On 26 November, two and a half weeks after the Cabinet decision, Lloyd George gave such a pledge to a larger inter-party deputation that waited upon him to express their support for it.[70]

The last four months of 1917 had demonstrated how much popular support there was. To enact the measure in a Parliament elected on pre-war issues and on a pre-war franchise was another matter. It was through the parliamentary process that sectional interests were now able to make their influence felt.

The first matter was the attitude of the local education authorities towards the administrative clauses. In the period between the last months of 1917 and the new session of Parliament in 1918, Fisher and the Board of Education held a number of discussions with delegations from the various associations representing the authorities.[71] As a result, in early January Fisher introduced amendments designed to meet their criticisms. The sections relating to provincial councils, the transference of powers from a smaller authority to a county council and the reference of certain educational questions to the Board of Education were all omitted. The terminology of other clauses had been rephrased and a new clause inserted to provide for deficiency grants where a Treasury grant did not meet 50 per cent of a local authority's approved expenditure. Other modifications sought to satisfy the Catholic community that the rights and privileges of religious denominations would be protected.[72]

L. I. Andrews has claimed that the government had yielded to pressure from the local education authorities because it had not felt strongly enough committed to the administrative provisions of the Bill.[73] This view needs some qualification. The changes satisfied the authorities but they also ran counter to the original 1913–14 idea of creating a national system of education in which the authority of the Board of Education would be strengthened and co-ordination between local education authorities facilitated. On the other hand, successful implementation of the Bill would depend on the co-operation of the local education authorities. Despite popular enthusiasm for the Bill, neither Fisher nor the Board was prepared to face unnecessary controversy. Concession seemed the safest course, as was to be demonstrated again on other, more important, clauses.

The debates on the second reading in the Commons took place from mid-March to mid-June 1918. On the surface the Bill's prospects appeared bright. Leaders of both the opposition parties gave it their approval. Asquith reminded the London Liberal Federation that before the war his government had been preparing to tackle the problem of a national system of education: '. . . we are all glad that it has been taken in hand now by so competent and liberal-minded a man as our friend Mr Fisher.'[74] Praise was translated into active support, and Fisher later told Gilbert Murray that he was deeply indebted to Asquith.[75] Speaking at a W.E.A. conference in May Arthur Henderson said his party welcomed the Bill as an instalment of overdue reforms, although Labour would not be satisfied until the fullest educational opportunities were open to every child. In the meantime it would watch and guard against industrial interests seeking to force Fisher to drop the proposed continuation classes on the false grounds of consideration for the incomes of working-class families.[76]

The commitment of the party leaders could not, apparently, guarantee the support of their backbenchers. The debates were poorly attended.[77] The major parliamentary critic of the Bill's shortcomings was the Liberal, J. H. Whitehouse, who echoed his pre-war views, arguing that it confined working-class children to elementary schools and continuation classes and so reinforced the class system in education. The proper reform, he claimed, would be to establish elementary schools as the 'natural avenue' to secondary and higher education.[78] Some Labour members backed his efforts to carry an amendment establishing a leaving age of sixteen with full maintenance allowances, but support was far from general.[79] The combination of Labour backbenchers and the Conservatives provided strong opposition.

The key issue was the hostility of both employers and employees to the continuation classes. After surveying 2,000 firms the Federation of British Industries (formed in 1917 to promote manufacturing interests) issued a memorandum accepting the raising of the school age to fourteen but rejecting the principle of compulsory continuation classes as creating unnecessary industrial disruption. Instead capable students should be selected to pass at the age of twelve from elementary education to secondary and junior technical schools. For the majority of juveniles, part-time vocational training in continuation classes could then be established in some industries.[80]

Similar obstruction came from within the ranks of labour. A United Textile Factory Workers' Federation delegation informed Fisher that, while they would not resist the raising of the school age, their union still opposed continuation classes. They argued that such a system would deprive adult workers of juvenile assistants necessary for the organisation of the mills, leading to a general loss of wages.[81]

To meet the cotton trade's objections the Lancashire Conservative member Sir Henry Hibbert suggested a compromise. Instead of eight hours' continuation classes a week for fourteen-to-eighteen-year-olds the government should allow local education authorities to establish continuation classes of approximately 600 hours a year for fourteen-to-sixteen-year-olds. It was expected that this scheme would cause far less disruption, as it would merely be an extension of half-time up to but not beyond sixteen. A deputation of Lancashire members urged Fisher to accept the amendment, Hibbert himself pointing out that as he and his colleagues had now accepted the abolition of half-time under fourteen Fisher should be satisfied, rather than trying to 'take two bites of the cherry'.[82]

Fisher rejected the compromise as unacceptable. He told the War Cabinet that, while it might be in the interests of employers, there would undoubtedly be opposition from employees, particularly if half-time meant half-pay. Rather than allow the proposal to operate in exceptional circumstances, Fisher suggested that the best way to meet the opposition of the Lancashire members was to postpone the establishment of continuation classes for sixteen-to-eighteen-year-olds. It had always been recognised, he claimed, that it would take time to organise continuation classes for everyone between fourteen and eighteen. There were 'distinct administrative advantages' in organising a scheme for fourteen-to-sixteen-year-olds first, since it would allow employers and industries time to adapt. It would also 'allay many fears' and go a long way to meet the difficulties of employers outside the textile industry. He admitted that confining continuation classes to fourteen-to-sixteen-year-olds for the time being would reduce the Bill's emphasis on full-time education, whether in secondary, junior technical or central schools, but if this was 'regrettable' it was 'inevitable'.[83]

Fisher therefore decided to make three concessions. The provision allowing local education authorities to increase the hours of continuation classes above the statutory limit of 320 hours a year was removed. Secondly, sixteen-to-eighteen-year-olds were to be excluded from the operation of the Act during its first seven years. Finally, during this initial period, a local education authority could reduce continuation classes from 320 to 280 hours a year.[84]

In justification he told Gilbert Murray that the Lancashire opposition had been 'solid', as Snowden and his Labour colleagues had sided with the employers. It could have been voted down, but the former educational Ministers McKenna and Runciman had warned that such a course could prove fatal to the Bill's prospects.[85] To Sir

Henry Miers, Vice-chancellor of Manchester University, Fisher explained that the concessions were less drastic than appeared on the surface. Spreading the Act over nine rather than four years would be more acceptable to the country, while administrative problems such as teacher supply would probably have forced the Board to accept the concessions anyway.[86]

This reasoning was in line with the case argued against the more ambitious measure proposed by the Reconstruction Committee. It again demonstrated that the thinking of Fisher and the Board was governed by caution about what was thought possible within the existing structure of society. On the other hand, the concessions also showed the strength of sectional interests in a Parliament elected on a pre-war franchise.

Once over the hurdle of continuation classes, the Bill had an easier passage. To satisfy other interests Fisher was prepared to yield some minor points. He appeased the drama lobby by agreeing to theatrical licences for children aged twelve to fourteen.[87] Of more significance, he satisfied Labour interests by accepting that no young person would be forced to attend a continuation school established in industrial works,[88] empowering local education authorities to grant maintenance allowances in elementary and secondary schools,[89] and finally allowing advanced education in the elementary schools up to the age of sixteen.[90] A last-ditch appeal to Lloyd George from the Catholic episcopacy seeking State aid for denominational continuation schools[91] failed, although Fisher reassured denominational and other interests by making concessions on public inquiries and conscience clauses.[92]

In the Lords the Bill passed almost without debate, although both Haldane and Salisbury tried unsuccessfully to include military training in the curriculum of continuation classes.[93] The only important amendments were to restrict the labour of children under fourteen to two hours on Sunday, and to forbid the employment of all children under twelve on schooldays.[94] The measure received the royal assent on 8 August 1918.

Along with the Representation of the People Act, the 1918 Education Act stands out as one of the two major pieces of domestic legislation enacted before the end of the war. Its passage was therefore bound to be related to hopes for the post-war world. Lord Gorell, recently appointed to administer the educational schemes of the army, told the

Lords that many of the troops regarded the Education Act as the 'first broad measure of reconstruction'.[95] *The Times*, a firm supporter of educational reform, also praised it as destined to 'influence for good the lives of countless men and women in the unknown future, and to play no inconsiderable part in the rebuilding of all that has been shattered in England during the past four years of violence and upheaval'.[96]

There was much praise for Fisher as the Minister who had carried the Act through Parliament. Lloyd George complimented him on his 'consummate Parliamentary skill'.[97] Herbert Lewis told the Prime Minister himself, 'Fisher has been wonderful. It was a happy day for me when you sent him to the Board of Education. He has been a magnificent Minister of Education & deserves every encouragement.'[98]

In keeping with a tradition of associating the main English education Acts with the Ministers who piloted them through Parliament, the 1918 measure has become known in popular parlance as the Fisher Act. In this case the influence of a man drawn from academic life to serve the cause of national education has appeared direct and immediate. Historians have reinforced the impression. Thus D. W. Dean has written, 'Although educational reform had been widely discussed even before the War, Fisher's contribution to it was a distinctive one, and the Education Act sprang from his specific viewpoint.'[99] Another student of educational policy during this period has claimed that 'the 1918 Education Act was allowed to be very much the personal creation of Fisher'.[100]

Titles, like appearances, can be deceptive. In 1902 it had been Morant rather than Balfour who had framed both the principles and the details of legislation. Lord Butler has made it clear that he relied upon the advice of his permanent officials in drawing up the Act of 1944.[101] So it was in 1917–18. As has been demonstrated, while wartime developments had an important influence upon its terms – notably the report of the Lewis committee and the appointment of Fisher himself – the Act cannot be understood in isolation from its pre-war origins. In the end it was an advance on what had been proposed then, though it was an advance in degree rather than in kind. The opposition of the smaller local education authorities had led to a modification and some weakening of the clauses concerned with administration. Of more importance, despite his claims to the contrary, by deferring compulsory continued education for sixteen-to-eighteen-year-olds Fisher had made a concession which meant that the Act did not immediately reach even the aims of the Lewis committee's report, let alone the proposals of the 1917 Reconstruction Committee. The principle of compulsory continuation classes for all fourteen-to-eighteen-year-olds was on the statute book, but implementation was now more doubtful than before. As Fisher himself had admitted to Gilbert Murray on his appointment in December 1916, enthusiasm for educational reform was unlikely to outlast the war. He was therefore throwing chance to the wind if he now believed that continuation classes could be extended at a future date.

Assessing the 1918 Act, it can be seen that the war had acted not as the source of reform but rather as the catalyst. As Sir George Kekewich wrote in 1920, there was nothing new in the proposed improvements, for 'there is not a single one which was not equally necessary, perhaps even more necessary, before the war'.[102] The 'chief merit' of the Act was that in regard to nursery, continuation and special schools it had 'translated the ideals of the past into more or less practical politics'.[103] There is much truth in this claim. By providing for the establishment of nursery schools, and increasing the powers of local education authorities in physical and medical education, the Act extended the aims of the 1906 School Meals Act and the creation of school medical service in 1907. Similarly, the regulation of the hours of employment for schoolchildren, the ending of half-time, the raising of the school age to fourteen, and, most of all, the provision for up to eight hours' continued education for fourteen-to-sixteen-year-olds, to be extended later to sixteen-to-eighteen-year-olds, were an attempt to ensure that supervision of the health and moral welfare of working-class children would be extended to the end of adolescence. Viewed in this way the 1918 Act contributed to the end of an era rather than the opening of a new world.

Yet it did not overcome all the old problems. It made no attempt to settle the grievances of the Nonconformists, the response to which in 1913 had provided the original impetus to the more general proposals for reform. The religious question was still very much a live issue. The General Committee of the National Liberal Federation welcomed the 1918 Act. However, its executive also called for an end to the 'grievances' of the 1902 Act for all publicly maintained schools to be 'controlled and managed by public bodies'.[104] Despite an appeal from one committee delegate that since the 1918 Act had been passed without religious controversy it should be given a chance to work without hindrance from denominational squabbles,[105] the executive would not accept this view. Its motion went through only with a rider calling for free education and other amendments demanding public authority control of all schools as in the 1918 Scottish Education Act.[106]

If the 1918 Act made no attempt to settle the disputes of the past, then neither did it live up to the ideals of those who represented working-class opinion. At a special conference in June the Labour Party adopted its general programme of social reconstruction entitled 'Labour and Social Order', which stressed the importance of collectivisation and national ownership. As part of this programme the resolution on education declared:

> That the conference holds that the most important of all measures of social reconstruction must be a genuine nationalisation of education, which shall get rid of all class privileges, and bring within the reach, not only of every boy and girl, but also of every adult citizen, all the training, physical, mental and moral, literary, technical and artistic of which he is capable.[107]

The party could not be content with a system which not only left the 'great bulk of the children to elementary schooling with accommodation and equipment far inferior to that of the secondary schools, in classes too large for efficient instruction, under teachers of whom at least one-third are insufficiently trained' but also reserved the endowed secondary schools and, even more, the universities to a 'small privileged class' whilst contemplating nothing better than eight weeks' continuation schooling a year for 90 per cent of English youth.[108]

Agreeing with this view, A. J. P. Taylor has seen the proposed establishment of continuation schools as a reactionary measure. 'The continuation schools would have provided a strictly proletarian education and so have made the class cleavage in education worse than ever.'[109] Contemporaries also realised that the difference in the education of adolescents would still be strongly emphasised. Spurley Hey, the director of education for Manchester, painted the picture well when he told the January 1919 meeting of the Incorporated Association of Headmasters:

> So far as he could judge, there was little real educational relationship between the secondary schools and the day continuation schools. They would be rather parallel systems, but really independent, separate, and quite distinct so far as much of their internal working organisation were concerned. In the secondary school one was expected to be sowing the seeds of a life of real culture; in the day continuation system there was little more

> than a nodding acquaintance with education beyond the elementary system. The two types of pupils were also very different and their aims in life were different. Every secondary school looked forward to sending some proportion of its pupils to the university. There was not much at present that the day continuation pupils could look forward to although one hoped they would eventually have contact with the higher technological institutions and even with the universities.[110]

Perhaps the 1918 Education Act should finally be judged not against ideals but in the terms of those who had framed it. It did not set out to restructure English education or create full educational opportunity. It built upon the earlier Act of 1902, by trying in part to eliminate some of the deficiencies revealed since. In educational terms, continuation classes were not the only form of adolescent schooling that it encouraged. The Act did allow for the development of other forms of post-primary education, provided local authorities accepted the duties and responsibilities imposed upon them. Selby-Bigge, who should be regarded as one of the main authors of the legislation, later wrote that the 'leading note of the 1918 Act was undoubtedly that of "systematisation" – the *"adequate" contribution* in every area to a *national system* of education accessible on a basis of equal opportunity to every person capable of profiting by it'.[111] As such, he pointed out, 'systematisation' was to be followed through local initiative reinforced by the supervisory power of the State.

> The Act of 1918 did not contemplate a 'national system' which would obliterate the characteristics of local organisation of education which had been built up since 1902. Indeed, it was careful to give the initiative in the construction of the national system to the Local Authorities. It rested on the modest proposition, reinforced by war, that in the national interests, the local inequalities which are incidental to 'decentralised administration' should be reduced, that the state had a right and a duty to see that the cheerful prospect of fruitfulness in one area was not spoilt by the sterility of other areas, and that the taxpayers' money which bore a large share of the cost of the local service, ought in equity to obtain more equal advantages for the youth of the country wherever they happened to live.[112]

To carry out this aim the Board of Education issued a circular early in 1919 pointing out that one of the most important purposes of the Act was to establish the principle of local authorities' providing for all forms of education. The Board required that each authority undertake a survey of educational needs in its area and draw up a scheme for the progressive development and organisation of its own provision in relation to both national and local requirements. Each authority was also encouraged to plan not only for the immediate future but to take a long-term view and establish a programme of educational development for a period of at least ten years.[113]

In this sense, then, the 1918 Act did contain potential. Whether the country would be prepared to take up the task remained to be seen.

Notes

1 Fisher, *An Unfinished Autobiography*, pp. 95–6.
2 *Daily News*, 20 April 1917, p. 2.
3 P.R.O., Ed 24/1491; Archbishop of Canterbury to Fisher, 24 and 25 January 1917 and Fisher to Archbishop of Canterbury, 26 January 1917.
4 Fisher told his wife that his predecessor Crewe also agreed that the religious question should be dropped. B.L., F.P., Box 5; Fisher to Mrs Fisher, 10 May [1917].
5 The original draft of the 1917 Bill along with a Board of Education memorandum explaining its terms and notes upon most of its clauses is to be found in P.R.O., Cab 24/13; War Cabinet Paper G.T. 757 of 16 May 1917. A slightly redrafted version is to be found in P.R.O., Cab 24/22; War Cabinet Paper G.T. 1651 of 30 July 1917. This second version was the Bill presented to Parliament and is the measure outlined in discussion here.
6 P.R.O., Cab 24/22; War Cabinet Paper G.T. 1651 of 30 July 1917.
7 *Ibid.*
8 *Ibid.*
9 *Ibid.*
10 *The Times Educational Supplement*, 19 July 1916, p. 426.
11 *Schoolmaster*, 27 May 1917, p. 594.
12 *Report of National Conference on Educational Reconstruction*, held at the Central Hall, Westminster, on Thursday May 3rd 1917, p. 4. (Pamphlet located in W.E.A. Library, London, Miscellaneous Pamphlets.)
13 *Ibid.*, p. 9.
14 *Ibid.*, p. 38.
15 *Ibid.*, p. 41. However, the noted supporter of child care, Margaret Macmillan, did protest that manual and intellectual development was related.
16 *Schoolmaster*, 27 May 1917, p. 594. See also P.R.O., Ed 24/1474; J. M. MacTavish to Fisher, 4 May 1917, enclosing the conference resolutions.
17 *The Highway*, May 1917, pp. 135–6.
18 P.R.O., Ed 24/1474; E. K. Chambers, Observations on W.E.A. Programme, 2 January 1917.

19 P.R.O., Ed 24/1911; Gilbert Murray, A conversation with members of the W.E.A. about the Bill, 28 April 1917.
20 Johnson, *Land fit for Heroes*, pp. 59–67.
21 P.R.O., Cab 24/19; War Cabinet Paper G.T. 1305 of May 1917.
22 P.R.O., Cab 24/13; War Cabinet Paper G.T. 757 of 16 May 1917.
23 P.R.O., Cab 23/2; War Cabinet Minute W.C. 150(4) of 30 May 1917.
24 P.R.O., Cab 24/19; War Cabinet Paper G.T. 1304 of July 1917.
25 *Schoolmaster*, 8 September 1917, p. 246.
26 B.L., F.P., Box 8(a), Diary entry, 14 January 1918.
27 P.R.O., Recon 1/85; Reconstruction Committee on Adult Education. See also Corfield, *Epoch in Workers' Education*, p. 172.
28 Ministry of Reconstruction, Interim Report of the Committee on Adult Education, Industrial and Social Conditions, *Parlt. Pprs.* 1918, IX, Cd 9107, p. 3.
29 *Ibid.*, p. 28.
30 *Ibid.*
31 For the views of Fisher on demobilisation see the description of the relevant Cabinet discussions in Johnson, *Land fit for Heroes*, pp. 398–401.
32 *Hansard*, Commons, 5th ser., XCVII, 10 August 1917, col. 800. Fisher also told an American reporter that mass education should be viewed in terms not solely of academic subjects but 'of teaching the people how to enjoy leisure.' *Schoolmaster*, 2 March 1918, p. 268.
33 P.R.O., Ed 24/657; Deputation from the Federation of British Industries, 6 February 1918. Gilbert Murray later wrote that, faced with the alternatives of raising the school age to fifteen or providing continuation classes to eighteen, Fisher 'unhesitatingly' chose the latter, because, while the former plan appeared democratic, the new Minister considered that by the age of eighteen adolescents had lost the discipline and training inculcated in the elementary schools. Murray, *Herbert Albert Laurens Fisher*, pp. 8–9.
34 P.R.O., Ed 24/720; E. K. Chambers, Note of July 1917.
35 For some of the reasons and debate behind the establishment of the Ministry of Reconstruction see Johnson, *Land fit for Heroes*, pp. 68–77.
36 Johnson, *Land fit for Heroes*, pp. 107–17 and 340–7.
37 P.R.O., Recon. 1/46; Minute by Vaughan Nash, 26 November 1917.
38 See *ibid.*; Addison to Fisher, 12 February 1918, and Fisher to Addison, 19 February 1918. Even George Newman, Chief Medical Officer at the Board and one of those who strongly supported the Ministry of Reconstruction's efforts to establish a Ministry of Health, could tell Vaughan Nash somewhat testily, 'I have looked upon the Reconstruction Ministry as a Ministry to serve in the first place as a "clearing house" preparatory to reconstruction, and secondly as an Advisory Department of Reconstruction. I take it, however, that it is not a Health Ministry or an Education Ministry either.' P.R.O., Recon 1/46; Sir George Newman to Vaughan Nash, 11 January 1918.
39 *Hansard*, Commons, 5th ser., XCVII, 10 August 1917, cols. 795–6.

40 *Ibid.*, col. 796.
41 *Ibid.*, cols. 799–800.
42 *Ibid.*
43 *Ibid.*, col. 814.
44 *The Times*, 11 August 1917, p. 7.
45 *Manchester Guardian*, 11 August 1917, p. 4.
46 *Daily Mail*, 11 August 1917, p. 2.
47 *Hansard*, Commons, XCVII, 10 August 1917, cols. 840–4. For analysis of parliamentary attendance and views see the report in *Manchester Guardian*, 11 August 1917, p. 5, and *Daily Telegraph*, 11 August 1917, p. 5.
48 *Ibid.*, cols. 816–9.
49 Fisher, *An Unfinished Autobiography*, p. 106.
50 P.R.O., Ed 24/704; Selby-Bigge to Archbishop of Canterbury, 11 and 15 May 1917, and Selby-Bigge, note of an interview with the Archbishop of Canterbury, 21 May 1917.
51 P.R.O., Ed 24/704; Archbishop of Canterbury to Fisher, 25 October 1917.
52 P.R.O., Ed 24/707; F. S. Meyer and J. Scott Lidgett, Secretaries, Free Church Council, to Fisher, 25 September 1917.
53 *Ibid.*, Memorandum of interview with J. Scott Lidgett, 4 January 1918.
54 P.R.O., Ed 24/705; Secretary, Catholic Educational Council, to Selby-Bigge, 26 April 1917.
55 P.R.O., Ed 24/1425; Report on the Effects on Industry of a Proposed System of Continued Education, 11 June 1917. See also P.R.O., Ed 24/1450; Note of an interview with T. L. Roberts, 24 May 1917.
56 *Manchester Guardian*, 3 September 1917, p. 8.
57 *Ibid.*, 26 September 1917, pp. 4 and 8. See also H. A. L. Fisher, *Educational Reform*, Address delivered at the University of Manchester on 26 September 1917 to the Association of Educational Societies, London, 1917.
58 As some examples see *Burnley News*, 29 September 1917, p. 6., and *Rochdale Observer*, 29 September 1917, p. 6. A general collection of Fisher's speeches is contained in H. A. L. Fisher, *Educational Reform Speeches*, Oxford, 1918.
59 B.L., G.M., 115(a); Fisher to Gilbert Murray, 28 September 1917.
60 Allan Bullock, *Life and Times of Ernest Bevin*, London, 1960, I, p. 85. See also Fisher, *An Unfinished Autobiography*, p. 107.
61 *Cardiff Times*, 13 October 1917, p. 4. For a general account of Fisher's tour in Wales see *The Times Educational Supplement*, 18 October 1917, p. 397.
62 Be.L., L.G.P., F/32/1/9; Herbert Lewis to Lloyd George, 17 October 1917. See also Fisher's own account of his tour. P.R.O., Cab 24/29; War Cabinet Paper G.T. 2370 of 20 October 1917.
63 Lloyd George, *War Memoirs*, II, p. 1992.
64 *The Times*, 25 October 1917, p. 3. The educationalist Michael Sadler also opposed any provisions that would centre authority in provincial associations. *Manchester Guardian*, 19 September 1917, p. 8.

65 B.L., F.P., Box 5; Fisher to Mrs Fisher, 16 October 1917.

66 *The Times*, 25 October 1917, p. 3.

67 H. A. L. Fisher, *Educational Reform Speeches*, p. 86. Fisher had earlier sought Cabinet approval that the Treasury would deal liberally with the educational provisions in the Bill. P.R.O., Cab 24/26; War Cabinet Paper G.T. 2060 of 18 September 1917. At its meeting on 19 September 1917 the War Cabinet agreed that Fisher could announce that the development of higher education would be 'liberally subsidised' by the Treasury. P.R.O., Cab 23/24; War Cabinet Minute 236(2) of 19 September 1917.

68 P.R.O., Cab 23/4; War Cabinet Minute W.C. 268(10) of 8 November 1917. See also the specific support from Barnes in P.R.O., Cab 24/30; War Cabinet Paper G.T. 2394 of 29 October 1917.

69 *Ibid.*

70 *The Times*, 27 November 1917, p. 3.

71 See P.R.O., Ed 24/733.

72 *Hansard*, Commons, 5th ser., CI, 14 January 1918, cols. 55–8. For favourable response from the local education authorities to the changes see *The Times*, 4 February 1918, p. 3.

73 L. I. Andrews, 'The 1918 Education Act', University of London, unpublished Ph.D. thesis, 1968, pp. 319–21.

74 *The Times*, 17 January 1918, p. 4.

75 B.L., F.P., Box 7; Fisher to Gilbert Murray, 8 June 1918.

76 *The Times*, 27 May 1918, p. 10. In early 1918 the central office of the W.E.A. had apparently met the Parliamentary Labour Party to discuss the Bill and proposed amendments. W.E.A. Library, London, 1918 Education Bill File; H. S. Lindsay to J. M. MacTavish, 4 February 1918, and J. M. MacTavish to R. H. Tawney, 9 May 1918. The W.E.A. also published a pamphlet putting forward its 1917 educational programme as proposed amendments to the Bill. See *The Choice before the Nation. Some amendments to the Education Bill by the Workers' Educational Association*, 1918.

77 An analysis of division lists shows that on no occasion did the total voting exceed 250 members, or less than half the House.

78 *Hansard*, Commons, 5th ser., CIV, 13 March 1918, cols. 400–2. A pacifist, Whitehouse was to be overwhelmingly defeated in the 1918 election, receiving a bare 504 votes out of a total poll of 16,000. Trevor Wilson, *The Downfall of the Liberal Party, 1914–1935*, Ithaca, N.Y., 1966, p. 175.

79 *Ibid.*, CVI, 29 May 1918, cols. 846–922. As Rodney Barker has recently pointed out, Labour in public maintained a facade of unified support for the general principles of the Bill, but behind the scenes many Labour Party members were apathetic or even opposed to the measure. Barker, *Education and Politics*, pp. 31–2. See also *Labour Party Conference Report*, June 1918, p. 22. The W.E.A.'s *The Highway* later noted that the absence of Labour members was 'one of the most remarkable features of the debate'. July 1918, p. 136.

80 Federation of British Industries, *Memorandum on Education*, January

1918.

81 P.R.O., Ed 24/667; Deputation from United Factory Workers' Federation of Lancashire, 21 February 1918.

82 P.R.O., Ed 24/670; Memorandum of interview, 30 May 1918.

83 P.R.O., Ed 24/652; War Cabinet Paper of 1 June 1918.

84 *Hansard*, Commons, 5th ser., CVI, 5 June 1918, cols. 1644–6.

85 B.L., F.P., Box 7, Fisher to Gilbert Murray, 8 June 1918. Fisher later wrote that he believed many of the Labour Party opposed educational reforms because 'such hard-bitten half-timers like J. R. Clynes' cherished a 'secret liking for the system under which they had been schooled for success'. Fisher, *An Unfinished Autobiography*, pp. 110–1. The comment on Clynes is hardly fair. Clynes has written of his early experiences in the mills. 'Often I fell rolling instinctively and in terror from beneath the gliding jennies . . . . Sometimes splinters as keen as daggers drove through my naked feet, leaving aching wounds from which dribbles of blood oozed forth to add to the slipperiness of the floor.' J. R. Clynes, *Memoirs, 1869–1924*, London, 1937, I, pp. 29–30. Hardly an experience one would wish to cherish.

86 P.R.O., Ed 24/1895; Fisher to Sir Henry Miers, 6 June 1918.

87 P.R.O., Ed 24/1457; Fisher to Sir George Cave, 15 July 1918.

88 *Hansard*, Commons, 5th ser., CVII, 10 June 1918, cols. 2007–8.

89 *Ibid.*, 3 July 1918, cols. 1800–2.

90 *Ibid.*, CVIII, 15 July 1918, cols. 784–91.

91 P.R.O., Ed 24/705; War Cabinet paper of July 1918.

92 *Hansard*, Commons, 5th ser., CVIII, 15 July 1918, cols. 771–4 and 803–8.

93 *Hansard*, Lords, 5th ser., XXXI, 1 August 1918, cols. 328–42.

94 *Ibid.*, col. 323.

95 *Ibid.*, col. 1155.

96 *The Times*, 10 August 1918, p. 7.

97 B.L., F.P., Box 8, Diary entry, 17 July 1918.

98 Be.L., L.G.P., F32/1/14; Herbert Lewis to Lloyd George, 17 July 1918.

99 D. W. Dean, 'H. A. L. Fisher, reconstruction and the development of the 1918 Education Act', *British Journal of Educational Studies*, XVIII, 3, 1970, p. 261.

100 L. O. Ward, 'The educational ideas and contributions of the British political parties, 1870–1918', University of London, unpublished Ph.D. thesis, 1970, p. 363.

101 R. A. Butler, *The Art of the Possible*, London, 1971, pp. 93–4.

102 Sir George Kekewich, *The Education Department and After*, London, 1920, P. 189.

103 *Ibid.*, p. 308.

104 National Liberal Federation, *Proceedings in Connection with the Meeting of the General Committee of the National Liberal Federation*, Manchester, 26 and 27 September 1918, London, 1918, p. 104.

105 *Ibid.*, p. 106.

106 *Ibid.*, pp. 107–8.

107 Labour Party Conference Report, June 1918, Resolution XV, p. 71. The important place that educational policy held in *Labour and the New Social Order* was due to Fabian and W.E.A. influence. Sidney Webb had composed much of the party platform. The Labour Party's Advisory Committee on Education, one of the policy-making bodies to emerge from Labour reorganisation, included R. H. Tawney as chairman, and the W.E.A. members MacTavish and Dallas, Margaret Macmillan and G. D. H. Cole. Labour Party, Transport House, Advisory Committee on Education, Minutes, 8 April 1918. This same group, along with Sidney Webb and Arnold Freeman, produced the *W.E.A. Yearbook*, the aim of which was stated to be to convince the public that 'no phase of Reconstruction so demands attention as Education'. *W.E.A. Yearbook*, London, W.E.A., 1918, preface.

108 *Ibid.*, pp. 71–2.

109 Taylor, *English History, 1914–1945*, p. 184.

110 *The Times*, 4 January 1919, p. 4.

111 Selby-Bigge, *The Board of Education*, p. 56.

112 *Ibid.*, p. 57.

113 Board of Education, Circular 1096, 7 March 1919.

VI

Return to peace

The 1918 Act was the main piece of educational legislation during the war and immediately after it. With its passage, most public attention soon shifted elsewhere. The Cabinet became preoccupied with post-war transitions, coping with peace-making abroad and, at home, industrial strikes and a heavy legislative programme which included measures to establish a Ministry of Health and the long awaited housing Bill. Fisher himself assumed increasing responsibilities, becoming chairman of the important Home Affairs Committee, established in mid-1918. He piloted the 1920 Home Rule Bill through Parliament and was later appointed a delegate to the League of Nations. Had he wished to embark upon major new directions in educational matters, which he did not, he would have found little available time. C. P. Scott noted in late 1919:

> Lloyd George has placed H. A. L. Fisher in charge of the preparation of the Home Rule Bill and asked me to go and see him before I left next day. He spoke in very warm terms of him – 'another Morley' he said, most popular also and influential in the Cabinet, and a thorough Liberal – evidently his chief support on the Liberal side.
>
> Went to see Fisher [on 1 December] by appointment at 12 o'clock. He is friendly but a little inexpressive, very unlike George's exuberance. Like everybody else in the Government he has too much on his hands and complains that there are not 'brains enough' available for the task in hand.[1]

The war had left its own legacies. There were immediate problems to be faced. The educational system had to be put in order, with teachers returning from the services, and adolescents being displaced from wartime jobs. Some difficulties were tackled only perfunctorily. As part of its general demobilisation programme the government decided to provide non-vocational courses for unemployed youths on the dole. Between December 1918 and February 1920 166 juvenile unemployment centres opened, the highest total attendance throughout the country being 17,000 in March 1919.[2] The centres were not generally popular with young people, and difficulties were encountered in co-ordination between the Board of Education and local education authorities.[3] The experiment did not augur well for the planned operation of continuation classes under the Act.

More substantial provision was enacted for teachers. Lack of new entrants to the profession had been a preoccupation before the war. The Board of Education now estimated that the demands of the 1918 Act would require up to 15,000 new trainees each year, an increase of almost 10,000 over the current intake.[4] In order to improve the supply, in August 1917 Fisher had outlined to the Cabinet a superannuation scheme which would cover elementary, secondary and technical staff. Much of the discussion had centred on the need to raise the 'quality' of the teachers and so remove discontent 'inasmuch as at present revolutionary movements were to no small degree fermented by dissatisfied school teachers'.[5] The eventual result was to be the 1918 Teachers' Superannuation Act, providing a fully State-financed pension for those in secondary, technical and elementary schools. The scheme included both certificated and uncertificated teachers and provided benefits of one-eightieth of the average salary received during the previous five years for each year of recognised service (up to a maximum of forty-eightieths) payable after forty years of service.[6]

Even here Fisher has been credited with an influence he did not exercise. It has been suggested that he himself had decided on a fully State-financed pension scheme.[7] Actually the Board of Education had proposed that insurance companies should run a scheme financed by a contribution of 10 per cent of salary provided equally by the teachers and the State.[8] Apparently disenchanted over the operation of national health insurance, the Treasury considered that a scheme of such size operated through insurance would meet strong opposition in Parliament. The Secretary of the Treasury, Sir Thomas Heath, put forward the plan for a State-supported superannuation scheme, and this was the provision finally enacted.[9]

Other action came with the difficult transition to peace. A report issued by a Board of Education departmental committee early in 1918 had urged local education authorities to form a common basis of principles upon which they could draw up salary scales.[10] Faced by strikes, and teacher unrest, including moves to affiliate with the

Labour Party,[11] organisations representing local authorities informed the Board that they were considering unified pay scales to prevent teachers pushing scales up.[12] Finally, acting on such appeals, Fisher called together a conference of the local education authorities and the National Union of Teachers. Out of it there emerged a standing joint national negotiating committee, composed of delegates from the teachers and their employers and chaired by the newspaper magnate Lord Burnham. What was to become known as the Burnham committee was originally instructed to decide upon minimum scales, carry-overs and war bonuses. Pending general agreement, strikes were to be referred to arbitration.[13] The initial report was to have important implications for all educational development.

The war also left a legacy of commitment. 'We must pay more attention to the schools,' Lloyd George declared in an important speech on post-war policy delivered at Manchester on 12 September 1918.

> The most formidable institutions we had to fight in Germany were not the arsenals of Krupp, or the yards in which they turned out submarines, but the schools of Germany. They were our most formidable competitors in business and our most terrible opponents in war. An educated man is a better worker, a more formidable warrior, and a better citizen. That was only half comprehended before the war.[14]

Some believed that, despite changes, the lesson had still not been learnt. The 1918 Act was an achievement, but it would have little impact on the curriculum of the secondary schools and universities. Apart from providing more education for the masses, the main concern in the ferment over 'reconstruction' in 1916 had been scientific and technical studies. Yet, since then, little had been done. Science still seemed to be neglected.

In the early post-war period the science lobby started to reorganise. In March 1919 a leading chemist, W. J. Pope, claimed that, despite the war work of his colleagues, 'small encouragement existed for those who desired to see pure and applied science flourish as it deserved in Great Britain'. The prospect of future economic competition made support even more necessary than in the past. 'The coming struggle for scientific and industrial position, on the results of which rest the whole future of our race, would call for far larger, greater, more persistent and more intelligent efforts than any we had hitherto exerted.'[15]

Two months later a group known as the League for the Promotion of Science in Education, the successor to the 1916 Neglect of Science

Committee, held a conference to 'direct attention to the continued neglect of science in the educational system of the country and its subsequent effects'. The conference was addressed by the industrialist Lord Leverhulme as well as by other notable figures such as the scientific propagandist Sir Richard Gregory, H. G. Wells, Philip Magnus and F. W. Sanderson, headmaster of Oundle.[16] Finally, in September, Professor Henry Armstrong criticised the Board of Education's Committee on Science, which had issued its report in 1918, generally focusing on recommendations to improve scientific teaching. Armstrong suggested that by neglecting other issues the report itself proved the 'necessity' of the 'reconstruction, root and branch, of the Board of Education so that it might become an active, alert and sympathetic body in touch with public needs and desires, governed by scientific method'.[17]

Much centred on policy towards the universities. Formerly caught up in scientific war work, they still seemed of prime national importance in the early post-war years. In September 1917 Fisher and Balfour had urged the War Cabinet to foster closer relations between universities in Britain and the United States.[18] By mid-1918 steps were under way to encourage American postgraduate students to attend British universities.[19] As part of its demobilisation plans the government implemented also a system of awards for ex-servicemen to train in universities and technical institutes. In its final form, as accepted by the Home Affairs Committee of the Cabinet on 10 March 1919, the scheme provided not only for British residents but also for Dominion officers and men in the United Kingdom and for United Kingdom officers and men overseas.[20] During 1919–20 over 30,000 ex-servicemen applied for assistance under this scheme, and 26,000 benefited, receiving a total expenditure of almost £8 million at an average cost of £140 a year for each student.[21]

The influx of ex-servicemen posed new problems for the universities. They had already suffered financially during the war. One estimate suggested that owing to lost income from student fees their wartime debt was £500,000.[22] The difficulties were brought to the attention of the government by a delegation that waited on Fisher and Bonar Law, Chancellor of the Exchequer, in November 1918. Introducing the delegation, the Vice-chancellor of Birmingham University, Oliver Lodge, made it clear what the universities expected. He urged a quadrupling of the pre-war State grant to the universities in order to meet the immediate problems of demobilisation and provide for both the expansion of university education in the future and the capital equipment for scientific research.[23] With the background of wartime participation still fresh, it was significant that many of the speakers who followed Lodge were anxious to assert not the traditional claims of academic freedom but rather the importance of the universities to the national interest. Sir Alfred Ewing from Edinburgh said that the nation was looking for 'Pioneers, for creators, for technical experts in immense numbers, for what I may call the scientific officers of the great army'. He reminded Fisher that the 1918 Act had created opportunities for 'promotion from the ranks of that industrial army'. The universities must be given resources to meet these challenges.[24] Professor Bragg of Leeds, a Nobel prize winner in physics, said that those who had participated in military science during the war had been impressed, first, by the amount of work achieved and the results, secondly by the fact that it had been done by 'armies recruited from University and college classrooms', and finally by the amount of time required to get work done in such fields as aviation and wireless.[25] In all these matters, however, those involved had been struck by the fact that there had been so few people to undertake such tasks. The nation had to realise the importance of science, and that it was the 'natural function' of the university to develop this work.[26]

A somewhat different appeal came from outside university circles. In a letter to *The Times* in April 1919 Arthur Henderson noted the inadequacy of State assistance for university education. The result was, he declared, that the universities were 'unable to meet the urgent demands which are being made upon them by new classes of students'. The awakening of the mass of the people to the value of higher education greatly increased the universities' responsibilities, and the State had to take the appropriate action. 'Universities ought to be national institutions serving the nation as a whole, not any class within it. And the nation should provide them with sufficient resources to enable them to discharge their growing liabilities.'[27]

Of importance in understanding government policy towards the universities was the attitude of Fisher. Robert O. Berdahl has suggested that one of the main factors making for the preservation of the independence and autonomy of British universities in the twentieth century has been the common outlook of government and university leaders.[28] Nowhere was this more clearly demonstrated than in Fisher's case. As former Vice-chancellor at Sheffield, he had an intimate knowledge and understanding of the universities' problems and demands. He also recognised the need for extra State finance. He told an audience in February 1918 that before the war Prussian universities received over £1 million a year in State funds, whereas English universities and technical institutions received only £378,000 from rates and taxes combined; the nation would have to realise that a better educational system required more finance.[29]

After meetings between Fisher and Austen Chamberlain, who became Chancellor of the Exchequer in January 1919, it was agreed to raise the sum total of university maintenance to £1 million in 1919–20. Secondly, there was to be a non-recurrent grant of £500,000 to help the universities return to pre-war efficiency. Thirdly, it was decided to set up a single committee for all British universities, which would both recommend the allocation of State grants and decide whether the State should distribute grants for capital expenditure on buildings.[30]

The course of events arising out of the last of these three recommendations has caused some confusion in the mind of at least one historian. As noted above, the committee on university grants to institutions in England, established in 1904, had been transferred from the Treasury to the administration of the Board in 1911. V. H. H. Green has recently written that, in reconstituting the body which now became formally known as the University Grants Committee, Fisher took 'deliberate action' to transfer it from the jurisdiction of the Board of Education to the Treasury in order to 'prevent partisan dictatorship by a Minister'.[31] The evidence does not bear out this claim.

In attempting to clarify this point, it should be said that, while Fisher certainly had no intention of interfering with the independence of the universities, he did see the State playing a stronger advisory role than in the past. Delivering an address on 'The Functions of Government in Relation to Education' in March 1919, he stressed that, as the universities would now be compelled to accept a larger measure of State assistance, there should be a committee to distribute grants, 'in the administration of which there would be some opportunity to give counsel to the Universities as to a particular line of development in the pursuit of which they were most likely to contribute to the common weal'. Within the next generation he hoped to see the completion of a public system of education which would preserve 'all the best elements' of their 'ancient freedom' along with a 'higher measure of efficiency and a great comprehension of the many scientific needs of modern life'.[32]

The Board of Education itself was anxious to ensure that, while there should be no interference in university teaching, its own status and interest in university policy were maintained.[33] As the ministerial head of education Fisher agreed with this viewpoint. The new grants committee was to be for the whole United Kingdom and not merely for England. Thus, in early April 1919, he met the Secretary of State for Scotland and the Chief Secretary for Ireland, the Ministers with some responsibility for university policy in those parts of the United Kingdom, to discuss the composition of the committee and decide its terms of reference.[34] Communicating the decisions of the meeting to Austen Chamberlain, Fisher made it clear that, while the three Ministers agreed about preserving the committee's independent status, they also considered it essential that the committee should also first act in consultation with their respective departments, which would in turn maintain the right to pass its reports and recommendations on to the Treasury.[35]

The final say came from the Treasury. Sir Thomas Heath, its secretary, informed Fisher that as the committee would be responsible for the whole United Kingdom it would have to be either a Royal Commission, which Austen Chamberlain was prepared to accept some time in the future, or a committee responsible to the Treasury, a form that would be more convenient for the present. He agreed that the Treasury should appoint the committee only after consultation with the respective education Ministers for England and Wales, Scotland and Ireland, and although its reports would go direct to the Chancellor of the Exchequer he would also communicate with and consult them about the reports.[36]

The supposed break with the past was therefore less dramatic than has often been portrayed. Rather than weakening the control of the Board of Education in the area of university policy, Fisher had sought to maintain some of its influence. It was the Treasury itself that insisted on retaining ultimate jurisdiction over the new committee. For the universities this was in one sense a disadvantage, for it ensured the pre-eminence of financial considerations. As early as September 1919 Austen Chamberlain indicated that, while the government would do its bit to aid the universities, support would be conditional on an equal response from local and private sources. 'It would be an evil day if the universities looked only to the government and not to the communities in which they were placed.'[37] The Chancellor also told Sir William McCormick, chairman of the newly constituted University Grants

Committee, that his committee should not approve for grant activities which were 'unwarranted in the national interest' or improvident on the part of a particular institution. The grants were to be applied only to activities 'clearly of university character'.[38]

Treasury conservatism was matched by Fisher's caution and sense of social values. In an address at Oxford University on 23 February 1919 he stated his own position on 'The Place of the University in National Life'. Setting out what he saw as the forces making for change, Fisher admitted that the circumstance of the past twenty years had brought the State into much closer relations with higher education. The growth of the newer universities, the Acts of 1902 and 1918, the expansion of the State secondary school system, the increase in the teaching profession, a new hunger for learning among the workers, even the promotion of industrial research – all revealed a new State responsibility towards learning and education.[39] The war itself had shown how much the universities and technical education had stood for in time of stress, for there had been 'Great drafts upon scientific brains' into government service.[40]

The result of all these forces promoting the interest of the State in education and research would mean, Fisher believed, that the universities would be drawn inexorably into the movement for change. They must therefore realise their new role and not only co-operate but review national needs and shape a national policy, and thus escape being directed by the State. The 1918 Act itself would affect the universities in three related ways: by fitting a much greater number of young men and women for university life, creating a bigger demand for teachers, and establishing a new clientele for extra-mural work.[41] In all these fields the universities had an important role to play, particularly in that of teacher training and the preparation of men and women for posts in the continuation schools – 'A new field of endeavour, half educational, half social, of enormous promise, but likely to be confronted by great difficulties and by reluctances only to be overcome if the new schools are staffed with men and women of the right stamp'.[42]

Fisher argued, however, that the growing responsibilities of the universities should not be allowed to repress what he saw as their real purpose and role. 'The business of a University is not to equip students for a professional post,' he stressed, but to 'train them in disinterested intellectual habits, to give them a vision of what real learning is, to refine taste, to form judgment, to enlarge curiosity, and to substitute for a low and material outlook in life a lofty view of its resources and demands.'[43] At Oxford and Cambridge the humanities were firmly entrenched, so much so that the muses of antiquity overshadowed pure and applied science. At the newer universities the situation was reversed. It was there that efforts should be made not to reinforce the position of science but to emphasise the claims of the humanities:

> The Sciences are now safe enough. They require more money; they require more recruits; they are susceptible of almost infinite developments; but there is very little danger that the needs of this side of intellectual activity will be neglected in our civic Universities. What does need emphasis is the value for a manufacturing community of an influence which, if it should be as widely diffused as one might desire, is capable in a thousand and one ways of altering for the better the general tone and temper of industrial life, both on the side of capital and on the side of labour.[44]

In this role for the newer universities, Fisher believed, Oxford and Cambridge would play an important part, particularly since they supplied most academic staff throughout England. The newer universities therefore could not be indifferent to the practice and purpose of the older ones, while Oxford and Cambridge themselves were being influenced by the new developments. 'In this interchange and intercommunion there are seeds of rich promise for the moral and intellectual development of the nation.'[45]

Although certain departments had accepted State aid before the war, the two senior universities had remained outside the general system of State grants. The war had made such isolation difficult if not impossible. Like other British universities, Oxford and Cambridge had suffered financially through loss of fee income while facing higher running costs due to inflation and the need for extra capital expenditure. Despite financial pressures, the governing bodies of both institutions wanted to maintain their special position and avoid formal relations with the State. What they sought was aid without interference. In response to an enquiry from Fisher, the Vice-chancellor of Oxford, H. E. D. Blakiston, proposed that the State should give favourable consideration to special applications for particular developments and provide a large sum of around £100,000 per annum from which Oxford and Cambridge could draw upon for capital grants.[46] Similarly the Vice-chancellor of Cambridge, noting the need for an extra £20,000 for stipends, £30,000 for maintenance of new departments, and £750,000 for capital grants in the chemical laboratory, called for a 'substantial grant from National resources provided that the conditions under which it is given do not interfere with the autonomy to which throughout the long history of the University the Senate has always attached the ultimate importance'.[47]

These conditions were simply unacceptable on financial or political grounds. Austen Chamberlain was prepared to make emergency grants of £30,000 out of the general sum already allocated for the universities, but only on condition that both the older institutions submitted to a full examination of their financial position. The government would be exposing itself to 'legitimate Parliamentary criticism' if it created a permanent grant without asking whether they were making efficient use of existing resources.[48]

The labour movement in particular wanted far-reaching changes at Oxford and Cambridge. R. H. Tawney argued that the older universities had to bear some responsibility for education's having divided the nation along class lines, for they had helped to create the 'alliance between learning and wealth'.[49] In June 1919 the Labour member William Graham, acting on behalf of his party, wrote to Fisher calling for a comprehensive inquiry into endowments, finance, government, expenses of college life, and the provision of scholarships at Oxford and Cambridge. The body of inquiry to be set up should include representatives of organised labour and of women, and 'any enquiry now should not be of a superficial character carried out merely to satisfy public opinion that the Grant was being made after proper public consideration'.[50]

While accepting the need for an inquiry, Fisher was unwilling to extend its terms of reference too widely. Because he felt that Oxford and Cambridge held a special and valuable place, he approached the question of a Royal Commission cautiously. To an Oxford deputation he held out the threat of a much fuller inquiry than a financial one, pointing out not only that Parliament maintained ultimate control over grants but that there were also demands for a Royal Commission irrespective of the question of State aid.[51] Faced by such pressure, the governing bodies of Oxford and Cambridge eventually agreed to an inquiry, albeit reluctantly.[52] Fears of undue interference in university affairs were, however, unfounded. Conservatism ran all through Fisher's submission to the Cabinet on the proposed Royal Commission's terms of reference and composition. The inquiry was to be limited to financial questions, though it would be necessary to consider the relation between the colleges and the central university authority. The complexity of the two universities, their individual characteristics and 'value to the intellectual well-being of the Nation' suggested that the commission should be constituted so as to 'ensure a sympathetic understanding of their spirit and conditions'. There should thus be enough members familiar with Oxford and Cambridge, others qualified to consider administrative and financial questions, and finally some representation for Labour and women.[53]

The limited terms of reference were reinforced by the selection of Asquith as chairman, a move guaranteed to ensure a favourable hearing for Oxford and Cambridge. As Roy Jenkins, his biographer, has admitted, Asquith was 'a natural conservative on most subjects outside politics. This was particularly so on anything touching both scholarship and his early life, and he led the Commission into producing an unadventurous report.'[54] Meeting for the first time in autumn 1919, the commission did not produce its report until mid-1922. The general tone and theme were designed to reassure the nation of the continuing value and purpose of Oxford and Cambridge. Although receiving submissions from the Labour Party, the W.E.A. and a group known as the Oxford Reform Committee, all of which wanted to increase the central authority of the universities over the colleges, and to cheapen the cost of living in college so as to provide greater opportunities for poor students,[55] the commissioners confined their attention strictly to their terms of reference. Their report contained two main proposals. Suggestions for improving the organisation and government of both universities confirmed a number of changes that had already been carried out at Oxford.[56] A recommendation that State grants for each institution should rise to £110,000[57] was not fully implemented, owing to the prevailing climate of economy.

After discussions with the university authorities Fisher presented to the Cabinet a draft Bill for a statutory commission to carry out the recommendations.[58] Even here he was anxious to ensure that reform came only with the universities consent. In particular, he insisted that on the question of admitting women to full status at Cambridge (an issue which the commission had considered) the university should be allowed to reform itself.[59] As a result, the measure which was to become the 1923 Oxford and Cambridge Bill made no provision on this score.[60] It was not until 1945 that Cambridge followed the step adopted voluntarily at Oxford in 1919 and admitted women to full status and degrees.

University policy was the main new educational development of the immediate post-war years. In comparison, other issues were of minor concern. Nevertheless, secondary and technical education and the general question of scholarships were all considered essential to the development of national education. Both the Addison committee in 1915 and the report of the Consultative Committee in 1916 had emphasised that the encouragement and development of scientific and technical education depended on the provision of further financial assistance for individual students, and a general expansion of opportunities in the secondary school system. On the other hand, the two curriculum committees on science and modern languages were disturbed to learn how far the scholarship system at Oxford and Cambridge had moulded the curricula of many secondary schools, particularly the independent and elitist public schools, in the interests of classics.[61] The issues of access to higher education and the nature of the curriculum in the secondary schools were thus related.

The situation was complicated by growing social pressures. Among the strongest was a continuing demand for places in the grant-aided secondary schools. The brief post-war economic boom stimulated it. By 1920–21 the number of secondary schools on the grant list had grown from 1,000 in 1913–14 to 1,205, while the number of pupils had expanded from a pre-war figure of 187,000 to 337,000.[62] The competition for existing places in secondary schools was so great that in 1919 local education authorities had to refuse 8,870 students who had won free places and 9,251 applicants for fee-paying positions.[63]

Matching social pressures was a growing awareness in the Labour movement that the extension of full-time secondary and university education was the only way to achieve social justice. Higher education, argued a paper prepared in May 1918 for the Labour Party's Advisory Committee on Education, was 'confined far too exclusively to a comparatively small class'. As a result 'the nation draws for its leadership in government and administration, science and other intellectual work, and even in industry, upon only a tiny fraction of the ability of the population in England'.[64]

Fisher later wrote that his aim in secondary education had been eventually to produce a secondary school population of 600,000.[65] If so it was slow, steady growth that he sought. Neither he nor the Board was prepared to contemplate a sudden large expansion of the secondary schools. Such a development would be as unwelcome as it was unnecessary, since the 1918 Act provided adequately for other forms of post-primary education. As Fisher told the Commons in August 1919,

> I believe that when the scheme, which is outlined in the Education Act of 1918, has been fully worked out – and it will take at least a generation to work it out – we shall find ourselves equipped with all the types of schools which are required to give every section of the children of the people that education which is best adapted to provide them with a good start in life, and furnish them with that measure of culture of which they are capable.[66]

Beneath this rather bland statement of educational opportunities suited to the abilities of all lay a view of secondary schools confined to the few. Fisher continued to oppose the principle of free secondary education. His secretary told Sir Henry Hibbert, of the Lancashire Education Authority, that the Minister himself believed that such a policy would 'tend to create a sharp line of social cleavage' between schools in the State system and the older, independent fee-paying sector.[67] He was similarly reluctant to insist on universal application of the 25 per cent free place rule in the secondary schools. One had to proceed cautiously in this area, he told the Commons. The 'avenue into the secondary schools is broad and is daily broadening' but a 'school is a delicate organism. You cannot at once introduce a number of pupils, educated upon different lines, into a school which had hitherto been recruited from pupils whose educational antecedents are entirely different.'[68]

Where Fisher was prepared to meet certain of the demands of Labour was on financial assistance for working-class children and adolescents. The Cabinet agreed in June 1919 to provide a 50 per cent grant to local education authorities towards maintenance allowances for all forms of higher education beyond the elementary level, with a maximum annual State expenditure of £787,500.[69] As a supplement to this provision, in autumn 1920 the Board inaugurated a scheme of 200 scholarships for students going from secondary school to university.[70]

The scholarships were to be awarded to students in the grant-earning secondary schools who had passed one of the secondary school examinations approved by the Board of Education. Awards were to be distributed among the seven examining boards of the universities, which were required to allocate an equal share to male and female pupils. This national scheme not only carried forward the 'systematisation' that was part of the intent of the 1918 Act, but also furthered the Board's pre-war aim of strengthening relations between the secondary schools and the universities. The State scholarship scheme complemented the earlier reform of the secondary examination system, as proposed in 1911 and carried out in 1917, and the extra grants for advanced secondary courses first provided in 1917. Behind the State scholarship scheme were also the aims and priorities of Fisher himself. Writing to Murray in July 1921, he claimed that his particular object here was to divert criticism from existing scholarship provision at Oxford and Cambridge:

> The disappearance of Greek from our system of humane studies would be so great a catastrophe, that we must do all we can here to help to procure for all students capable of profiting from Greek studies a free and easy access to them. I am particularly anxious that the funds expended in Oxford and Cambridge on Classical scholarships should not be diminished. Indeed, it was mainly to this end that I planned the new State scholarships.[71]

His claim to have 'planned' the scholarship scheme is, of course, an exaggeration. The Board had been thinking along these lines before the war, and both the Addison committee and the Board's Consultative Committee had recommended such a scheme. Nor was the scholarship scheme instituted in the way Fisher had proposed. To protect existing scholarships at Oxford and Cambridge he had wanted to supply awards in the sciences and modern humanities that would be open not only to the grant-aided secondary schools but to the public schools as well.[72] In the end the idea was dropped. What is important to note, however, is that Fisher had revealed his own predilections on the curriculum of the secondary schools. His respect for Oxford and Cambridge was founded on the strength of classics in those universities. Moreover, while others believed that the experience of war had emphasised the claims of scientific and technical education, Fisher believed the opposite. He saw the war leaving a harmful legacy. As he told an American audience in 1923,

> Very few of the effects of War can be described as good. For the most part its influence is to depress the intelligence of the societies which have fallen victims of the fever of militarism. One of the results of the War in England was to enhance the value attached to studies having a direct practical bearing, and to lower the importance of those forms of discipline less directly connected with the needs of everyday life, to exalt modern studies as opposed to ancient studies, applied science as opposed to pure science, and in general, knowledge as a source of national power at the expense of knowledge as an ideal motive and as an end in itself. This has been the general tendency. Despite the wonderful discoveries in the field of Hellenic scholarship and archaeology comparable in range and interest with the conquests of the Italian Renaissance, Greek, once the staple and glory of

English education, beats a rapid retreat, and some fears are expressed that Latin may follow in the receding footsteps.[73]

In public Fisher was a man of compromise, seeking to strike a balance between ancient and modern studies. Commenting on the reports of the science and modern languages committees, he had told an audience in mid-1918 that he would like to see

> more students learning Greek, but fewer learning it in compulsion, more science, but fewer scientists devoid of the humanities, more scholarships at the old Universities in the newer branches of study, but little or no reduction in the rewards offered for real proficiency in the study of Greek and Latin.[74]

Behind the scenes he was more alarmist. His policy aimed at preserving classics from what he saw as a dangerous threat, particularly after 1919, when Oxford abolished Greek as a compulsory matriculation subject. Part of his strategy was to mould the curriculum of the State secondary schools so that it would become even more like that of the public schools. During 1919 a delegation from the Headmasters' Conference had approached the Board and suggested that well endowed public schools could voluntarily accept a certain percentage of elementary school boys along the same lines as State-aided schools. (The aim was to preserve the status of lesser endowed public schools, which feared they would have to accept State grants or lose staff to State-aided schools which enjoyed the benefits of the 1918 Superannuation Act.)[75] The offer was rejected. As Selby-Bigge noted, the public schools could not be considered part of the public system unless they all accepted State inspection.[76] Nevertheless, Fisher was still anxious to promote a closer relation between the independent public schools and the State secondary schools. In January 1920 he told the Incorporated Association of Assistant Masters that the State and public schools were growing closer.

> Under the pressure of a variety of forces these two groups of schools were gradually approximating one to one another; the old schools were developing modern studies, scientific and literary, while some of the other schools had shown that they could produce classical work of as high quality as that which was found in the best of the older schools. Economic forces were also bringing more of the older schools within the circle of those institutions which received aid from the State. He hoped that the modern schools would develop the study of the humanities with the same breadth, knowledge, and accuracy as the study of classical languages had been organised in the best of the older schools, and that the grants of the Board

> of Education in aid of a definite course in secondary schools would assist in that purpose.[77]

In 1919 a memorandum prepared by four inspectors of the Board of Education had pointed out that the position of classics in the secondary schools was more precarious and ill defined than that of any other subject in the curriculum. Of the 20,488 candidates in the first school exam in 1918, only 6,560 had offered Latin (despite the regulations providing for it as a second language) and 970 Greek. An inquiry was called for to advise on how to maintain and encourage classics.[78]

In the circumstances Fisher requested and received approval to establish a committee of inquiry under the authority of the Prime Minister, so granting it the status accorded in 1916 to the committees on science and modern languages.[79] Appointing the Marquess of Crewe as chairman, Fisher made it clear where his own priorities and motives lay. 'I am of the opinion that it is more important that the case for the Ancient Languages should be temperately stated now than that attention should be directed to the growing needs of the Sciences and the Humanities. There is a real danger of a debacle in Hellenic Studies unless something is done.'[80]

The report of the classics committee appeared in 1921. Its conclusions concurred strongly with Fisher's views. Although admitting that classics had held a privileged position in the past, it argued that there was now a change of emphasis, particularly in the secondary schools and the newer universities, which threatened the very future of ancient studies.[81] Among other proposals the committee recommended that all students should have the opportunity to study both the classical languages, and that in public exams and the curricula of the universities and secondary schools Greek should be an alternative to Latin.[82]

Only after the publication of the report and the issue of a departmental study of English teaching did the Board of Education itself decide to make its own post-war statement on the secondary school curriculum. The circular issued in December 1922 (after Fisher had left office) revealed just how much continuity with pre-war policy remained. Following the model of immediate pre-war policy statements, the circular did not set out to lay down firm guidelines but it did indicate the main attitude of the Board. Thus the nucleus of the curriculum was still to be regarded as general in character, although schools could exercise their own discretion in allocating timetables and even omitting some subjects. The general principle of at least some science and one foreign language was to be maintained, while Latin was still regarded as an important element in general education and should continue to be the main second language. In accordance with the views of Fisher and the classics committee it was also stated that provision for the study of Greek should be regarded as a necessary part of secondary education, and in order to pursue studies in this subject students should be allowed if necessary to transfer to other schools.[83]

Related to secondary and university education were technical studies. The experience of war had demonstrated not only the importance of scientific and technological research but also the part played by technical training. In February 1920 Sir James Currie, head of the Department of Industrial Training at the Ministry of Labour, pointed out how wartime organisation associated with the Ministry of Munitions had been extended into the post-war period. As part of a training scheme for the disabled, the government had entered into negotiations with the employers and trade unions. National Trade Committees, in some cases affiliated with the Whiteley councils (formed in 1918 to promote co-operation between labour and industry), had devised training courses that would provide six to eighteen months in a technical school or instructional centre and a further eighteen months in a works. Local technical advisory committees had been formed. From 1919 the government decided to take up the scheme on a large scale, and it was estimated that as many as 80,000 disabled soldiers would require training.[84]

General policy seemed to give further encouragement to technical education. By mid-1919 the government was moving towards a policy of trade protection, the eventual result of which was to be the Safeguarding of Industries Act of 1921. In July 1919 Auckland Geddes, President of the Board of Trade, informed Fisher that, as part of this policy, Lloyd George wanted steps taken on technical instruction.[85] The Board of Education responded by pointing out that there were two areas of difficulty. While local education authorities were responsible for providing technical studies, few of them had either technical instruction committees or advisory committees comprising employers and workmen. Moreover there had been no 'organised demand' for technical education, and both employers and trade unions were ill informed. It was suggested that departmental committees be formed to investigate the needs of each industry, and the machinery of the Whiteley councils utilised.[86]

Carrying forward its pre-war aim of creating course work in technical education, the Board entered into direct negotiations with industry. In June 1920 officials of its technological branch, including Frank Pullinger, met representatives of the Institution of Mechanical Engineers.[87] The result was the inauguration of the 'national certificate' scheme providing for the certification of mechanical engineers who had passed a qualifying examination after part-time study of three years (for the Ordinary National Certificate) or five years (for the Higher National Certificate) at a local technical college. There were also to be national diplomas awarded after full-time study. The system was later adapted in other fields, including chemistry, electrical engineering, naval architecture, building and commerce.[88]

Despite this important development, a number of factors retarded technical education. Partly it was the attitude of the Board itself. One particular issue was the position of the junior technical schools, for which regulations had first been laid down in 1913. By 1918 the number of such schools had expanded to sixty-one from a pre-war figure of thirty-seven.[89] In October 1917 a deputation from the North East Coast Institution of Engineers and Shipbuilders had urged the Board to alter its regulations to allow students from these schools to pass on to higher educational schools and even university.[90] The committee on science had also shown an interest in them, suggesting that they should concentrate on promoting 'aptitude and liking for occupations in or related to industrial applications of science', so providing for the 'material increase in the supply of students qualified for study and investigation in pure science and for more advanced technical education, as provided in the higher technical institutions and in the scientific departments of universities'.[91] The committee recommended 'room in our scheme of education for those between the ages of 12 and 16 for schools where no foreign language should be compulsory and where a definite bias is given towards practical education in connection with Science and Mathematics'. These schools, it was stressed, should be regarded as 'part of our secondary system' and the existing junior technical schools 'strengthened and developed into such a form of secondary education.'[92]

Although the terms of the 1918 Act sought to encourage various forms of post-primary education, the science committee's proposal ran counter to the pre-war regulations of the Board that junior technical schools must be regarded as preparing their students only for a trade and not for higher technical instruction. In the Board's eyes it was the secondary schools that should provide the avenue to higher technical institutes and the universities. Fisher reaffirmed this policy to a delegation from the N.U.T. in 1917, and there was to be no departure from the official view in the immediate post-war period.[93]

A further facet of Board policy was that its view of technical education was rather academic in outlook. Sir James Currie argued that the provision for continuation classes, as contained in the 1918 Act, would succeed only if the instruction offered was 'largely vocational' and 'along lines which will appeal to the working classes, both parents and actual recipients, as being of direct practical bearing upon their occupation'.[94] Stressing the importance of assuring the goodwill of the trade unions in any plans for technical education, he emphasised the need for Board officials who 'shrink from the prospect of hearing temples of learning echoing with the din of industrial disputes' to realise that education itself had always been the 'subject on which the whole world draws knife'.[95]

Like Fisher, the Board's officials were unimpressed by purely vocational ends. Their aim was that the continuation schools would meet the ideal of a 'balanced culture' as discussed by Morant, Pullinger and Chambers in 1909–11. Such views come out strongly in a pamphlet entitled *Humanism in the Continuation School*, prepared by Dover Wilson under the direction of Frank Pullinger. In a notable passage Dover Wilson proclaimed how those who directed technical and further education at the Board saw its purpose:

> It is not technical instruction we stand in need of so much as an informed humanism, which welcomes and understands the results of technical achievement, faces them boldly, and declares that the work of man's hand, even in these grimy days, deserve the blessing which, up to the advent of industrialism, poetry, art and culture have always rejoiced to bestow upon them. For the first time in history a fatal schism has arisen between culture and the crafts, with the result that modern culture tends to be trivial, esoteric, dillentane, while the crafts, from which poet and artist turn away in disgust, are left mean, ugly and formless. In the continuation schools of the future we have an opportunity of doing something to bring these natural allies together once more, and so to lend our assistance, however feeble, to the re-establishment of our civilisation upon a sound basis.[96]

The official Labour view was also antagonistic to utilitarianism. C. T. Cramp, a railway union delegate and leading spokesman in the T.U.C. parliamentary deputation to the Board in 1919, told Fisher that

Labour was now approaching education in a 'different spirit', with concern for instruction and the curriculum, not merely technical efficiency and better economic opportunities.[97] Similarly, Labour's Advisory Committee on Education took the view that 'wisely directed' continuation classes could become the 'greatest training ground of democracy which the world has seen'. 'Perverted by a short-sighted subordination to economic interests', they would not only leave young persons little better educated but could be 'positively harmful by using the school to reinforce the mechanical discipline of the factory'.[98] For the present continuation classes had to be regarded as the 'secondary school and university of the vast majority of working-class children'.[99] Labour would oppose the formation of works schools and any emphasis on specialised technical training. 'Continued education is simply part-time secondary education, and its first object must be not to cultivate economic aptitude, but to give a broad physical, moral, and intellectual training.'[100]

These suspicions cast a shadow across the development of technical education. Amidst post-war industrial unrest there seemed little chance of ensuring the goodwill of the unions in any State-sponsored plan. By the end of 1919 the general Whiteley councils, established on State initiative to promote harmonious industrial relations, had broken down in mutual acrimony between capital and labour.[101]

While the hostility of Labour was a negative factor, there was a much wider and continuing uncertainty. Despite wartime experience, the place of technical education in the educational system remained unclear. As a later departmental committee of the Board admitted, 'technical education represents a debatable country with limits not very clearly defined lying upon the borders of secondary and University education'.[102] The answer to that claim had still to be formulated.

By the end of 1919 the legacies of war were being overtaken by the priorities of peace. In September 1917 Fisher had told one audience,

> It would be a disgrace if the country came to the conclusion that some form of continued education for its adolescents was a good thing, but it was not prepared to disburse what is spent in 30 hours of war. The war has taught us that the nation is rich enough and powerful enough to pay for anything it really wants.[103]

Many now believed that the lesson of peace was that the nation could not always afford all it might want. Even before the Armistice, a committee of the Treasury had urged that the main priority should not be further expenditure on social reform but immediate steps to reduce the national debt and preserve the international position of sterling.[104] Faced by uncertain demobilisation plans, the government had opted initially for a post-war policy of economic boom and a continuing programme of social reform.[105] The bubble soon burst as inflation and industrial unrest overtook its plans. In July the Chancellor of the Exchequer, Austen Chamberlain, presented to the Cabinet a paper outlining government commitments and gloomily predicting a total budgetary deficit of £200 million for 1921–22.[106] As a major area of social policy, there was now much scrutiny of educational costs.

The main concern centred on the first report of the Burnham committee, issued in late 1919. Going beyond its initial brief, the committee had recommended not only a national standard of salaries but provisional minimum scales, and increments. For certificated male teachers the minimum would be £160 a year, rising to £300, and for females £150, rising to £240. Uncertificated males would receive a minimum of £100, rising to £150 (or £180 if appointed before April 1914), and uncertificated females £90, rising to £140 (or £150 if appointed prior that date).[107]

Fisher admitted to Chamberlain, who was alarmed at the cost of the Burnham recommendations to the national exchequer, that he had expected the committee to confine its attention to the worst-paid areas and so provide a year of grace. The representatives of the local education authorities on the Burnham committee, influenced largely by the need to attract teachers, had 'moved rather faster and further' than he had anticipated. The national salary agreement would have a wider application than expected and the cost would consequently be greater, although he also argued that the process would be spread over several years and the effect would not be felt in the educational estimates until 1921–22. On the other hand, he urged that there was no reason to regret the results, for 'You will readily appreciate the influence of the teachers in the country and the effect which a discontented body of over 160,000 teachers may easily have in keeping alive increasing social and industrial unrest.'[108]

The Board pointed out too that little of the growing education bill was directly due to the reforms that had been carried out during the war and the post-war period. Although the educational estimates had increased from £19,335,000 in 1918–19 to a projected £43,570,000 in 1920–21, £19 million of this £24 million increase had been due first to devaluation as a result of wartime inflation and secondly to the increase in the salaries of teachers. Devaluation alone had added over £4 million to the cost of various items in the current educational estimates. The major projected increase was £15 million in teachers' pay, but it was argued that it was impossible to distinguish between increases in this area owing to devaluation and the necessary levelling up of salaries. The Board admitted, however, that the main causes of the increase in grants 'have not yet spent their force'. A long list of items, including teachers' pensions, maintenance allowances and scholarships, would all add to the educational budget. The biggest increase, however, would come from the operation of the 1918 Act, particularly the abolition of half-time and the raising of the school age to fourteen, the establishment of the continuation classes, and the provision for nursery schools. The cost of these three reforms was expected to total over £10,500,000. Undaunted, the Board argued that future rises in the cost of education would depend not only on price trends, the energy of local education authorities and the 'liberality' of successive Parliaments, but ultimately 'upon the degree of determination shown by the people of this country to establish the best national system of public education they can afford'. Recognising that developments under the 1918 Act would be gradual, it urged that the government should also take a liberal attitude to educational costs, for 'it is a form of expenditure which serves lofty ends rather than the purpose of immediate gain, and so far as it is profitable, is profitable from a generous and far-sighted conception of public good'.[109]

The case was well argued. It was undoubtedly true that inflation made comparisons with pre-war education budgets difficult. By 1920 the purchasing power of the £ had more than halved compared with 1914.[110] More significantly, the proportion of total government revenue spent on education in 1920–21 was actually less than half that of 1910–11 (4·5 compared with 9·8 per cent).[111] The point here, of course, was that total government revenue had increased considerably since 1914. However, in contrast with 1916–18, when all segments of social policy were considered as interdependent parts of 'reconstruction', education was now not only in competition for financial resources with other aspects of social welfare, such as housing, health and pensions, but the Exchequer was saddled with interest payments on a national war debt which was, even allowing for inflation, five times the pre-war burden. At least the Prime Minister was on the Board's side. 'I hope you will not become unreasonable through sheer fear and cut down education,' Lloyd George appealed to the Commons in October 1919. 'There is nothing more that this War has demonstrated more clearly than the value of education, especially on the technical side, in peace and war.'[112]

Table 4 *Government revenue, expenditure and debt (£ million)*

Date	*Revenue*	*Main heads of expenditure*				*National Debt*
		Defence	*Education (U.K.)*	*Health labour and insurance*	*Pensions*	
1900	140	121	13	—	—	628·9
1910	204	67	19	—	—	713·2
1920	1,426	292	54	73	110	7,828·8

Source: David Butler and Jennie Freeman, *British Political Facts, 1900–1967*, London, 1968, pp. 228 and 230.

But Lloyd George was no longer the powerful wartime leader who had promised Fisher in December 1916 that financial support for educational reform would be forthcoming. He was bound by the results of the 'coupon' election which had left him as Premier in a coalition government dependent upon the support of an overwhelmingly Tory back bench.[113] There were also voices within the Cabinet which took a line quite opposite to that which he publicly espoused.

The Treasury provided the main reply to the Board's defence. As far as the prospects of implementing a programme of educational reform were concerned, the winter of 1919–20 marks a turning point. The Treasury was clear in its priorities. It insisted that the Board should consider: the need for firmer control over the expenditure of local education authorities; the possibility of securing a larger contribution from the rates; and the postponement of any further developments until the country could better afford them. The Treasury argued that the growth in educational costs was 'an outcome of policy' and not, as the Board suggested, the 'inevitable result of a natural law'. The increase in teachers' salaries would remain, and their purchasing power would therefore be 'enormously greater' than before the war. The fact that, under the grant system instituted in 1917, the

Exchequer paid 60 per cent of teachers' salaries merely reduced the disposition of local authorities to resist pay demands. The rise in salaries, however, was only a beginning. To the Treasury the prospect of further expenditure on planned educational reform was even more alarming. It estimated that by 1927–28 education costs could be as high as £86 million. Steps had to be taken to prevent such a situation arising. If the Board was prepared to appeal to the liberality of successive Parliaments, then the Treasury had its reminder: 'Another factor will be the degree of resistance which successive Chancellors of the Exchequer offer to the demands of successive Ministers of Education'.[114]

The Treasury's response was an indication of how far priorities had changed. Education was now not so much a means of improving society and increasing productivity as a costly item which the nation, now facing the repayment of a high war debt, could ill afford. As Paul Johnson has written, all plans for social reform now faced the scrutiny of the cost factor. 'Remembering the economy drive of 1922, one watches as the case for economy obtrudes itself in 1919. It is clear, even with hindsight fully discounted, that by the end of 1919 economy had established a primary claim on the statesmen.'[115] For education too the signs of the future were already there.

Notes

1 Diary entry, 30 November–1 December 1919, Wilson (ed.), *The Political Diaries of C. P. Scott*, p. 379.
2 P.R.O., Ed 24/1349; Juvenile Unemployment Centres, Historical Note.
3 R. Pope, 'Adjustment to peace: educational provision for unemployed juveniles in Britain, 1918–19', *British Journal of Educational Studies*, XXVII, i, 1979, pp. 69–80.
4 Board of Education, Circular 1124, 2 August 1919.
5 P.R.O., Cab 23/3; War Cabinet Minute, W.C. 217 (20) of 17 August 1917, and P.R.O., Cab 24/22; War Cabinet Paper G.T. 1601 of 1 August 1917.
6 See Gosden, *The Evolution of a Profession*, pp. 139–40.
7 J. Vaizey, 'Teachers' superannuation in England and Wales', *British Journal of Educational Studies*, VI, 1957–58, pp. 14–5.
8 P.R.O., Ed 24/847(a); Main Outlines of Proposed Legislation, to establish a Comprehensive Scheme of Pensions for Teachers, 1 December 1917.
9 *Ibid.*; T. L. Heath to Selby-Bigge, 11 January 1918; and Note of

Conference, 16 January 1918.

10 Report of the Departmental Committee for Enquiring into the Principles which should Determine the Construction of Scales of Salary for Teachers in Elementary Schools, *Parlt. Pprs*. 1917–18, XI, Cd 8939.

11 Thompson, *Professional Solidarity*, p. 213. See also Sidney Webb, *The Teacher in Politics*, Fabian Tract No. 187, 1918.

12 P.R.O., Ed 108/23; Notes of an Interview between the Secretary of the Board of Education and Representatives of Association of Education Committees, 14 March 1919.

13 *Ibid*.; Resolutions passed at a Meeting of the Constituent Committee representing Associations of Local Education Authorities and the National Union of Teachers, 12 August 1919.

14 *The Times*, 13 September 1918, p. 18.

15 *Ibid*., 28 March 1919, p. 14.

16 *Ibid*., 1 May 1919, p. 10. See also Jenkins, 'The Thompson committee and the Board of Education, 1916–1922', pp. 80–2.

17 *The Times*, 11 September 1919, p. 15.

18 P.R.O., Cab 23/4; War Cabinet Minute 263(3) of 19 September 1917.

19 Eric Ashby, *Community of Universities*, Cambridge, 1963, pp. 19–20.

20 P.R.O., Cab 26/1; Home Affairs Committee, Minute 22(4) of 10 March 1919. For origins of the scheme see P.R.O., Recon 1/78; Officers Resettlement, Training and Financial Assistance, 27 November 1918, and P.R.O., Cab 24/69; War Cabinet Paper G.T. 6277 of 14 November 1918.

21 Report of the Board of Education, 1921–22, *Parlt. Pprs*. 1923, X, Cmd 1896, p. 6.

22 P.R.O., Ed 24/1970; Universities and Colleges; Particulars as to Income, 1914–18.

23 P.R.O., Ed 24/1970; Memorandum of Proceedings of Representatives of the Universities of the United Kingdom and of certain other Institutions, 23 November 1918, pp. 9–15.

24 *Ibid*., p. 21.

25 *Ibid*., p. 29.

26 *Ibid*., p. 32.

27 *The Times*, 8 April 1919, p. 8.

28 Robert O. Berdahl, *British Universities and the State*, Berkeley, Cal., 1959, p. 167.

29 *The Times*, 1 February 1918, p. 8. See also *Nature*, 7 February 1918, pp. 452–3.

30 P.R.O., Ed 24/1968; Memorandum of Interview, 30 January 1919.

31 V. H. H. Green, *The Universities*, London, 1968, p. 184.

32 *The Times*, 20 March 1919, p. 7.

33 P.R.O., Ed 24/1968; L.A.S.B. [L. A. Selby-Bigge], Minute, 6 February 1919. See also P.R.O., Ed 24/1964; L.A.S.B., Minute, 22 November 1918 and A. H. K. [A. H. Kidd], University Grants, 13 March 1918.

34 P.R.O., Ed 24/1964; Memorandum of Interview with Secretary of State for Scotland and Chief Secretary for Ireland with respect to the

Committee on Government Grants, 4 April 1919.
35 *Ibid.*, Fisher to Chamberlain, 9 April 1919.
36 *Ibid.*, Sir Thomas Heath to Fisher, 3 May 1919. See also Ashby and Anderson, *Portrait of Haldane*, pp. 150–2.
37 *The Times*, 18 September 1919, p. 12.
38 Report of the University Grants Committee on the Financial Needs of the Universities of the United Kingdom, and on the Application of Parliamentary Grants, 1921, *Parlt. Pprs.* 1921, XI, Cmd 1163, p. 17.
39 H. A. L. Fisher, *The Place of the University in National Life*, London, 1919, pp. 3–5.
40 *Ibid.*, p. 6.
41 *Ibid.*, p. 9.
42 *Ibid.*, p. 10.
43 *Ibid.*, p. 12.
44 *Ibid.*, p. 13.
45 *Ibid.*
46 P.R.O., Ed 24/1970; H. E. D. Blakiston to Fisher, 20 November 1918.
47 Thomas C. Fitzpatrick to Fisher, 20 December 1918, in *Royal Commission on Oxford and Cambridge Universities*, London, 1922, p. 224.
48 P.R.O., Ed 24/1968; H.F., Minute for Sir William McCormick, 24 March 1919.
49 R. H. Tawney, 'The public schools and the older universities,' in J. H. Whitehouse (ed.), *The English Public School*, London, 1919, pp. 73–4.
50 P.R.O., Ed 24/1190; William Graham to Fisher, 5 June 1919.
51 *Ibid.*; Memorandum of Interview, 15 May 1919.
52 The Dean of Christ Church told Gilbert Murray, 'We have been badly swindled by the Board in this matter, I think – at any rate if we can suppose that they have had any guiding purpose in their relation with us. *We were forced into applying for a grant*, and then we were induced to accept the principle of enquiry into finance – but not, as the Labour people wanted, into the whole structure and character of the University. I expect the Commission would probably have come in any case, but it could hardly have been forced upon us in a more unpleasant fashion.' B.L., G.M.P., 115(a); Thomas B. Strong to Gilbert Murray, 10 July 1919.
53 P.R.O., Cab 23/11; War Cabinet Paper G.T. 7874 of 22 July 1919.
54 R. Jenkins, *Asquith*, London, 1964, p. 483, note 1. Even Albert Mansbridge, one of the two working-class representatives on the commission, looked as much to the past as to the future. He later wrote, 'I was, as in duty bound, a convinced advocate of reforms, but was determined, so far as in my lay, to secure the re-expression of the ideals and practice which were inherent in both universities, but which owing to the incursions of the state and of forceful social tendencies had been overlooked or forgotten.' Mainsbridge, *The Trodden Road*, p. 121.
55 *Royal Commission on Oxford and Cambridge Universities*, Appendices, pp. 10–17, and 60–71.
56 At Oxford the governing Hebdomadal Council became more open to

democratic election, the powers of Congregation (those in University teaching and administration) were increased, the faculties and their boards had been reconstituted and a General Board of Faculties created to co-ordinate teaching, while a Board of Finance had also been set up. Compulsory Greek had been abolished and women admitted to full membership of the university. C. E. Malet, *A History of the University of Oxford*, London, 1929, III, p. 486.

57 *Report of the Royal Commission on Oxford and Cambridge Universities*, pp. 220–44.

58 P.R.O., Cab 24/137; Cabinet Paper C.P. 4065 of 26 June 1922.

59 P.R.O., Cab 24/136; Cabinet Paper C.P. 3973 of 15 May 1922.

60 A free vote in the Commons on this issue was defeated by 150 votes to 124. *Hansard*, Commons, 5th ser., CIXVI, 20 July 1923, cols. 2754–6.

61 Report of the Committee appointed by the Prime Minister to Enquire into the Position of Natural Science in the Educational System of Great Britain, *Parlt. Pprs.* 1918, IX, Cd 9011, p. 13, and Report of the Committee appointed by the Prime Minister to Enquire into the Position of Modern Languages in the Educational System of Great Britain, *Parlt. Pprs.* 1918, IX, Cd 9036, p. 5.

62 Lowndes, *The Silent Social Revolution*, pp. 89–90.

63 Report of the Departmental Committee on Scholarships and Free Places, *Parlt. Pprs.* 1920, XV, Cmd 968, p. 68.

64 Transport House, Labour Party Archives; Advisory Committee on Education, Memorandum on Maintenance Scholarships, May 1918, p. 1. The author of this memo was undoubtedly R. H. Tawney.

65 Fisher, *An Unfinished Autobiography*, p. 112.

66 *Hansard*, Commons, 5th ser., CXIX, 12 August 1919, col. 1234.

67 P.R.O., Ed 24/1640; N. D. Bosworth Smith to Sir Henry Hibbert, 12 September 1918.

68 *Hansard*, Commons, 5th ser., CXIX, 12 August 1919, col. 1230.

69 P.R.O., Cab 23/10; War Cabinet Minute 548(8) of 24 June 1919.

70 Report of the Board of Education, 1919–20, *Parlt. Pprs.* 1921, XI, Cmd 1451, pp. 84–5.

71 B.L., F.P., Box 7; Fisher to Gilbert Murray, 21 July 1921.

72 P.R.O., Ed 24/1530; H.F., University scholarships, 1 January 1918. Fisher had written this minute after he learnt that Magdalen College, Oxford, had transferred a number of its scholarships from classics to science. *Ibid.*; Herbert Warren to Fisher, 8 December 1917. However, Selby-Bigge had pointed out that there would be strong objections to any direct allocation of State scholarships, particularly if they were provided to Oxford and Cambridge without full parliamentary control. P.R.O., Ed 24/1570; L.A.S.B., Minute, 7 November 1918. Despite efforts to reach a compromise nothing eventuated on open awards. But see P.R.O. Ed 24/1181; H. A. L. Fisher, Appointment Minute, 23 January 1919, and P.R.O. Ed 24/1534; Report of the Committee appointed to prepare a Scheme for the award of State-provided Scholarships tenable by young Men and Women at Universities, 19 January 1920.

73 H. A. L. Fisher, 'Six years of education in England', *Yale Review*, 1922–23, pp. 519–20.

74 *The Times*, 23 July 1918, p. 3.

75 P.R.O., Ed 24/877; Deputation from the Headmasters' Conference and Headmasters' Association, 3 April 1919, and C. A. Aldington to Fisher, 16 May 1919. See also Frank Fletcher, *After many Days*, London, 1937, p. 272.

76 *Ibid.*; L.A.S.B., Minute, 28 May 1919.

77 *The Times*, 3 January 1920, p. 14.

78 P.R.O., Ed 24/1188; Memorandum on question of Committee for Classical Studies.

79 *Ibid.*; Fisher to Lloyd George, 13 September 1919, and enclosed memorandum, 12 September 1919.

80 C.U.L., C.P., Box C/15; Fisher to Crewe, 17 September 1919.

81 *Classics in Education*, Report of the Committee appointed by the Prime Minister to Inquire into the Position of Classics in the Educational System of the United Kingdom, London, 1921, p. 43.

82 *Ibid.*, pp. 269–70.

83 Board of Education, Circular 1294, 8 December 1922.

84 Currie, *The War and Industrial Training*, p. 3.

85 P.R.O., Ed 24/1863; Auckland Geddes to Fisher, 21 July 1919.

86 *Ibid.*; Board of Education, Proposals for Developing the National System of Technical and Commercial Instruction.

87 S. R. Craddock. 'The inception of the National Certificate scheme', *The Vocational Aspect of Further and Secondary Education*, XIII, 1961, pp. 48–9. See also W. H. G. Armytage, *A Social History of Engineering*, London, 1961, pp. 257–8.

88 F. E. Foden, 'The National Certificate', *The Vocational Aspect of Further and Secondary Education*, III, 1951, pp. 38–46.

89 B. Doherty, 'The education of the adolescent, 1918–1928. Policy and opinion', University of Manchester, M.Ed. thesis, 1960, p. 19.

90 P.R.O., Ed 24/1859; Deputation of North East Coast Institution of Engineers and Shipbuilders, 18 October 1917.

91 Report of the Committee appointed by the Prime Minister to Enquire into the Position of Natural Science in the Educational System of Great Britain, Cd 9001, p. 41.

92 *Ibid.*, p. 43.

93 Doherty, 'The education of the adolescent', pp. 28 and 178–80.

94 Currie, *The War and Industrial Training*, pp. 6–7.

95 *Ibid.*, p. 8.

96 *Humanism in the Continuation School*, Board of Education, Educational Pamphlets, No. 43, p. 6. See also Dover Wilson, *Milestones on the Dover Road*, pp. 88–90.

97 P.R.O., Ed 24/1384; Deputation from the Trades Union Congress Parliamentary Committee, 12 March 1919.

98 Labour Party, Memoranda prepared by the Advisory Committee on Education, *Continued Education under the New Education Act*, London, 1918, p. 2. (Pamphlet located at Transport House, Labour

Party Archives.)

99 *Ibid.*, p. 5.

100 *Ibid.*, p. 7.

101 Henry Pelling, *A History of British Trade Unionism*, London, 1963, p. 160.

102 Report of the Departmental Committee on Scholarships and Free Places, Cmd 968, p. 6.

103 *The Times*, 17 September 1917, p. 5.

104 P. Cline, 'Reopening the case of the Lloyd George coalition and the post-war economic transition, 1918–1919', *Journal of British Studies*, X, 1970, pp. 164–5.

105 *Ibid.*, pp. 166–75.

106 Johnson, *Land fit for Heroes*, p. 445.

107 Report of the Standing Joint Committee representative of the County Councils, the Municipal Corporations Association, the Association of Education Committees and the London County Council and the National Union of Teachers, *Parlt. Pprs.* 1919, XXI, Cmd 443, p. 4.

108 P.R.O., Ed 108/32; Fisher to Chamberlain, 17 November 1919.

109 P.R.O., Cab 24/95; Cabinet Paper C.P. 239 of 23 December 1919.

110 David Butler and Jennie Freeman, *British Political Facts, 1900–1967*, London, 1967, pp. 222–3.

111 Figures extracted from Education, 1900–1950, Cmd 8244, p. 250.

112 *Hansard*, Commons, 5th ser., CXX, 30 October 1919, col. 983.

113 J. M. McEwan, 'The coupon election of 1918 and Unionist members of Parliament', *Journal of Modern History*, XXXIV, 1962, pp. 296–306. Cf. D. Close, 'Conservatives and coalition after the first world war', *Journal of Modern History*, XLV, 1973, pp. 240–60.

114 P.R.O., Cab 24/97; Cabinet Paper C.P. 512 of 27 January 1920.

115 Johnson, *Land fit for Heroes*, p. 444.

VII

Post-war education

From the beginning of 1920 the forces for change were already muted. The idealism and unity of war had faded. The nation had passed beyond the uncertainty of a difficult peace to the prospect of industrial depression and high unemployment which would be the distinguishing features of the inter-war years. Tensions from the pre-war world too obtruded themselves into educational debate. Wartime consensus soon gave way to sectarian concerns. Just as the moves towards educational reform in 1911 had originated from the political need to satisfy the Nonconformists, so the fate of much of the pre-war and wartime planning now rested in the hands of the religious sects.

A major defect of the 1918 Act had been its failure to tackle the issue of the denominational schools. Despite this deliberate omission the terms of the legislation required local education authorities to co-operate with the denominational sector over teacher supply and the use of buildings so as to develop educational schemes for an area as a whole. Such co-operation was particularly crucial to the encouragement of advanced forms of elementary education and central schools. Because of this perceived need some historians have suggested that Fisher was now forced to act. Marjorie Cruickshank has written, 'as his measure was evidently in danger of becoming a dead letter Fisher in 1919 decided to re-open the religious issue'.[1] In effect, moves towards a religious settlement originated from outside and not within the Board of Education.

During the war Randall Davidson, the Archbishop of Canterbury, and the moderate Nonconformist leader, J. Scott Lidgett, had met to try and resolve the differences between their respective communities, particularly over the religious question in elementary education.[2]

Without official sanction such efforts proved fruitless. By mid-1919, after approaches from the Archbishop of Canterbury, Fisher had agreed to call a private conference between leading representatives of the Anglicans and the Nonconformists.[3] They met secretly at the Board of Education on six separate occasions from July 1919 to February 1920. The actual proposals for settling the religious question were drawn up not by Fisher but by J. Holland, secretary of the Anglican National Society, though Fisher presented them to the conference as his own.

There were four major points. Local education authorities were to appoint, promote and dismiss all teachers. No teacher was to be required to give religious instruction unless specially appointed for the purpose. Local education authorities were to have the use of denominational school premises for educational purposes. Finally, local education authorities were to be obliged to make adequate provision for religious instruction in all elementary schools. No privilege of contracting out of these arrangements was to be conceded to any one denomination which was not open to others.[4]

At its meeting on 19 November the conference reached substantial agreement on the proposals.[5] Yet their successful implementation was always dubious. From the outset the Board and Fisher were lukewarm. As Selby-Bigge told the conference, the Board's attitude was 'we can get on well with the dual system'.[6] Fisher himself admitted that 'nothing would be more troublesome for me than having to defend this in the House of Commons'.[7] He was prepared to do it because of the enormous advantages but warned the conference that the government would take up any such large scheme only if it was 'assured of a very substantial measure of agreement'.[8] It would certainly shrink from controversy, and he himself would not proceed if it became clear that opinion was 'acutely divided'.[9]

If lack of commitment from the government was one drawback, another was the nature of the conference itself. It included no delegates from the Roman Catholic Church, an obvious weakness. Once made aware of the proposals, the Catholic hierarchy soon made it clear that there were serious objections from their side. In particular the proposals did not provide security for Catholic supervision or religious atmosphere, or for the appointment of Catholic teachers.[10] On the other hand, neither the Anglican nor the Nonconformist representatives were prepared to accept special contracting-out arrangements for the Roman Catholics.[11]

The supposed agreement between the Anglican and Nonconformist positions was also unreal. The influential and important Baptist leader John Clifford, who had led the non-payment of rates campaign with Lloyd George in 1902–04, had withdrawn at an early date. He told Fisher that 'the general effect of the changes suggested will be to give us an entirely denominational system of State education, and so carry out the aims of those who have been seeking for many years to "capture the Board" or "Council" schools for ecclesiastical institutions'.[12] Despite Fisher's efforts to convince him otherwise, Clifford was to maintain this stand.[13]

The odds were therefore weighted against the settlement even before Fisher publicly announced its terms at the Kingsway Hall, London, on 27 March 1920. Guarding himself, Fisher indicated that the government could not proceed with the proposals in the 'absence of general agreement'.[14] The initial purpose was therefore to ascertain the prospect of agreement. The storm of protest that followed showed how far this was lacking.

The strength of Nonconformist resistance was a particular indicator of how shaky the consensus of the conference had been. The politically active National Education Association called a conference of Dissenters, labour groups and teachers to organise opposition to the proposals.[15] Even those who had participated in the discussions at the Board were now forced to take a different stand. Introducing a delegation from the Free Church Council, Scott Lidgett told Fisher there were three objections to the scheme: on the proposal for religious teaching in the schools, on religious tests for teachers and on a fear of creating a local demand for religious teaching.[16]

Equally crucial was the attitude of the teachers. A deputation from the executive committee of the N.U.T. made it clear that its opposition was firm. James Yoxall, the president of the union, told Fisher that the teachers were 'strong and unflinching' in opposing denominational teaching in council schools. They would also oppose the compulsory transfer of denominational schools or any provision to allow Catholic schools to contract out of a national agreement.[17]

In the face of such intractable opposition Fisher allowed the proposals to lapse. The failure of this attempt to settle the religious question revealed that the national consensus, particularly the agreement between the major religious bodies, which had played an important part in the passage of the 1918 Act had not outlasted the war. It also demonstrated the limitations of the Act itself, for the measure had left untouched a legacy which would still hinder educational change for another twenty years.

The *impasse* over the religious question showed how firm the hold of the past could remain. The trend of development from early 1920 was to dash other hopes of educational change.

Of major concern were the provisions for continuation classes in the Act. Fisher had assured Parliament in 1918 that the introduction of continuation classes would take place only at the 'end of the war'.[18] The phrase was to be interpreted by the Board itself in legalistic terms to mean not merely the conclusion of hostilities but rather the formal termination of war as fixed by order-in-council after the signing of all the peace treaties.[19]

As a result the Board was prepared to allow local education authorities to proceed at their own pace rather than give a direct lead. To some observers such inactivity was irresponsible. At the National Union of Teachers' conference in April 1919 Sir Cyril Cobb, chairman of the London County Council, and Spurley Hey, director of education in Manchester, both firm advocates of continuation classes, called upon the Board to name the 'appointed day' for the appropriate sections of the Act to come into operation as soon as possible.[20] In August Fisher did indicate to the Commons that he had written to all authorities urging the establishment of continuation classes on a voluntary basis,[21] but it was not until the following October that he actually named 1 April 1920 as the day on which the relevant clauses would come into operation.[22]

Similarly, the Board was prepared to point out the logistic problems of setting up continuation classes, but its policy stopped short of any further direct action. One major issue was teacher supply. An initial office report of the Board had emphasised that because most pupils in the continuation schools would be in employment, their teachers would require particular qualifications and backgrounds substantially different from those of teachers in the elementary and secondary schools. The committee expected that up to 16,000 teachers would be required during the first seven years of continuation classes. It recommended that teachers should be recruited from four groups: university graduates, people with experience of industrial or commercial life, specialists in technical subjects, and instructors in physical education. In the period of transition emergency steps should be taken to create part-time courses for experienced teachers and establish training centres.[23] Acting on this report, the Board issued a circular in April 1919, pointing out the importance of teaching in continuation schools as a form of social service, and calling on local education authorities to make plans for training teachers and establishing continuation schools on a voluntary basis so as to encourage entrants to the profession.[24]

To one Board official, advice alone was not enough. Aware of the problems of supply that were already threatening to overcome the government's housing programme,[25] in June 1919 J. B. Owen, a staff inspector, urged the Board to do something positive and establish teacher training courses itself, while allowing local education authorities to employ selected persons from the commencement of training. Despite possible Treasury objections and the risk of inadequate standards and qualifications, Owen argued, perhaps prophetically, 'I contend that the choice before us is not between an ideal system and an imperfect one, but between an imperfect and none at all.'[26]

Here was a far-sighted recognition of the need for action, yet his plan was simply shelved. In particular, Selby-Bigge objected that he himself had always doubted whether the development of continuation schools would be as rapid as enthusiasts had wished or expected. He did not think there was much likelihood of their being established before the autumn of 1921, and so local education authorities would be unlikely to make systematic provision for teacher training until the autumn of 1920. It would be wrong for men to be trained and then find no employment. Eventually the Board might have to bear the whole cost of training, but it was unlikely that the Treasury would approve grants of more than 75 per cent. On the whole, Selby-Bigge concluded, it was unfortunate that there would be such a gap between the demobilisation of the army (from where potential teachers could be recruited) and the opening of continuation schools, but it was in general unavoidable.[27]

This was a short-sighted attitude, even though it was consistent with his general caution towards educational administration. In the immediate post-war period local education authorities faced general problems of teacher recruitment and training without the added and special question of providing for the proposed continuation schools. By mid-1920 the whole area of financing teacher training had begun to break down under the weight of increased costs and an inadequate distribution of the burden between local education authorities.[28] In the circumstances some positive action by the Board might have been expected. There was, after all, a precedent. Despite objections from some in the teaching profession,[29] the Ministry of Labour had established emergency teacher training schemes for disabled soldiers, while some local education authorities had also created special training courses for other discharged men.[30] The Board itself, however, took no such steps. In late 1919 it attempted to encourage a number of teachers involved in army education schemes to take up a career in continuation schools,[31] but action seems to have been taken too late, as by then most were in other civilian employment.[32]

Matching the rather half-hearted attitude of the Board towards the actual establishment of the continuation schools was a general lack of commitment throughout the country. Analysing the available draft educational 'schemes' of almost half the counties, and over a quarter of county boroughs, a 1923 study indicated that in 40 per cent of counties and towns the continuation school was seen as a transitory form of education, and only 9 per cent of the counties and 13 per cent of towns regarded it as a permanent feature.[33] What many local education authorities wished to encourage and develop was the principle of full-time education in the secondary schools and the higher form of elementary education in what were known as central schools.[34]

Tacit support for full-time adolescent schooling came from the Board of Education itself. A departmental committee had been set up in mid-1919 to consider the whole question of free places and maintenance allowances in the secondary schools. Its report, published in 1920, argued that section 4 of the Act of 1918 'effects a revolution and looks forward to a new order,'[35] since it established the principle of making adequate provision for children to receive the education to which they were suited. The committee considered that up to 75 per cent of all children were probably intellectually able to undergo full-time instruction to the age of sixteen but urged an immediate aim of doubling the population of the secondary schools.[36] It proposed a regulation of 40 per cent of free places in the secondary schools and acceptance of the principle of free secondary education.[37] Perhaps more important, the committee indicated that it took a wide view of the meaning of 'secondary education', which it conceived of as being 'not only the normal secondary schools and such variant types as are being, or may be developed, but also Junior Technical and similar schools, distinguished administratively from the others but in one aspect an alternative to them'.[38]

By late 1920 sections of the Labour movement had also begun to review the whole purpose of secondary education. In January 1921 the Advisory Committee on Education of the Labour Party appointed R. H. Tawney to prepare a memorandum.[39] The result was to be *Secondary Education for All*, propounding the view of full-time free primary and secondary education as successive stages of development for all children and adolescents. As Tawney argued, continuation classes were not an answer to the question of adolescent education. The continuation school should be 'a continuation not of primary but of secondary education, and it will find its proper place in the years between seventeen and eighteen when the majority of boys and girls will have entered some branch of industry but ought still to be in touch with education'.[40]

While some rejected continuation schools as too limited in aim, others saw them as too costly. Early in December 1920 a deputation from the Unionist Social Reconstruction Committee waited on the Prime Minister to press for the suspension of all clauses of the 1918 Act involving extra expenditure.[41] Equally firm opposition came from the Treasury. Alarmed by the growth of the education estimates, Austen Chamberlain proposed that the Act be suspended for two or three years.[42] Concern over the cost was part of a much wider Treasury attack on all government expenditure. The priorities of finance now held firm sway. At its meeting on 8 December 1920 the Cabinet resolved generally that 'except with fresh Cabinet authority all schemes involving expenditure not yet in operation are to remain in abeyance'.[43]

This decision put the whole future of the continuation schools in jeopardy. By December the Board had given approval for the operation of continuation schools in eight areas, but only in two – Stratford on Avon and Rugby – had classes actually begun. The fate of the other six areas was therefore uncertain.[44]

In early December Fisher was away in Geneva.[45] The most impassioned defence of continuation schools came from the Board's Parliamentary Private Secretary, Herbert Lewis. After a conference between the Treasury and Selby-Bigge and himself, he wrote to Lloyd George to say how 'appalled' he was to hear that Chamberlain believed approval for continuation schools in the six nominated areas should be rescinded. This meant, Lewis claimed, 'a complete scrapping of the Fisher Act for an indefinite time'. The nation was trying to save adolescents from 'hooliganism' and make them good citizens, and it was 'deplorable that for the sake of temporary political expedience their future should be damaged'. The reactionaries were trying to stop all educational development, whatever the result. He implored the Prime Minister, 'I pray you do not let them do this wrong.'[46]

To reinforce his appeal he drew up a memorandum addressed to Fisher but also sent on to Lloyd George. It was a reminder of past ideals:

> The Act of 1918, passed with the fullest assent of Parliament and the nation, was not only a pledge to the private soldier who fought for us, but to civilisation. It was a vow made when the country was in desperate straits and if it is now abandoned for the sake of temporary political expediency, I cannot imagine anything more likely to embitter for good and all the minds of the men who composed our Armies. They fought for a better England and the Act of 1918 was an instalment – perhaps the first in point of time, certainly the greatest in point of quality – of the payment of the nation's debt, and it seems to me inconceivable that, in these circumstances, the Government should be ready to officially and before the world in effect to abandon entirely the core of the Act in response to a temporary panic.[47]

Lewis and Lloyd George were old Welsh political allies and friends. Their relationship may have had some bearing on what followed, particularly since Lewis added a letter threatening resignation.[48] After a meeting between Austen Chamberlain and Fisher,[49] back from Geneva, the Cabinet agreed on 23 December that unless a local authority applied to withdraw its scheme continuation schools would be allowed to go ahead in the six areas where approval had been granted.[50] Lewis wrote to thank Lloyd George for the support he had apparently given Fisher. 'I am *most grateful* to you. Generations of boys and girls will have reason to thank you for that decisive word.'[51]

He had spoken too soon. The Cabinet decision may have helped to save the continuation schools temporarily but, denied official encouragement, there was little chance of their survival in the harsh climate of economy. By early 1921 one local authority, Birmingham, had already closed its continuation schools. Those that decided to carry on faced difficulties. The major case in point was London. The London County Council had provided for twenty-two compulsory schools to open in January 1921, with a rapid build-up to a projected final total of 120,000 students.[52] By the middle of the year financial considerations led the council to reduce the compulsory leaving age at the schools from sixteen to fifteen.[53] Local industry was also far from co-operative, and the attitude of many parents became hostile, particularly since numerous employers preferred to hire juveniles living outside London in districts where continuation schools were not operating.[54] The general unpopularity of the London schools was one of the factors behind the election in 1922 of the Municipal Reform Party, which was pledged to review the whole situation. As a result, by the end of 1922 London had abandoned its compulsory continuation schools. A number of classes remained open but mainly to provide for unemployed youths.[55]

The situation in the capital was reflected elsewhere. Continuation schools opened in West Ham, Stratford on Avon and Swindon, but none was successful. The one exception was at Rugby. Owing to the support of local industry, a continuation school was maintained there until after 1945.[56]

By early 1921 the 'anti-waste' campaign to cut educational and other government costs was well under way. As a result of the December 1920 Cabinet decision deferring all future schemes of expenditure without specific approval, Fisher agreed that until financial conditions improved all local education authorities were to show why they should incur any new expenditure.[57] A circular was issued directing them not to undertake new commitments without submitting specific proposals and estimates of cost to the Board.[58] Despite protests from the Labour movement, including efforts organised by the W.E.A., the campaign grew in strength.[59] On 2 August 1921 Fisher noted that Lloyd George had proposed in Cabinet a business committee under Sir Eric Geddes to recommend economies. 'I oppose so does Churchill very vehemently. Baldwin also. However the thing is comical. The fact is that the P.M. is dead tired and wants to throw a sop to Anti-Waste before the recess.'[60]

The reports of the Geddes committee, issued in early 1922, went far beyond mere restrictions on expenditure to propose wholesale reductions. Although recommending economies in all areas of government spending, its major cuts fell on the defence services and education. Of the total savings of £86 million, the estimates for the army, navy and air force were to be reduced by £46,500,000, and education in England and Wales by £16,500,000.[61] Indicative of the change in climate since the war, the Geddes committee made little or no attempt to assess the national importance of the social services. Nor did it try to analyse the impact and significance of inflation during the war and after. Its concern was to reduce the growth of total government expenditure, and all other considerations were subordinate.

In its first interim report the committee took particular exception to the percentage grant system for local services, which in education had arisen out of the Kempe committee report of 1914 and had been introduced in 1917. Where the Board of Education had seen this reform as the foundation of change, the Geddes committee regarded it as 'a money-spending device' for local authorities.[62] It pointed out that the Board's estimates had grown from £14,369,000 in 1912–13 to £50,600,000 in 1922–23: an increase of 239 per cent in the proportion contributed by national taxes to education, compared with a rise of only 101 per cent in the rates.[63] To redress the balance the Geddes committee wanted to replace the percentage grant formula. In the short run, however, it concentrated on means of reducing current educational expenditure. By raising the lower limit of the school age to six, closing small schools, increasing the pupil – teacher ratio to fifty to one in urban areas, and paying teachers less, the Geddes committee hoped to cut the total cost of elementary teaching from £45 million to £36 million.[64] Cut-backs in other areas would mean further savings of over £4 million in elementary education, while the committee also recommended that elementary grants be limited to a maximum of 50 per cent of local costs, saving the taxpayer £10 million.[65] In secondary and other higher education, pointing out that the budgets of local authorities had grown from £4,402,000 in 1913–14 to £16,200,000 in 1922–23, it wished to limit grant payments to merely £11 million of that expenditure. It also proposed a restriction on maintenance allowances and an end to State scholarships to the universities.[66] Finally, along with other recommendations for savings in administration, the committee proposed that the existing superannuation scheme for teachers should be reformulated to provide a contributory 5 per cent levy from the teachers themselves.[67] Added together, all these savings would reduce the educational State grant estimates for 1922–23 to only £34,678,000.[68]

If fully implemented, the major recommendations of the Geddes committee would have meant not merely a halt to the growth of expenditure but a general crisis throughout the educational system. A later estimate concluded that up to 43,000 teachers would have had to be dismissed.[69] Since contraction of local expenditure could not have come overnight, the burden of finance would have shifted drastically from taxes to the rates. That it did not happen was due to a number of factors. In the first place, Fisher threatened resignation if the Cabinet

PRUNING THE ORCHARD.
JOHN BULL: I say! Do be careful with that tree. It's one of the few trees that bear fruit in this orchard.

The Geddes 'axe' cut across all government spending. Education was not spared, although after the wartime changes many believed that it should remain sacrosanct. (From *Western Mail*, 10 January 1922)

accepted the Geddes recommendations.[70] After a series of Cabinet conferences he put forward a figure of £45 million for the 1922–23 education estimates, below which, he claimed, the government could not go, on either political or educational grounds.[71]

Political circumstances ran in his favour. At two by-elections in February 1922 government candidates were defeated in campaigns which seemed to show public opposition to the Geddes proposals.[72] There was also the influence of 150,000 teachers to consider. In November 1921 J. H. Yoxall, president of the N.U.T., had warned McCurdy, the government chief whip, that teachers and local education authorities would unite in opposition to cuts in salaries.[73] Lloyd George himself made it clear to Fisher that he opposed any salary cuts, and he gave a pledge to a teachers' delegation that there would be no interference in the Burnham scales, although he did appeal to them to support the principle of contributory pensions and accept voluntary restrictions on pay.[74]

Eventually the Cabinet committee, set up to consider the Geddes report decided to impose reductions in educational spending of only £5,700,000. This lowered the budget for 1922–23 to £44,900,000, a fraction less than the figure Fisher had put forward as the absolute minimum.[75] Yet the cuts were still severe, and they lasted for two years, until the election of the Labour government in 1924. A firm hand was laid on free places and maintenance allowances in secondary schools, and the university scholarships provided by the State disappeared, although they were to be restored in 1924. Any attempt to develop continuation schools nationally was abandoned. Despite strong opposition from the teachers the government also forced through a Bill that revised the superannuation Act of 1918 by stipulating pension contributions from both the teachers and the local education authorities.[76] Finally, in late 1922, in the face of moves to abandon the Burnham scales by many local authorities, the teachers voluntarily accepted a 5 per cent cut in pay.[77]

The Geddes report and its aftermath has a significance quite apart from the details of its recommendations. It indicated where priorities would lie for governments of any political colour between the wars. Although defence no longer consumed a large portion of the national budget, as it had before the war, the major shift in government expenditure between 1914 and the mid-1920s had been not towards the social services but towards servicing the national debt.

Table 5 *Government expenditure (%)*

	1913–14	*1925–26*
Defence	44	19
Social services	19	24
Debt service	14	46
Other	23	11

Source: E. V. Morgan, *Studies in British Financial Policy*, London, 1952, p. 98.

Under the pressure of war debt, financial orthodoxy insisted on a balanced budget as the means of preserving Britain's international credit, so necessary for a major trading nation and for the special position of the City in the world money market. A nation with overseas commitments and a significant proportion of its population out of work could ill afford a costly programme of social reform. It was the Treasury view which therefore remained the prime determinant of social policy. Despite its commitment to a new order in society, even Labour in office was to adopt the principles of financial conservatism, as the events of 1931 were to demonstrate so well.

Leaving office on the defeat of the coalition government in October 1922, Herbert Fisher sat down to draft a letter. Setting out his appreciation of service under his now revered political chief, he outlined what he saw as the educational achievements of the previous five and a half years.

> I cannot allow you to lay down your office without writing to express to you the gratitude which I feel to you for the opportunity which you gave me in 1916 of serving the cause of Education and for your continued help and support through the whole period of your Premiership. Whatever may happen in the future, National Education has made an advance during the past five years from which there can be no retreat. The whole Teaching Service has been lifted out of the pit and placed upon a securer level of comfort. There has been a great development of secondary education, a systematic review of the main subjects in the school curriculum with a view to the introduction of modern and enlightened methods of teaching and this quite apart from the legislative enactments of 1918 which abolish Half time, introduce the principle of adolescent education for all, and link up the Elementary school with every other part of the educational system. I believe that in time to come your two Administrations will be held in honour by the friends of Education all over the world for the examples which they have set and the results they have achieved.[78]

What is one to make of this assessment? Of all the work done while he was in office, Fisher seems to have been most proud later of what was achieved for teachers. As he wrote in his autobiography, 'Hereafter the teacher in the state-aided schools might consider himself to be a member of one of the liberal professions. He was relieved of grinding poverty, of the prospect of a sad and anxious old age.'[79] Much was due to the establishment of the Burnham scales. Initially, as has been pointed out elsewhere, these scales had barely met post-war inflation and in 1920 teachers had been only slightly better off than before the war.[80] But with the fall in prices from 1921 onwards they gained substantially. With an average salary of about £400 for graduates and £300 for non-graduates, during the inter-war years, but particularly during the 1920s, teachers joined that select eighth of the population which earned over £250 a year.[81]

Table 6 *Average salaries of teachers, 1914–30 (£)*

	Graduates			*Non-graduates*		
	Men	*Women*	*Men and women*	*Men*	*Women*	*Men and women*
1914	225	151	194	165	123	139
1922	451	343	400	357	272	301
1923	461	359	413	376	289	319
1924	442	348	399	365	382	310
1930	436	366	420	384	297	326

Source: P. H. J. H. Gosden, *The Evolution of a Profession*, p. 54.

The situation was dampened somewhat during the slump of the 1930s with a 10 per cent pay cut for all public-sector employees in 1931, but it was restored in 1934–35. In general, the increasing attraction of teaching as a profession was shown by the constant demand for places in the training colleges and the subsequent oversupply of trainees. Teaching had become respectable, drawing many of its recruits from a middle-class background, its members playing important roles in public office.[82]

Improved pay was only part of the picture. The superannuation scheme introduced in 1918 provided a security denied to most of the population. With the prospect of a fairly comfortable retirement teachers could use their higher income to sample the material delights that inter-war Britain could offer its middle class – better housing, consumer durables, even a motor car. As one member of the salaried middle class later wrote, 'In 1939 I had a salary of £300 a year. We ran a small car, we lived in a modern flat, we had all the cigarettes we wanted, we could even enjoy an occasional pub crawl.'[83] If nothing else, the war had helped raise the living standards of the teaching profession.

Fisher's other point, that the Board's policy had played a part in the development of the secondary schools, also has some truth. Such development had been along lines consistent with pre-war aims. The reform of the secondary school examination system in 1917 led to the establishment of the general school certificate and eventually the higher school certificate. In the words of H. C. Dent, 'They gave the schools precise academic targets; set what were at the time very high academic standards; compelled steady, restrained, systematic and disciplined work; and offered tangible, and relevant, rewards for success.'[84] As a corollary, between 1917–18 and 1924–25 the number of advanced courses in secondary schools grew from 127 to 469. Similarly while in 1908–09 a total of 695 boys and girls had proceeded from State secondary schools to university, by 1920–21 their numbers had expanded to 1,674 and 1,214 respectively.[85]

The first flush of growth in advanced secondary school work soon slowed. The number of secondary school sixth-formers increased from under 10,000 in 1912 to 20,000 in 1926 and to almost 40,000 in 1937, but their proportion in the secondary school population remained much the same throughout the inter-war years.[86] On the other hand, the Secondary Schools Examination Council (set up to administer the reform of secondary school exams), composed as it was mainly of university representatives, has been seen as weighting the secondary schools towards an academic emphasis and away from the moves to more vocational subjects that had been evident before 1914.[87]

As before, it continued to be the middle rather than the working class that benefited from the expansions of the secondary schools. Among boys born in the years 1910–29, about two-fifths of those from the middle class went on to a secondary school, four times the proportion of working-class children. Similarly, 8½ per cent of middle-class boys born in 1910–29 attended university, but only 1½ per cent from the working class.[88]

This imbalance of educational opportunity, which had been changed little by the policy pursued during the war and after, had consequences not only for social justice but for the nation as a whole. It was calculated in the 1930s that 73 per cent of children of high intelligence were trapped in the elementary schools, while 49 per cent of fee-paying pupils in secondary grammar schools were not of sufficient intelligence to benefit from such education.[89] Viewed in this light, there is some substance in A. J. P. Taylor's claim that 'class differences were not only maintained. They were made clearer and more effective than before.'[90] Increasingly, class also entered the classroom. Under guidance from the Board the old system of pupil-teachers was ended and teachers were drawn almost exclusively from the secondary schools.[91] The middle-class grammar-school background of most elementary school teachers was often at odds with the culture of their predominantly working-class pupils.

Unlike their teachers, working-class adolescents still had no contact with the education system past the age of fourteen. There was to be no attempt to revive the idea of compulsory continuation classes (although the Act of 1944 contained provision for part-time day continuation education). After the Hadow report on adolescent education in 1926 most educational opinion focused on the aim of universal secondary education, with a break between primary and secondary level at the age of eleven. Consequently, as a further development of pre- and post-war trends, some reorganisation did take place in the upper reaches of the elementary schools. By 1937–38 the proportion of the adolescent population in England and Wales between the ages of fourteen and eighteen attending State-aided schools had grown to just under 15 per cent compared to under 10 per cent in 1920–21.[92] Even here there were obstacles because of what had not been settled during the war years. In particular, despite the 1918 Act's provision for educational schemes and co-operation between local authorities, the distinction between Part II and Part III authorities continued to hamper the organisation of post-primary education.[93] Similarly, attempts to raise the school age to fifteen, as a necessary corollary to reorganising on the basis of universal primary and secondary education, faced the religious difficulties which Fisher had failed to resolve. In 1931 the Labour Minister Charles Trevelyan introduced a Bill that would have established a school leaving age of fifteen. The measure was later dropped, having not only raised the opposition of certain sections of Trevelyan's own party, who feared for the financial position of Catholic schools, but also the suspicions of the Nonconformists regarding a new religious settlement.[94] Many of the denominational schools, particularly those of the Church of England, were old and decaying. Little building was done by the Anglican sector and many schools closed. When Butler and the Board of Education came to tackle educational reconstruction during the second world war they had to face the problems of administrative arrangements and finance for denominational schools – legacies left over from the inadequate planning in the first.[95]

Provision for the mass of adolescents had been one of the two main pressures for change during the pre-war and wartime periods. The other was the demand for more scientific and technical education. Of this Fisher had said little in his 1922 letter to Lloyd George. Nevertheless he had made it clear on numerous occasions in 1919–20 that science and technological education had been secured by the events of war. As we have seen, most of his interest in higher education had been to counteract a stress on utilitariansim and reinforce the position of the classics. Yet in the long depression between the wars his bland and confident assertion that scientific and technical studies would flourish was not substantiated. If population changes are taken into account, the increase in enrolments for evening class technical students between 1911 and 1931, expressed in terms of the fifteen-to-twenty-four age group, was under 2 per cent. The proportion of day students in technical classes only rose from 2½ per cent in 1921 to under 4 per cent in 1937.[96]

The situation in the universities was similar. Between the wars the Treasury continued to maintain its pre-1914 view of State grants being for recurrent, not capital, expenditure. In 1938–39 the total non-recurrent grant for building and related expenditure was less than £1,500,000.[97] Science and technology were hampered. Between 1922–23 and 1938–39 the proportion of science students in the universities actually fell. By 1939 there were only 10,278 reading science and technology as compared with 9,852 in 1922.[98]

What the full picture reveals is limited change. The Great War cannot be described as a turning point in English education. The opportunities that were there were either missed or, because of stagnation in the economy, failed to develop. In the crisis of another world conflict the nation would again face much the same problems and issues.

Notes

1 Cruickshank, *Church and State in English Education*, p. 115. See also G. K. A. Bell, *Randall Davidson*, Oxford, 1935, II, pp. 1125–6.
2 See J. Scott Lidgett, *My Guided Life*, London, 1936, pp. 251–6.
3 P.R.O., Ed 24/1493; Fisher to Archbishop of Canterbury and Scott Lidgett, 19 June 1919. A copy of this letter and a brief account of the resulting meetings also appears in Bell, *Randall Davidson*, II, pp. 1125–8.
4 P.R.O., Ed 24/1494; L.A.S.B., Minute, 13 November 1919, and 'Establishment of a National System of Education', 19 November 1919.
5 P.R.O., Ed 24/1494; Conference on Religious Education, 9 November 1919.
6 *Ibid.*; Conference on Religious Education, 19 November 1919, p. 16.
7 *Ibid.*
8 *Ibid.*
9 *Ibid.*, p. 17. Fisher noted in his diary that Lloyd George was 'very much adverse' to any commitment in relation to the proposed religious

settlement. B.L., F.P., Box 8(a); Diary entry, 19 March 1920.

10 P.R.O., Ed 24/1497; H.F. Memorandum of an Interview with Bishop Bidwell, 27 January 1920, and L.A.S.B., Proposals for the Establishment of a National System of Education, 12 February 1920.

11 The conference on 28 January 1920 centred on means of including the Roman Catholics. P.R.O., Ed 24/1493; Conference on Religious Education, 28 January 1920.

12 P.R.O., Ed 24/1499; John Clifford to Fisher, 26 January 1920.

13 See P.R.O., Ed 24/1496; Fisher to Clifford, 29 January, 10 and 21 February and 21 March 1920.

14 Owing to an uproar from protesting teachers the speech was not actually delivered but was released to the press. *The Times*, 29 March 1920, p. 8.

15 National Education Association, *Hands off the Schools*, Report of the Proceedings of Progressive Educationalists, 15 April 1920 (pamphlet located in Dr Williams Library, Ms.207.8).

16 P.R.O., Ed 24/1500; Deputation from National Free Church Council, 7 May 1920.

17 P.R.O., Ed 24/1504; Deputation from Executive Committee of the National Union of Teachers, 24 April 1920.

18 *Hansard*, Commons, 5th ser., CVIII, 26 July 1918, col. 963.

19 P.R.O., Ed 46/14; E. K. Chambers, Minute, 24 February 1920.

20 P.R.O., Ed 46/15(6); newspaper cutting from *The Schoolmaster*, 26 April 1919.

21 *Hansard*, Commons, 5th ser., CXIX, 12 August 1919, col. 1235.

22 *Ibid.*, CXX, 28 October 1919, col. 492.

23 P.R.O., Ed 46/19; Report of the Committee on the Supply of Teachers for Day Continuation Schools, 20 August 1918.

24 Board of Education, Circular 1102, 4 April 1920.

25 See, in particular, Johnson, *Land fit for Heroes*, pp. 434–43, and P. Abrams, 'The failure of social reform', *Past and Present*, No. 24, 1963, pp. 55–7.

26 P.R.O., Ed 46/19; J.O., Minute, 5 June 1919. Unusually for Board officials, Owen was an inspector of working-class background. See Dover Wilson, *Milestones on the Dover Road*, p. 82.

27 *Ibid.*; Minute, L.A.S.B., 28 July 1919.

28 Prior to 1919 the Board of Education had met 90 per cent of the operating costs of local education authority training colleges. However, under the 1918 Act provision was made for only a 50 per cent grant for all higher education. Hence local education authorities providing colleges (about sixteen) were suffering, particularly since only a small percentage of students in the colleges came from the respective l.e.a. area. Eventually the Board was to establish a departmental committee whose report in 1925 laid the basis for the future of all teacher training. For further discussion see Gosden, *The Evolution of a Profession*, pp. 266–7, and J. L. Dobson, 'The training colleges and their successors, 1920–1970', in History of Education Society, *Education and the Professions*, pp. 56–9.

29 In September 1921 the National Federation of Class Teachers passed a

resolution depreciating the efforts of the Ministry of Labour as a recruiting force. *Manchester Guardian*, 24 September 1921, p. 12.

30 As well as the disabled some 711 other discharged soldiers underwent training. P.R.O., Ed 24/1799; H. Ward, Report of Special Scheme for Training Certain Discharged Sailors and Soldiers to be Certificated Teachers, 15 December 1922.

31 Board of Education Circular 1132, 30 September 1919.

32 P.R.O., Ed 24/1902; Lord Gorell to Fisher, 27 October 1919.

33 E. A. Waterfall, *The Day Continuation School in England*, London, 1923, p. 75. See also D. W. Thoms, 'The emergence and failure of the day continuation school experiment', *History of Education*, 4, 1, 1975, pp. 36–50.

34 Doherty, 'The education of the adolescent', pp. 81–135.

35 Report of the Departmental Committee on Scholarships and Free Places, *Parlt. Pprs.* 1920, XV, Cmd 968 pp. 7–8. The committee had been set up at the urging of Selby-Bigge. P.R.O., Ed 24/1187; L.A.S.B., Minute, 18 June 1919.

36 *Ibid.*, p. 9.

37 *Ibid.*, p. 10.

38 *Ibid.*

39 Transport House, Labour Party Archives; Advisory Committee on Education, Minute, 25 January 1921.

40 *Secondary Education for All*, London, n.d., p. 103.

41 *The Times*, 7 December 1920, p. 12.

42 P.R.O., Cab 27/71; Finance Committee Minute F.C. 29(4) of 7 December 1920.

43 This decision was communicated to local education authorities on 17 December 1920. Board of Education, Circular 1185, 17 December 1920.

44 P.R.O., Ed 46/15(b); Note upon the History of Continuation Schools, p. 3. The names of the authorities and the formal appointed day were as follows: Warwickshire (as regards Stratford on Avon), 12 April 1920; Warwickshire (as regards Rugby), 13 April 1920; Wiltshire (as regards Swindon), 20 September 1920; West Ham, 1 October 1920; London, 27 October 1920; Southend on Sea, 2 November 1920; Kent (only as regards juveniles resident in Kent and employed in London), 11 November 1920.

45 Fisher did write to Maurice Hankey, Secretary of the Cabinet, requesting that no action be taken before he returned from Geneva. P.R.O., Cab 23/117; Cabinet paper C.P. 2346 of December 1920.

46 Be.L., L.G.P., F32/1/22; Herbert Lewis to Lloyd George, 13 December 1920.

47 Be.L., L.G.P., F32/1/23; Herbert Lewis, Minute, 20 December 1920.

48 *Ibid.*; Herbert Lewis to Lloyd George, 20 December 1920.

49 P.R.O., Cab 24/117; Cabinet Paper, C.P. 2344 of December 1920.

50 P.R.O., Cab 23/23; Cabinet minute 76/20 (6) (b) of 23 December 1920. The provision for withdrawal of continuation school schemes was related to the precedent at Birmingham, where the city council had

asked the government on 7 December 1920 not to enforce the clauses of the 1918 Act pertaining to continuation schools.

51 Be.L., L.G.P., F32/1/24; Herbert Lewis to Lloyd George, n.d. [but late December 1920].

52 Maclure, *One Hundred Years of London Education*, p. 118.

53 P.R.O., Ed. 46/15(b); Note upon the History of Continuation Schools, p. 5.

54 Maclure, *One Hundred Years of London Education*, pp. 118–19. Fisher later wrote that this particular difficulty could have been overcome if the Act had contained a provision that all children employed in an area in which compulsory continuation classes were operating had to produce a certificate of school attendance. B.L., F.P., Box 19; Newspaper cutting from *Teachers' World*, 17 December 1930.

55 From 1922 to 1923 the numbers attending voluntarily actually grew from 4,071 to 4,941, but by mid-1924 only four centres remained open. Maclure, *One Hundred Years of London Education*, p. 119.

56 See P. T. Kitchen, *From Learning to Earning*, London, 1944. Some industries continued to maintain their own continuation schools. There were seventy-two in 1926 and 42,000 students in 1939. Armytage, *Four Hundred Years of English Education*, p. 310.

57 P.R.O., Ed 108/34; H. A. L. Fisher, Memorandum, 29 December 1920; Chamberlain to Fisher, 30 December 1920; and Fisher to Chamberlain, 31 December 1920.

58 Board of Education, Circular 1190, 11 January 1921.

59 Brian Simon, *The Politics of Educational Reform, 1920–1940*, London, 1978, pp. 34–6.

60 B.L., F.P., Box 8(a); Diary entry, 2 August 1921.

61 Third Interim Report of the Committee on National Expenditure, *Parlt. Pprs*. 1922, IX, Cmd 1589, pp. 168–9.

62 First Interim Report of the Committee on National Expenditure. *Parlt. Pprs*. 1922, IX, Cmd 1581, p. 105.

63 *Ibid*., p. 107.

64 *Ibid*., pp. 108–11.

65 *Ibid*., p. 112.

66 *Ibid*., pp. 117–18.

67 *Ibid*., p. 120.

68 *Ibid*.

69 Selby-Bigge, *The Board of Education*, p. 107.

70 Be.L., L.G.P., F16/7/77; Fisher to Lloyd George, 10 January 1922. Herbert Lewis also appealed to Lloyd George to support the cause of education. 'I have worked under you for over 30 years but I do not remember any question of domestic politics which has caused me so much anxiety, for if this reduction is approved, I fear that the damage will be beyond the power of this generation or even of the next to repair.' Be.L., L.G.P., F16/7/77; Herbert Lewis to Lloyd George, 17 January 1922.

71 Be.L., L.G.P., F16/7/80; Fisher to Lloyd George, 21 February 1922, enclosing details of educational estimates.

72 Simon, *The Politics of Educational Reform*, pp. 46–7.
73 P.R.O., Ed 108/59; J. H. Yoxall to C. A. McCurdy, 21 November 1921.
74 B.L., F.P., Box 8(a); Diary entry, 18 January 1922, and Diary entry, 2 February 1922.
75 P.R.O., Cab 24/133; Cabinet paper C.P. 3785 of 28 February 1922.
76 The government was defeated on the second reading of this Bill after charges of breach of contract. See *Hansard*, Commons, 5th ser., CLIV, 16 May 1922, cols. 263–327. The measure was later resubmitted and passed the House but a select committee of inquiry was also set up, leading to the 1925 Pensions Act. See Vaizey, 'Teachers' superannuation in England and Wales', pp. 16–9.
77 Gosden, *The Evolution of a Profession*, p. 51; and Selby-Bigge, *The Board of Education*, pp. 269–70.
78 Be.L., L.G.P., F16/7/91; Fisher to Lloyd George, 20 October 1922. In February 1922 Fisher had told Tom Jones that on assuming office in 1916 he had several objects in mind and had at least realised some: (1) raising the level of the teaching profession, (2) increasing the provision and availability of secondary schools, (3) adolescent education, (4) the Royal Commission on Oxford and Cambridge, (5) medical treatment for young children. Diary entry, 1 February 1922, in Middlemas (ed.), *Thomas Jones Whitehall Diary*, I, *1916–1925*, p. 192.
79 Fisher, *Unfinished Autobiography*, p. 104. Once Fisher had retired, Dover Wilson also asked him what he considered his greatest achievement. Fisher replied, 'what I was able to do to increase the salaries of elementary school teachers, thus making it possible for the first time for women teachers, at any rate, to travel; for I cannot imagine a more educative experience or one more likely to influence education as a whole.' Dover Wilson, *Milestones on the Dover Road*, p. 87.
80 Tropp, *The School Teachers*, p. 212.
81 Sean Glynn and John Oxborrow, *Interwar Britain. A Social and Economic History*, London, 1976, p. 47.
82 Tropp, *The School Teachers*, pp. 227–8.
83 Cited in Glynn and Oxborrow, *Interwar Britain*, p. 50.
84 Dent, *1870–1970: Century of Growth in English Education*, p. 96.
85 Report of the Board of Education, 1923–24, *Parlt. Pprs*. 1924–25, XII, Cmd 2443, p. 27.
86 Edwards, *The Changing Sixth Form in the Twentieth Century*, p. 17.
87 R. J. Montgomery, *Examinations*, London, 1965, pp. 135–6. See also Banks, *Parity and Prestige in English Secondary Education*, pp. 85–93.
88 D. V. Glass, 'Education and social change in modern England', in Morris Ginsberg (ed.), *Law and Opinion in England in the Twentieth Century*, Berkeley and Los Angeles, Cal., 1959, pp. 330–1.
89 Sanderson, *The Universities and British Industry*, p. 278.
90 Taylor, *English History, 1914–1945*, p. 171.
91 Gosden, *The Evolution of a Profession*, pp. 273–6.
92 Education 1900–1950, Cmd 8244, p. 257.
93 See Gosden, *The Development of Educational Administration in England and Wales*, pp. 153–5.

94 D. W. Dean, 'The difficulties of a Labour educational policy. The failure of the Trevelyan Bill, 1929–31', *British Journal of Educational Studies*, XVII, 1969, pp. 286–300.
95 Butler, *The Art of the Possible*, pp. 96–107 and 119–20.
96 Cotgrove, *Technical Education and Social Change*, p. 68.
97 Argles, *South Kensington to Robbins*, p. 77.
98 Perkins, *Key Profession*, p. 78.

Conclusion

Much had happened in English education during the years 1911–20 and much had remained the same. Despite the prospects of wide-scale change there was a still higher degree of continuity.

In part the failure to achieve change was due to the political priorities of the immediate post-war period. Administrative difficulties were equally significant. As in the case of housing, the problems of setting up continuation classes were vast and perhaps never fully thought out. Their establishment depended too much on an active response at the local level. Immediately after the war local education authorities faced more than administrative problems: a conflict of priorities. In September 1919 the Director of Education for Gloucestershire informed Selby-Bigge that in an agricultural area such as his, without pressure or assistance from industry, 'it will be very difficult to get Day Continuation Schools going on a voluntary footing – and any other footing is quite unthinkable at the moment'.[1] Writing in 1920, Sir George Kekewich argued that the Act of 1918 had 'set out to conquer a kingdom without the means of even taking a province'. He suggested that if Fisher had studied the past he would have first secured the passage of an enabling Act, and only when its provisions had taken root would he have introduced compulsion.[2] Instead, once faced by difficulties and opposition, the Board, and particularly Selby-Bigge, readily abandoned the idea of continuation classes.[3]

To explain continuity, however, one must start not with the problems of 1920 and beyond but with the planning back in 1911. As with electoral reform, education might be regarded as part of the 'unfinished business' of the Edwardian era.[4] The priorities of

Asquith's pre-war government were mixed. The first commitment had been to satisfy the Nonconformists. The other direction for sweeping change originated principally from the initiative of Haldane. Actual proposals for reform, however, derived mainly from the Board of Education. It was not only ideas but a general programme, including an important legislative measure, that had been drawn up before the war. This programme formed the basis of the policy measures that were enacted and implemented during the war and immediately after. The war provided a major impetus to immediate change, as well as altering priorities in educational policy and pushing advance forward, but it did not restructure the major outlines or shapes of what the policy-makers had decided upon as necessary before August 1914. Where war added new demands, particularly in the proposals of Lloyd George's 1917 Reconstruction Committee and, from a different standpoint, the claims of the scientific community, the policy-makers not only failed to respond but actively resisted.

An initiator of reform before the war, the Board became a conservative force during it. In part this was to be expected. It reflected past behaviour. Sir Robert Morant had been a dynamic educational administrator – perhaps the last of the great 'statesmen in disguise'. Unlike such departments as the Local Government Board, the Board of Education before 1914 held a position of some prestige in Whitehall.[5] The legacy of active policy-making remained. Christopher Addison later wrote of his experiences at the Board,

> Some of the chief officials, I think before we got to understand one another, were a little inclined to resent a Parliamentary Secretary who was active on matters of policy, and who was not disposed to be content with answering questions in the House in the words given to him on the day appointed and otherwise be seen occasionally and not heard.[6]

On the other hand the circumstances surrounding Morant's departure left a desire within the Board to avoid too much controversy. It has been suggested that during the nineteenth century the great educational statesman Kay-Shuttleworth was replaced by administrators linked by a common educational pattern and regarding the civil service as a career.[7] The pattern may have been repeated in the early twentieth century. Rather than attempt to create a new system, as Morant had, Selby-Bigge sought to administer what already existed, to co-operate as far as possible with local administration and the teachers, and thus to protect and increase the position and influence of the Board. Much of the planning for the measure which was to become the 1918 Act was aimed at this end. Whatever the circumstances, response was often cautious. Frustrated by what he considered unnecessary obstruction, Haldane complained in 1916 that the permanent secretary of the Board was a 'black-browed man, very jealous, and full of red tape and sealing wax'.[8] For Selby-Bigge at least, the crisis of war added little to the priorities that would apply in peacetime.

Finally it should be noted that the Board itself had the advantages of continuity. Unlike other areas of social policy, such as housing and health, there existed prior to 1914 a framework of educational policy administered by a coterie of experienced civil servants. While their political masters came and went, the Board officials remained committed to their own viewpoint. Moreover few in the corridors of power were prepared to challenge them. In 1911–14 Pease was more concerned politically with the religious question than with any other educational topic; in terms of educational administration and general policy he was prepared to rely on the advice of the permanent officials. Through no fault of his own Arthur Henderson in 1915–16 was a weak and ineffective President of the Board. Even those politicians who took an active part in framing policy did not disagree fundamentally with the aims of the Board officials. In drawing up a programme for developing scientific and technical education Christopher Addison built upon and used the established plans of the bureaucrats. Haldane argued with Selby-Bigge over procedure in 1916, but did not dispute the general framework of the programme both he and the Board's permanent secretary had done so much to further before the war.

Despite appearances to the contrary, the appointment of H. A. L. Fisher did little to alter policy. Coming from a similar social and educational background, he relied generally on the advice of his officials, particularly Selby-Bigge. It may be that Fisher cannot be neatly fitted into a category such as has been suggested for those dealing with reconstruction who 'really looked forward to the new world or to rebuilding the old'.[9] What can be said is that many of his values were drawn not so much from the Edwardian as from the Victorian era. Sceptical in outlook, he was really a late nineteenth-century liberal. As his friend Gilbert Murray later wrote, his historical vision as expressed in the later published multi-volume *History of Europe* was a 'definitive utterance of a certain Weltanschauung or faith . . . the spirit of liberalism among realms of thought, of Great

Britain among nations, of the nineteenth century among the ages'.[10] Change was desirable, but not too much; State intervention was necessary, but only to widen the liberty of the individual. Even then, individuals might have to be willing to accept their place in society. Fisher told the Commons in August 1917 that the extension of the franchise and the improvement of education were linked together. At a time when 'problems of national life and world policy' were becoming 'exceedingly complex and difficult', an intelligent response from the populace could be expected only if steps were taken to 'form and fashion the minds of the young'.[11] Continuation classes in particular would 'give to the industrial character of our people just that additional measure of stability which it so pre-eminently lacks'.[12]

His cautious liberal reformism thus complemented the approach of the Board. Perhaps Fisher's main contribution to policy was in higher education. Here his views were predominantly conservative, defending what he saw as the essence of university life epitomised in the study of the classics. Even then his views were not at odds with the Board's. As Crewe told Asquith in June 1916, not only the 'scientific fanatics' but the 'Quite moderate evangelists of science teaching' distrusted the Board of Education because its high officials 'even on the technical side are, without an exception, Arts Men'.[13]

What, then, of the general relation between war and social change? Of the four modes posited in Marwick's model, at least two had some relationship to education, though not in the way that he has generally suggested. The war did have a destructive effect on English education. The concern which arose, however, allowed the educational planners at the Board to push forward their own worked-out programme of reform. Secondly, the war did put English education to the test in a number of ways. But the educational challenge from Germany had been there long before; ever since the late nineteenth century. Two issues had been prominent: lack of provision for the mass of English adolescents, and the inadequacies in scientific and technical studies. The first deficiency was recognised by most of the nation during the war and partly tackled through the 1918 Act (although sectional interests could still force concessions; even wartime consensus had a fragile base). The second evoked far less awareness. It could even be said that it was strongly and successfully resisted by both Fisher and the Board.

Of Marwick's other modes, there was much greater participation in educational discussion and debate during the war. Under the guidance of the W.E.A. the labour movement became committed in principle to large-scale 'educational reconstruction'. As witnessed by increasing secondary school enrolments, the war also brought greater consciousness of education as an agent of social mobility. At another level, the universities and the scientific community were caught up in national war work. Because of the war scientists could speak and act with greater authority.

Despite increased 'participation', the decisions still rested in the same hands as before 1914. Fisher and the Board locked out views and priorities not in accord with their own. It is significant that they were able to do so effectively despite the rhetoric of change and increased 'outsider' participation so associated with the Lloyd George government of 1916–18. In general, such notions as the military participation ratio do not apply to the first world war and English education. There were no great educational gains for the masses. To the extent that there was a relation between the war and education it could be suggested that part of the 1918 Act, particularly the provision for compulsory continuation classes, was intended to restrict the freedom adolescents had found as wartime wage-earners. The major beneficiaries were the teachers. Even their gains became real only in the years of deflation.

Finally, if war was a psychological and emotional experience, as Marwick suggests, then it would seem that many such effects on post-war England were short-lived. The country could never be the same again, but many hoped that it would. After all, despite wartime concerns and fears, Britain had emerged victorious; Germany had been defeated. The lessons no longer seemed so pressing.

As a final contribution to any theory of the relation between war and social change, it might be said that one theme does stand out in this study. There had been a concern with 'national efficiency' embracing education which stretched back to Edwardian days and forward into wartime. The concern was not universal but it had been the most persistent. It took shape from the German threat. It helped unite diverse interests. It might even be possible to talk of a 'national efficiency ratio' of change, with concern reaching its peak as the crisis of war deepened during 1916 but lessening greatly as the danger receded. In the end the temporary removal of the German threat (to be replaced perhaps by the fear of international communism) tended to destroy what credibility the national efficiency campaign might have had.

In effect, military victory had obscured the real situation. The defeat of Germany on the battlefield did not confirm British superiority. Quite the contrary. The war had not only shown up deficiencies in economic and social life, it had weakened the country in human and material terms. To overcome these problems required greater effort and foresight than ever. Instead there was a retreat to the protection of existing resources and structures.

The general result in education was therefore an uncertain half-way house. Some advances were made, but much was left undone; others were not attempted or only partly developed. It may be said that the consequences of failure then are still being felt.

Notes

1 P.R.O., Ed 24/1902; H. W. Household to Selby-Bigge, 11 September 1919.

2 Kekewich, *The Education Department and After*, pp. 307–8.

3 Dover Wilson claims that upon his own resignation in 1924 Selby-Bigge informed him that he regretted the failure of the continuation classes but added, 'I told Mr Fisher that if we kept them in the Act we should all be hanging from lamp posts.' Dover Wilson, *Milestones on the Dover Road*, p. 94.

4 Pugh, *Electoral Reform in War and Peace, 1906–18*, p. ix. The term 'unfinished business' has, of course, also been used by Peter Rowland in his history of *The Last Liberal Governments*.

5 Roy Macleod points out that, in contrast to Morant's 'fresh enthusiasm', the pre-war Local Government Board lacked active leadership. R. Macleod, *Treasury Control and Social Administration*, Occasional Papers on Social Administration, No. 23, 1958, p. 39 and also p. 54.

6 Addison, *Politics from Within*, I, p. 61.

7 Richard Johnson, 'Administrators in education before 1870: patronage, social postiion and role', in Sutherland (ed.), *Studies in the Growth of Nineteenth Century Government*, pp. 110–38. See also Gillian Sutherland, *Policy Making in Elementary Education, 1870–1895*, Oxford, 1973. Cf. Henry Roper, *Administering the Elementary Education Acts, 1870–1885*, Educational Administration and History Monographs, No. 5, Leeds, 1976.

8 C.U.L., C.P., Box M.8(3); Haldane to Crewe, 29 August 1916.

9 Gilbert, *British Social Policy, 1914–1939*, pp. 121–2.

10 Murray, *Herbert Albert Laurens Fisher*, p. 13.

11 *Hansard*, Commons, 5th ser., XCVII, 10 August 1917, col. 810.

12 *Ibid.*, cols. 810–11.

13 C.U.L., C.P., Box M/8(3); Crewe to Asquith, 28 June 1916. The background of Pullinger, a scientist, belies this claim in part.

Bibliography

Primary sources

1. *Official*

(*a*) Unpublished

Public Record Office

Cab 23, War Cabinet and Cabinet minutes
Cab 24, War Cabinet and Cabinet papers
Cab 26, Home Affairs Committee
Cab 37, Pre-1916 Cabinet papers
Ed 12, Secondary Schools files
Ed 13, 'Schemes' under 1918 Education Act
Ed 23, Finance
Ed 24, Board of Education private office papers
Ed 46, Implementation of 1918 Act (continuation classes)
Ed 108, Teachers' salaries
Recon 1, Reconstruction Committee and Ministry of Reconstruction

Department of Education and Science Library, London

Papers contained in bound volume *T Revision Memoranda*

(*b*) Published

Two of the major sources of published official material were Hansard and the annual reports of the Board of Education. A further source was the circulars issued by the Board of Education (numbers of which are located in the Board of Education files or the Department of Education and Science Library). However, listed below, in chronological order, are the other major published official reports and histories used in this study.

Final Report of the Royal Commission on Local Taxation. *Parliamentary Papers* 1901, XXIV, Cd 638.

Report of the Interdepartmental Committee on Physical Deterioration. *Parliamentary Papers* 1904, LXXXII, Cd 2175.

Report of the Consultative Committee of the Board of Education upon the Attendance of School Children below the Age of Five. *Parliamentary*

Papers 1908, LXXXII, Cd 4529.

Report of the Consultative Committee of the Board of Education on the question of Devolution by County Education Authorities. *Parliamentary Papers* 1908, LXXXII, Cd 3952.

Report of the Consultative Committee of the Board of Education on Attendance, compulsory or otherwise, at Continuation Schools. *Parliamentary Papers* 1909, XVII, Cd 4757.

Report of the Interdepartmental Committee on Partial Exemption from School Attendance. *Parliamentary Papers* 1909, XVII, Cd 4791.

Report of the Royal Commission on the Poor Laws and Relief of Distress. 3 vols. London: H.M.S.O., 1909.

Report of the Consultative Committee of the Board of Education on Examinations in Secondary Schools. *Parliamentary Papers* 1911, XVI, Cd 6004.

Final Report of the Royal Commission on the University of London. *Parliamentary Papers* 1913, XI, Cd 6718.

Final Report of the Departmental Committee on Local Taxation. *Parliamentary Papers* 1914, XI, Cd 7315.

Interim Report of the Consultative Committee on Scholarships for Higher Education. *Parliamentary Papers* 1916, VIII, Cd 8291.

Report of the Committee for Scientific and Industrial Research, 1915–16. *Parliamentary Papers* 1916, VIII, Cd 8336.

Final Report of the Departmental Committee on Juvenile Education in Relation to Employment after the War. *Parliamentary Papers* 1917–18, IX, Cd 8512.

Report of the Departmental Committee of Enquiry into the Principles which should Determine the Constitution of Scales of Salaries for Teachers in Elementary Schools. *Parliamentary Papers* 1918, IX Cd 8939.

Report of the Committee appointed to Enquire into the Position of Natural Science in the Educational System of Great Britain. *Parliamentary Papers* 1918, IX, Cd 9011.

Report of the Committee appointed to Enquire into the Position of Modern Languages in the Educational System of Great Britain. *Parliamentary Papers* 1918, IX, Cd 9036.

Ministry of Reconstruction, *Juvenile Employment during the War and After*. London: H.M.S.O., 1918.

Ministry of Reconstruction, Interim Report of the Committee on Adult Education. Industrial and Social Conditions in Relation to Adult Education. *Parliamentary Papers* 1918, IX, Cd 9107.

Second Interim Report of the Committee on Adult Education of the Ministry of Reconstruction. Education in the Army. *Parliamentary Papers* 1918, IX, Cd 9225.

Third Interim Report of the Committee on Adult Education of the Ministry of Reconstruction. Libraries and Museums. *Parliamentary Papers* 1918, IX, Cd 9237.

Final Report of the Committee on Adult Education of the Ministry of Reconstruction. *Parliamentary Papers* 1919, XXVIII, Cmd 321.

Report of the Standing Joint Committee Representative of the County

Councils Association, the Municipal Corporations Association, the Association of Education Committees and the London County Council and the National Union of Teachers. *Parliamentary Papers* 1919, XXI, Cmd 443.

Report of the Departmental Committee on Scholarships and Free Places. *Parliamentary Papers* 1920, XV, Cmd 968.

Report of the University Grants Committee on the Financial Needs of the Universities of the United Kingdom, and on the Application of Parliamentary Grants, 1921. *Parliamentary Papers* 1921, XI, Cmd 1163.

Humanism in the Continuation School. Board of Education pamphlet No. 43.

Classics in Education. Report of the Committee appointed by the Prime Minister to inquire into the Position of Classics in the Educational System of the United Kingdom. London: H.M.S.O., 1921.

Report of the Royal Commission on Oxford and Cambridge Universities. *Parliamentary Papers* 1922, X, Cmd 1588.

Royal Commission on Oxford and Cambridge Universities. Appendices. London: H.M.S.O., 1922.

First Interim Report of the Committee on National Expenditure. *Parliamentary Papers* 1922, IX, Cmd 1581.

Third Interim Report of the Committee on National Expenditure. *Parliamentary Papers* 1922, IX, Cmd 1589.

History of the Ministry of Munitions. 8 vols. London: H.M.S.O., 1922.

Secondary Education, with special Reference to Grammar Schools and Technical High Schools. London: H.M.S.O., 1938.

Education 1900–1950, Report of the Ministry of Education, 1950. *Parliamentary Papers* 1950–51, XI, Cmd 8244.

2. *Unofficial*

(*a*) Unpublished

(i) Private papers

Beaverbrook Library: Lloyd George papers (now in House of Lords Library)

Bodleian Library: H. A. L. Fisher papers, Gilbert Murray papers

British Library of Political and Economic Science: Passfield papers

National Library of Scotland: R. B. Haldane papers, J. Dover Wilson papers

Nuffield College Library, Oxford: Gainford papers

University of Cambridge Library: Crewe papers

University of Leeds Library: Brotherton Collection: Haldane–Gosse correspondence

University of Wales Library: Thomas Jones collection, Herbert Lewis papers

(ii) Other archives

Labour Party Archives, Transport House: minutes and memoranda of the Advisory Committee on Education

Department of Health and Social Security Library: unpublished diary of Sir George Newman

National Liberal Club: manifestoes of political candidates

National Union of Teachers Library: pamphlet collection
Dr Williams Library (London): National Education Association pamphlets, 207.8
Workers' Educational Association Library: file on 1918 Education Act, pamphlet collection

(*b*) Published

(i) Reports
Labour Party annual reports
National Union of Teachers annual reports
Trades Union Congress reports
(ii) Newspapers
Major sources: *The Highway, The Schoolmaster, The Times, The Times Educational Supplement.* Other national and local newspapers consulted: *Bradford Daily Telegraph, Burnley News, Cardiff Times, Daily Mail, Daily News, Daily Telegraph, Manchester Guardian, Rochdale Observer.*

Published books, articles and pamphlets

Andrews, I. O., *Economic Effects of the War upon Women and Children in Great Britain.* Carnegie Endowment for International Peace, Preliminary Economic Studies of the War. New York, 1918.
Best, R. H., and Ogden, C. K., *The Problem of Continuation Schools and its Successful Solution in Germany.* Introduction by Dr Georg Kerchensteiner. London, 1914.
Beveridge, W. H., *Unemployment. A Problem of Industry*, London, 1909.
Bowley, A. L., *Prices and Wages in the United Kingdom, 1914–1920.* Economic and Social History of the World War, British Series, Oxford, 1920.
Continuation Schools in England and Elsewhere. Introduction by Michael Sadler. Manchester, 1907.
Currie, Sir James, *The War and Industrial Training.* Paper read before the Royal Society of Arts, 25 February 1920 (located in W.E.A. Library, London).
Education, Scientific and Humane. A Report of the Proceedings of the Council for Humanistic Studies. Edited by F. G. Kenyon. London, 1917.
Education after the War. Report of Proceedings at the Annual Conference of the National Education Association, 11 May 1916 (located in Dr Williams Library, London).
The Elements of Reconstruction. Introduction by Lord Milner. London, 1916.
Ellis, G. S. M., *The Poor Student and the University.* A Report on the Scholarship System, with Particular Reference to Awards Made by L.E.A.'s. London, 1925.
Farrow, T., and Cotch, W. W., *The Coming Trade War.* London, 1916.
Federation of British Industries, *Memorandum on Education.* February 1918.
Fisher, H. A. L., *Educational Reform.* Address delivered at the University of

Manchester on 26 September 1917 to Association of Educational Societies. London, 1917.
—— *Educational Reform Speeches*. Oxford, 1918.
—— *The Place of the University in National Life*. London, 1919.
—— *Political Prophecies*. Oxford, 1919.
—— Six years of education in England, *Yale Review*, XII, 1922–23, pp. 510–27.
—— What England has learned from war, *The Outlook*, 3 January 1917, pp. 22–3.
—— Ten millions for schools, *The Outlook*, 10 January 1917, pp. 64–5.
—— The universities and civic patriotism, *The Outlook*, 17 January 1917, pp. 108, 112–3.
The Government's Record. London, 1913.
Gray, H. B., and Turner, S., *Eclipse or Empire*. London, 1916.
Haldane, R. B., *Education and Empire*. London, 1902.
—— *National Education*. Speech delivered by Viscount Haldane, Manchester, 1913. London, 1913.
—— *The Student and the Nation*. Address delivered at the University of London, 23 March 1916.
Kekewich, G., *The Education Department and After*. London, 1920.
Kerchensteiner, Georg, *The Schools and the Nation*. Translated by C. K. Ogden. London, 1914.
Labour Party, Memoranda prepared by the Advisory Committee on Education. *Continued Education under the New Education Act*. London, 1918 (located in Labour Party Archives, Transport House).
Lockyer, Joseph Norman, *Education and National Progress*, London, 1906.
Mactavish, J. M., *What Labour wants from Education*. Workers' Educational Association. 1916.
Mansbridge, Albert, *An Adventure in Working Class Education*. London, 1920.
Masterman, C. F. G., *The Condition of England*. [Edited with an introduction by J. T. Bolton.] London, 1970.
Report of National Conference on Educational Reconstruction. Held at the Central Hall, Westminster, May 3rd 1917 (located in Workers' Educational Association Library).
National Education Association, *First Principles and other Matters*. 17 February 1914. Report of the Annual Conference of the National Education Association (located in Dr Williams Library, London).
—— *Hands off the Schools*. Report of the Proceedings of Progressive Educationalists. 15 April 1920 (located in Dr Williams Library, London).
National Education. Speeches delivered by Marquess of Crewe, Viscount Haldane and J. A. Pease at the Eighty Club, 4 April 1913. London, 1913.
National Liberal Federation. *Proceedings in Connection with the Meeting of the General Committee of the National Liberal Federation*. Manchester, 26 and 27 September 1918. London, 1918.
The Neglect of Science. Report of Proceedings at a Conference 3 May 1916 (pamphlet located in Crewe papers, Box M/8(3), in University of Cambridge Library).

N.U.T. (National Union of Teachers), *War Record, 1914–1919*. London, 1920.

Lord Riddell, *More Pages from my Diary, 1908–1914*. London, 1934.

Scobell Armstrong, J. W., *The Trade Continuation Schools of Germany*. With an introduction by Lord Haldane. London, 1914.

Secondary Education for All. London, n.d.

Tawney, R. H., 'The public schools and the older universities', in *The English Public School* [edited by J. H. Whitehouse]. London, 1919.

—— *The Attack and other Papers*. London, 1953.

Unionist Social Reform Committee, *Schools and Social Reform*. London, 1914.

Waterfall, E. A., *The Day Continuation School in England*. London, 1923.

Webb, Sidney, *The Teacher in Politics*. Fabian Tract No. 187. Fabian Society, September 1918.

Webb, Sidney and Beatrice, *Industrial Democracy*. London, 1902.

Webb, Sidney, and Freeman, Arnold, *Great Britain after the War*. London, 1916.

Whitehouse, J. H., *A National System of Education*. Cambridge, 1913.

Workers' Educational Association, *The Choice before the Nation*. Some Amendments to the Education Bill. London, 1918.

W.E.A. Yearbook. London, 1918.

Index